Images
of the
Church
in Mission

Books by John Driver

(By Herald Press unless otherwise identified)

Comunidad y Compromiso (Buenos Aires: Certeza, 1974)

Community and Commitment (1980)

Militantes para un Mundo Nuevo (Barcelona: Ediciones
Evangélicas Europeas, 1978)

Kingdom Citizens (1980)

Becoming God's Community (Elgin, Ill.: Brethren Press, 1981)

El Evangelio: Mensaje de Paz (Zaragoza, Spain: Mostaza, 1984)

Understanding the Atonement for the Mission of the Church (1986)

La Obra Redentora de Cristo y la Misión de la Iglesia (Buenos Aires:
Nueva Creación, and Grand Rapids: Eerdmans, 1994)

Contra Corriente: Ensayos Sobre la Eclesiología Radical (Guatemala:
Semilla, 1988)

How Christians Made Peace with War (1988)

Como los Christianos Hicieron Paz con la Guerra (Guatemala:
Semilla, and Bogotá: Clara, 1991)

Pueblo a Imagen de Dios: Hacia una Visión Bíblica (Guatemala:
Semilla, and Bogotá: Clara, 1991)

El Espíritu Santo en la Comunidad Mesiánica (Guatemala: Semilla,
and Bogotá: Clara, 1992)

Images of the Church in Mission (1997)

La Fe en la Periferia de la Historia (Guatemala: Semilla, and Bogotá:
Clara, 1997)

Imágenes de la Iglesia en Misión: Hacia una Eclesiología de
Transformación (Bogotá and Guatemala: Ediciones Clara-
Semilla, 1998)

Images

of the Church in Mission

JOHN DRIVER

HERALD PRESS
Scottdale, Pennsylvania
Waterloo, Ontario

Library of Congress Cataloging-in-Publication Data
Driver, John, 1924-
        Images of the church in mission / John Driver.
            p. cm.
        Includes bibliographical references.
        ISBN 0-8361-9058-0 (alk. paper)
        1. Missions—Biblical teaching. 2. Church—Biblical teaching.
    I. Title.
    BV2073.D75 1997
    262'.7—dc21

                                                                              97-4928

All Bible quotations are used by permission, all rights reserved, and
unless otherwise indicated are from the *New Revised Standard Version
Bible,* copyright 1989, by the Division of Christian Education of the
National Council of the Churches of Christ in the USA.

IMAGES OF THE CHURCH IN MISSION
Copyright © 1997 by Herald Press, Scottdale, Pa. 15683
    Published simultaneously in Canada by Herald Press,
    Waterloo, Ont. N2L 6H7. All rights reserved
Library of Congress Catalog Number: 97-4928
International Standard Book Number: 0-8361-9058-0
Printed in the United States of America
Book design by James Butti
Art on cover and divider pages by Gwen M. Stamm: "From Desert to
Firstfruits"

06 05 04 03 02 01 00 99 98 97 10 9 8 7 6 5 4 3 2 1

In memory of my parents,
the first to share with me
a vision of a church called to mission

Contents

THE CHURCH IN MISSION

Foreword

In these closing years of the twentieth century and the end of the second millennium since Jesus Christ, it is appropriate and indeed urgently necessary that Christians take stock of Christian reality. This is a particularly good moment to do so because of the varied perspectives available to us. The past several centuries have been tumultuous, resulting in great change for the church as well as in the wider culture.

The outward movement in mission from the historical Christian heartland in Europe, has resulted in burgeoning growth of the churches outside the West. In the West we have had revival movements and endless organizational tinkering, but the overall trend has not been positive. Decay from within and assaults from without have dogged the course of the church. Theological and ecclesiastical dry rot has been a constant source of threat in the modern period. Secularization and anti-religious ideologies have aggressively confronted the church in modern culture. While many churches in Asia, Africa, and Latin America—only one or two generations old—are enjoying the vitality of youth, the churches in Europe and North America appear to be tired and institutionally stymied.

John Driver's *Images of the Church in Mission* is written with a persuasive awareness of our historical moment, especially the position of the church in the West; he pleads passionately for the renewal of the church. But his four decades of ministry in Latin America and Europe have sharpened and shaped the agenda he pursues. This is a biblical study painted on a broad historical and cultural canvas. Driver argues for renewal of the most basic kind. Several points are worth underscoring.

The choice of method is critical. Driver could have given us one more study of the church using categories from systematic theology or approaches favored by biblical scholars. But he has declined those options and, consequently, we have in hand a pioneering study, one that has been sorely needed for a long time. Driver's long cross-cultural experience has made him "methodologically suspicious." All methods are freighted with cultural baggage. Methods developed in a culture that has been in the position of economic and political dominance for several centuries inevitably are biased in favor of power. To help free us from such cultural blinders, Driver has chosen to study the church by using images.

In the first place, the Bible does not offer a definition of the church or provide us with a doctrinal basis for understanding it. Instead, the Bible relies on images and narrative to disclose the meaning of the church. Second, the symbolic language of images introduces richness and variety. The Bible employs nearly one hundred different images for the church, thus developing a composite picture that, like a great painting, is filled with inexhaustible meaning. The third reason favoring this approach is that images have universal appeal and validity. These images are infinitely translatable. The use of images helps expose the cultural biases and blind spots we all have while inviting us to rethink the contextualization of the biblical message in our time and culture.

The thrust of this study is radical. John Driver has long been committed to going to the *radix,* to the root of the matter, laying bare God's intention for our discipleship. In this book he helps us recover the biblical meaning and function of images of the church while peeling away the historical layers of (mis)interpretation and (mal)practice that have concealed from us the fuller meaning of God's intention. It becomes clear that the church in the West is suffering from an advanced case of syncretism. Christians of all theological persuasions have, often unwittingly, sought to minimize the tension between themselves and the world in one of two ways.

One response has been to seek accommodation with the world, to be acceptable. The alternative approach has been to attempt to withdraw from the world, to avoid facing the question altogether. Both reactions are evasions of the covenantal responsibility God entrusted to the church; they must be rejected. The biblical vision of mission assumes—indeed requires—a people who embody and represent what they proclaim. The modern themes of individualism and specialization seriously distort our understanding of the corporate nature of mission and evangelization.

What we are given, then, is a compelling challenge to Christian discipleship that can only be expressed in living and being God's mission to the world.

—*Wilbert R. Shenk*
 Fuller Theological Seminary
 Pasadena, California

Preface

Thank God for the church. In its story are episodes of true greatness. The Catholic tradition has produced models of contemplative spirituality. Many of its saints have been selfless in their service, following Jesus in solidarity with the poor and the suffering. Catholicism has nurtured courageous exponents of peace and justice.

The Protestant tradition, invigorated by a Reformation triumph of grace, has inspired many with new spiritual vitality and vision. Throughout the centuries, both Catholics and Protestants have given birth to movements in which the gospel of the kingdom has been freed from its human enslavements. That gospel is bringing radical renewal to the life and mission of the church.

However, Catholic Christendom as well as Protestant has throughout much of its history perceived the church as a self-concerned community of salvation—an end in itself. This has led to a clear separation between its own church life and its calling to mission. Whenever interest in mission did arise, it often was carried out by Christians on the fringes, outside the structures of the church. In Catholicism, there are the missionary orders. In Protestantism, there are the mission agencies.

This dichotomy between the church and its mission has become even more pronounced among the established Protestant groups in Christendom than in their Catholic counterparts. The church has existed without mission, and mission has been carried on outside the church, resulting in the impoverishment of the church and the deformation of mission. The church's calling to share salvation has been betrayed, its practice of mission has withered, and its power to transform has been seriously compromised.

In the Bible, the people of God originated out of their calling to serve God's mission in the world. God's people occupied a fundamental place in the divine strategy to restore humanity. The church is not only an instrument for proclaiming the kingdom of God. It is also a visible and concrete demonstration of that kingdom. The church is God's "experimental plot," planted in the midst of human history and pointing to the ultimate "universal restoration" (Acts 3:21). In its mission the messianic community, like its Lord, finds true life in willingness to lay down its life for others. "Those who find their life will lose it, and those who lose their life for my sake will find it" (Matt. 10:39).

The church, by the very nature of its calling, must be in mission. Here is the thesis of this book. The church is the human community that experiences and communicates the saving intention of God. Often this vital sense of identity, inspired by the biblical images, is missing; then the church's vision dries up, its missional activity is deformed, and it falls short of following God's saving purpose for all creation.

The Bible employs a rich variety of metaphors that illumine our understanding of the identity and the mission of the church. Images can communicate a vision with power. They reflect the sense of identity which characterized the early Christian communities. Images also inspire the church and challenge it to live up to its real reason for being. The images we use reflect what we are; they also largely determine what we will become.

The chapters that follow contain theological and historical

studies of twelve biblical images of the church. These images have been chosen to represent the wide range of metaphors for God's people that appear in the Bible. They include pilgrimage images, new-order images, popular images of peoplehood, and images of the church as a community of transformation.

This project was brewing in the early 1980s, during a period of ministry among a network of radical Christian communities in Spain. The images chosen for study include metaphors that these Christian communities found to be especially useful in their search for more true evangelical expressions of church life and mission. In the years that followed, most of the research and writing was done at the Centro Menonita de Estudios Biblicos in Montevideo, Uruguay. Many of the themes were shared with students at the Center.

Finally, in the mid 1990s the project has come to fruition, thanks to an invitation by the Seminario Anabautista Latino-americano to teach a course in ecclesiology. This provided the opportunity to share with brothers and sisters in Central America, where social conditions are often like those in the early church. Their enthusiastic response encouraged me to see the project through to completion. These images especially inspired the imagination of the indigenous believers from the Panamanian Darien. Their worldview is notably more like the biblical view than the traditional understanding dominant in modern Western Christendom.

The main part of this book is made up of biblical studies interpreting the images, not only in their literary context but also in their sociohistorical contexts in ancient Israel and in the messianic communities of the first century. Focused in this light, the images are quite relevant for understanding and projecting the life and mission of the church in our time, especially where Christians live and witness in contexts similar to those experienced by the early church.

The poem that follows was written by the Guatemalan poetess, Julia Esquivel. Due to her deep Christian convictions and her prophetic commitment to the cause of Christ and his kingdom in her native land, Doña Julia was forced to live in exile for almost a decade. This poem offers a notable example of the power of images to communicate a vision, call us to reflection, awaken our imagination, and inspire us to action. Her metaphors and images communicate with extraordinary power; mere prose, depending largely on rational explanation and logic, often lacks vigor to inspire and transform.

THE CHURCH

Pure virgin
waiting for her spouse,
vigilant and anxious
sealed fountain
and vigilant heart.
Beautiful as the moon.

Prostitute
surrendered to her lovers
She, from whose mouth
the One who is madly in love with her
will perpetually remove
the name of Baal.

Virgin, prostitute
very deep within us
making the option with Jesus, or against Him
in our relations with the poor.

—Julia Esquivel, *The Certainty of Spring*
(Washington, D.C.: EPECA, 1993)

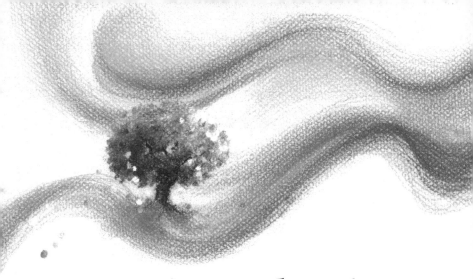

Introduction

1

Images of the Church in Christendom

The Bible nowhere gives us a concise, dictionary-style definition of the church. Instead, it paints a series of complementary images of the people of God. "The people of God" is one of the principal metaphors for the church in the NT (New Testament).

Paul Minear, in his well-known *Images of the Church in the New Testament* (see bibliography), has identified nearly a hundred images which clarify the essential identity and role of the church. Images are powerful vehicles for carrying a vision. They can reflect the self-understanding of the church as it is. In addition, they challenge God's people to become what they are called to be. The images which the church uses for its self-understanding will largely determine what the church will actually become.

Rather than merely using prosaic language, the NT is full of pictures, analogies, and images. Furthermore, NT use of imagery is solidly rooted in salvation history. These writers consistently reach back into the OT (Old Testament) for images to communicate the meaning of the life and mission of the church. Practically all of the NT images of the church are anticipated in one way or another in the OT story.

Metaphorical language can communicate more powerfully and imaginatively than abstract language. This is true of the images with which the apostolic writers proclaimed the church's basic identity and role. Images serve to communicate the church's self-understanding; they are also powerful forces for creating an authentic sense of identity and mission. These images are rooted in specific experiences of salvation history. When authentic experience fades, the images tend to lose their meaning and become abstract. However, images need to be understood in their formative settings, in their social and religious contexts of origin. Then they are a powerful resource for calling God's people back to their roots in God's saving intention for his people and for all humanity.

In its history of nearly two thousand years, the post-NT church has often failed to perceive its identity as the original Christian community saw itself. In using NT images, the church has frequently given them unbiblical twists to carry its deformed self-understanding.

As early as the third century, the church was facing problems arising out of internal disciplinary practices. Leaders compared the church to the ark of Noah, with unclean as well as clean animals (Gen. 6–8). Such a misuse of the biblical image led the church to accept unholiness in the lives of its members. This was notably different from the NT vision of a church of holy people, "a holy nation" (1 Pet. 2:9).

In the fourth century, problems arose out of the Constantinian detour. The church ceased to be a persecuted minority; it came to be tolerated in the Roman empire and even became popular. Hence, the church saw itself like a field in which weeds and wheat are left to grow together until the end of the age

(Matt. 13:24-30, 36-43). Here again, the image tended to create a church quite different from the apostolic community, which understood that "the field is the world" rather than the church (13:38).

Sadly, the Christian church has a history of twisting biblical images out of their settings and primary intentions. These images have been recast to serve as vehicles of the church's distorted self-understanding. Instead, they should be pictures of what, by God's grace, the church can become.

However, there is a far greater problem. The church often draws the controlling images of its self-understanding from secular society rather than from the NT. Even so, the church has generally continued to articulate its vision of self-identity and role with the traditional images. But those images have been wrenched out of their context and twisted from their primary intention.

One of the results of the fourth-century Constantinian shift is that the church began to draw its models from the Roman empire. In a gradual and largely unconscious process, changes were instituted until the church's hierarchy began to look much like the bureaucracy of the Roman government. The church's chief ministers came to be called "princes of the church." The bishop of Rome became a serious competitor of the Roman emperor, imitating his secular power and prestige. The use of the empire image for the church's self-identity has inflicted a blow to the church from which it has never fully recovered.

In the Middle Ages, the church adopted feudal models for its self-understanding. After all, in the eleventh century the church controlled more than a third of all the land in Germany. So the church naturally thought of itself in feudal terms. The church's ministers became feudal lords, and the church blended into a feudal society, reflecting its ethics and practices.

During this period Anselm developed the penal-satisfaction theory for understanding the atonement. This theory was based on a feudal view which rated the enormity of each sin according to the rank of the person against whom it was committed. Satisfaction was deemed necessary to requite the offended honor of God. Anselm's influence still continues today. In parts of Latin America, the Christian church is emerging from a feudal type of social structure. The church's self-understanding still suffers the results of this feudal image of the atonement.

The great century of Protestant missionary activity was also the century of imperial expansion. The predominantly Protestant powers of the northern hemisphere ruled throughout what has since come to be called the third world. Not unexpectedly, the imperial model has colored the church's self-understanding of its nature as well as its mission.

The civilizing role of the church seemed to be a legitimate and essential part of its mission. To civilize is literally to build cities. But in the Bible, that is a characteristic of Babel rather than of Abraham and his spiritual descendants (Gen. 11–12). In the biblical vision, God will build the eschatological city of the new creation, the new Jerusalem (Rev. 21–22).

However, in keeping with the rather secular model of the period, the church in its own way became an ecclesiastical empire builder. The mission agencies emerging at that time became the church's counterparts of the foreign office. Interchurch relationships were maternal or even bluntly colonial. Those located in the metropolis ("the mother city-state") perceived overseas bodies as daughter churches. This imperial image has unconsciously contributed in a major way to the church's self-identity in the northern hemisphere as well. In the last century and a half, the church has often treated the missionary enterprise as a way to dominate others. In some circles this vision persists.

During the colonial period in North America, churches borrowed from the democratic model of social organization. That image has largely shaped their self-understanding. The church took the form of a voluntary society, with membership based on a social contract. The organizational elements which the church borrowed from the democratic model included town-meeting ways of making decisions, mediating differences, balancing powers, having representatives, voting, electing leaders, raising money, and preserving freedoms. In some circles Protestantism is still viewed as a democratic way of being the church.

More recently the corporate business model has become a prominent image for the church's self-understanding in North America. Management techniques have slowly but surely left their marks on church administration. The congregation's performance is evaluated in commercial terms of gain or loss. The church program is run with one eye on competition (the congregation down the street) and the other eye on keeping customers (its own members) satisfied.

Evangelistic strategies and techniques are strikingly similar to those modeled by commercial sales campaigns. Popular demand largely determines how the gospel is packaged and dispensed. According to this model, the church's ministries are no longer charismatic, as shown in the NT (1 Cor. 12–14; et al.). Back then the church was perceived as God's gifted community; now the church is composed of management and staff, essential elements in the operation of God's enterprise.

The images with which the church understands its identity and role are mostly drawn from surrounding society rather than from the church's rootage in true biblical tradition. These examples of images (given above) have largely determined the church's self-understanding during its history. In addition, we can considerably expand the list of images which currently stir the church's imagination.

Some churches' chief claim to uniqueness is their amiable nature ("the friendliest church in town") and their relaxing and inspiring atmosphere ("good people to know"). They depend on a country-club model for their identity and role. The chief energy of many churches is directed toward making an impact on the viewer, either in person or through electronic media. They rely on an image drawn from the entertainment industry.

Various congregations receive their imagination from therapy groups of one type or another. In other churches formal Bible study is so prominent that it almost becomes an end in itself. They draw their model from the educational field. Some churches, if one judges from their programs, see themselves largely as supermarkets or cafeterias where essential goods can be picked up at low cost. Still others have perceived their life and mission in terms of a saving army, and more recently as Christian crusades, campaigns, or liberation movements.

Both the biblical record and Christian history remind us that the church needs images for understanding its identity and role. However, the church's story also stands as an eloquent reminder of the constant temptation to draw such images from secular culture. The church is also beguiled into twisting the meaning of biblical images to fit more easily into the actual forms which the life and mission of the church has taken. In both instances the images which the church has adopted have simply confirmed it in a deformed and unfaithful life and mission.

If the church is to recover the integrity of its life and mission, it must have adequate images to capture and inspire its imagination. Models drawn from secular society have invariably betrayed it into the hands of the enemy. Even biblical images have often failed to reorient the church in apostolic faithfulness. The church has allowed its understanding of those images to be conditioned by the prevailing ethos in which it participates.

Biblical images must be read and interpreted afresh, freed from traditional and current ecclesiastical practices. That new reading comes to us as a gift from the Spirit of God. The images must be grasped in the context of the faith community, committed to obedience. This is the realm in which God's will can be most fully discerned (John 7:17). We need to make a self-conscious attempt to remove those Constantinian grids through which we all, consciously and unconsciously, look at reality in the "Christian" West.

In the Bible the final goal of God's saving intention is the transformation of all creation. The biblical vision calls the people

of God first to live out this new reality in its own midst. The anti- /
social and corrupt systems of society—with coercive violence,
the desire to dominate, and economic greed—cannot be attacked
more decisively than by the formation of a countersociety in its
midst. Simply through its existence, this new society is an effective attack on the old structures for transforming the world. The
church as this new society can work much better than any of the
many brilliantly conceived programs, carried out at no personal
cost (Lohfink: 95; see bibliography).

During its history the church has constantly been tempted to
interpret the NT from the perspective of its own level of conduct. The church has often toned down the obvious meaning of
primitive Christian testimony because it could no longer imagine it possible to take the gospel with such seriousness. This is
a sad commentary on the church's hermeneutics.

In reality, the biblical images of the church can only be radically understood in a church committed to be God's contrast-
society in the world. This calls for interpreting the biblical images with authentic and intentional naiveté. Such unsophisticat-
ed simplicity is characteristic of God's kingdom and its values. It
is essential if we are going to break out of the stranglehold of the
world's inverted system of values.

The following studies of biblical images of the church are
signposts along the way in the church's quest to understand its
true identity and role. The images upon which these studies focus are a sampling drawn from about a hundred images which
the NT community used to articulate its self-understanding. If
we open ourselves to the power of the Holy Spirit, these metaphors of *pilgrimage*, of *the new order*, of *peoplehood*, and of *transformation* can deeply stir our imagination. They will become God's
instruments for our restoration to more authentic life and mission as God's community of transformation.

2

A People in Mission: The Biblical Record

The biblical history of salvation is essentially the story of a people—the people of God who live by faith. It is the story of this community's faith, life, and mission in response to God's salvific initiative. The mission of God's people is deeply rooted in God's saving alternative—in its vocation to holiness as God's contrast-community.

The Call of Abraham

The biblical story begins with creation, a creation which culminates in the formation of a human community bearing God's image. The primitive community is composed of man and woman. But this fleeting glimpse of humanity as God willed it soon fades with the loss of communion with God and his creation. Although sin brings death, the story ends with hope for the future. Human life will continue on the earth (Gen. 3:20).

The drama of the Fall is repeated in the story of Cain and

Abel. But this tragic episode also ends with a note of hope. Cain receives the visible mark of God's grace (Gen. 4:15-16). The story of Noah is a symbol of God's mercy which prevails in the midst of judgment. Finally, in the story of Babel, humankind's lust for power reaches its climax. Ironically, fallen humanity's efforts carry within themselves the seeds of the problem which it seeks to avoid. Those who attempt to build a city and to make a name for themselves, lest they "be scattered abroad upon the face of the whole earth" (Gen. 11:4), have in effect already anticipated their own fate (11:8). Humanity's attempts to dominate end in confusion.

All of the preceding stories which symbolize humanity's rebellion—the Fall, Cain's evil, and the Flood—end with a glimmer of hope. God has not abandoned his original purpose expressed in the creation of human community. However, all hope is missing from the Babel story, and on this negative note the first chapter of salvation history closes.

The story of Abraham's call is set precisely in this context of hopelessness. In reality, the creation of a new people of faith is God's word and act of grace in response to human rebellion. In the call of Abraham, God creates a new saving alternative, a people who bear his name. In the life of the people of God, hope is reestablished for fallen creation.

If we are to understand the biblical meaning of peoplehood and of our mission, we must grasp the creation of this concrete new saving alternative. There is to be a people which reflects God's character and expresses, albeit imperfectly, his salvific intention. We cannot recover a biblical view of mission apart from a radical return to peoplehood as God intended.

> Now the Lord said to Abram, "Go from your country and your kindred and your father's house to the land that I will show you. I will make of you a great nation, and I will bless you, and make your name great, so that you will be a blessing; . . . and in you all of the families of the earth shall be blessed." (Gen. 12:1-3)

The abortive attempt to create human society at Babel was based on the power to dominate, and it ended in confusion. God's answer to this quest is community freely given to those who will obey him in confident faith. This is God's community of blessing to all of humankind. Blessing, according to the biblical vision, includes infinitely more than mere words of well-wishing. God's blessing is conceived as the real communication of his power and life. In early Israel, blessing was viewed as the bearer of material and spiritual well-being. Concretely, God's sovereignty over his people was the realm of blessedness, the sphere in which the wholeness of God's salvation was experienced in the fruitfulness and the abundance of nature, and in social relationships characterized by peace and righteousness.

God's people are his new creation. In the call of Abraham, history begins anew. The people of God is clearly viewed as a new alternative rising up in the midst of humankind. This implies a radical break with the old. The call to Abraham to "go from your country and your kindred and your father's house" points to more than a mere change of geography. It implies the recognition of "the Lord, the God of Israel," in contrast to the "other gods" of the Chaldeans (Josh. 24:2).

A Jewish document from the intertestamental period reports,

These people are descended from the Chaldeans. At one time they lived in Mesopotamia, because they would not follow the gods of their ancestors who were in Chaldea. . . . They had abandoned the ways of their ancestors, and worshiped the God of heaven, the God they had come to know. (Judith 5:6-8)

So the call of Abraham carries both religious and moral dimensions. Ur was a prime center of agricultural, industrial, commercial, and religious achievements in the ancient world. To follow the Lord, the God of Israel, they are called to abandon Ur and its gods for a life of pilgrimage under the guidance of God. In short, it is a call to radical moral and spiritual nonconformity to Chaldean society and its values.

To know the God of Israel is to reorder all of life and its values in accord with his nature. God's call to Abraham is an invitation to become a contrast-society. The identity of God's people arises out of God's grace and providence. This is undoubtedly the point at which the contrast with Babel and its heirs is the sharpest. Confusion will always follow the selfish exercise of power to dominate and to perpetuate this domination. Whenever Israel has this vision of its distinctive identity as God's contrast-society in sharpest focus, then it will most faithfully fulfill its mission to serve for the blessing of all the earth's families.

Exodus-Sinai

The Exodus-Sinai experience in the life of ancient Israel is another point at which the saving purpose of God becomes especially clear. The Lord gives Moses a message for the Israelites:

Now therefore, if you obey my voice and keep my covenant, you shall be my treasured possession out of all the peoples. Indeed, the whole earth is mine, but you shall be for me a priestly kingdom and a holy nation. (Exod. 19:5-6a)

For you are a people holy to the Lord your God; the Lord your God has chosen you out of all the peoples on earth to be his people, his treasured possession. It was not because you were more numerous than any other people that the Lord set his heart on you and chose you—for you were the fewest of all peoples. It was because the Lord loved you and kept the oath that he swore to your ancestors, that the Lord has brought you out with a mighty hand, and redeemed you from the house of slavery, from the hand of Pharaoh king of Egypt. . . . Therefore, observe diligently the commandment—the statutes, and the ordinances—that I am commanding you today. (Deut. 7:6-8, 11)

The distinctive character of the children of Abraham keeps them from simply being absorbed into Egyptian society in spite of their four-hundred-year sojourn in Egypt. The "charismatic principle," characteristic of the ancient Hebrews, enables them to resist assimilation (De Dietrich: 46). They are a people called to live faithfully (as well as survive) by the grace of God. Their character is to bear the stamp of the God they serve. Thus they can be a countersociety, a perpetual stranger and sojourner.

Israel understood that it owed its identity to God's gracious election. Later Israel came to misunderstand this divine election in terms of special status and privilege. Yet as we have already noted in the vocation of Abraham, election is to service—to mission. This is also implied in Exodus 19:5-6 and Deuteronomy 7:6-11. In response to God's redeeming grace, Israel is simply expected to hold fast to the covenant relationship which God has established with his people in order to be God's "possession out of all the peoples."

The biblical term translated "treasured possession" in these passages refers to a portion withdrawn from the whole property and designated as a special donation (De Dietrich: 54). This accounts for the accompanying clause, "indeed, the whole earth is mine" (Exod. 19:5c). Israel is chosen as God's special possession, not by its own merits but in relation to God's saving intention for all nations. Israel's identity hinges on the fact that it is chosen from among all peoples to be different from the nations so it can be a faithful sign of God's saving intention for all the nations.

The holiness which characterizes Israel gives them no grounds for pride. It is, rather, the concrete spiritual and social shape of their vocation. Insofar as Israel, due to its relationship to God, is different from the nations,[1] it will be an effective sign of God's purpose for all humanity. It is not simply that at Sinai God set his people apart. It is probably more correct to say that through the covenant God establishes the identity of his people. As Israel confesses in its creed, God makes a people of those who were no people (Deut. 26:5-9; cf. Hos. 2:23). This people of

God stands in marked contrast to the "nations."

These passages underscore the fact that Israel's conduct must correspond to the character and action of Yahweh, who has chosen Israel from among the nations and saved it from Egypt. To be God's holy people is to adhere to a concrete social order which distinguishes it from all other nations. Israel's holiness rests essentially on two grounds. First, it is due to the electing love of God. Second, Israel's concrete holiness depends on whether it really lives according to the social order which has come to it as a gift of God's covenant grace. This is a social order standing in sharp contrast to those which characterize all other nations. "You shall be holy to me; for I the Lord am holy, and I have separated you from the other peoples to be mine" (Lev. 20:26).

The Monarchy

Following the occupation of the land of promise and its distribution among the families of Israel, the book of Joshua closes with the renewal of the Mosaic covenant at Shechem. Two things stand out in this passage. The first is the strong emphasis on the salvific initiative of God on behalf of his people. God called Abraham. God liberated Israel from Egyptian bondage. And God gave his people a land.

Second, although the covenant is Yahweh's gift to this people, they can freely choose to make it theirs, committing themselves to obedience (Josh. 24:15, 22). The kind of covenant-renewal ceremony we find described in Joshua 24 was probably an essential element in Israel's missionary witness among other tribes inhabiting the land. Covenant renewal became the formal structure through which new peoples were incorporated into the people of God. Some believe that this rite may have become an annual event in Israel (Bright: 149-150, 164-165).

However, this vision of an Israel different from the nations—a contrast-society serving as a sign to the nations—was not to endure for long. Israel's request for a king "like other nations" is clearly a step of unfaithfulness and counted as a rejection of God's provident rule. There is a transition from peoplehood under the rule of God with charismatic leadership (as seen in the judges and prophets) to kingship. This is a change of far-reaching consequences.[2] There is pathos in the repeated phrase, "appoint for us, then, a king to govern us, like other nations . . . that we also may be like other nations" (1 Sam. 8:5, 20). This pathos is especially striking because the very reason for Israel's existence, rooted, as it is, in the call of Abraham and the Exodus-Sinai experience, is its uniqueness, precisely in order to be a blessing to the nations. Even though the monarchy is established, reforming elements in Israel try valiantly to make kingship in Israel different (Deut. 17:14-20).

David personally illustrates the pathos and contradictions of kingship in Israel. His checkered career is a mixture of virtue and human weakness. However, King David initiates Israel into the politics of the nations. From the perspective of the Abrahamic and Sinaitic covenants, the history of the monarchy is a sad story. Solomon's reign is a prime example of what kings in Israel should not be (cf. Deut. 17:14-20). In asking for a king "like other nations," God's people have actually become like the nations around them.

Just as Samuel warned, the kings of God's people become warlords with imperial dreams. They use their subjects for military purposes and tax them almost beyond endurance to support royal programs. Israelite kings become the oppressors more often than the shepherds of their people (1 Sam. 8:10-18). The violence and oppression which God's people experienced before the Exodus return to haunt them under the monarchy. And the peace and justice which the Sinai covenant assures to God's people is shattered by human greed and selfish power-grabbing. Israel has, indeed, become like all the nations. There is no longer a difference which can contribute to the blessing of the other families of the earth.

The Prophetic Vision

This is the scenario within which the great prophets of Israel appear. They bring God's message to a people who have long since ceased to be a contrast-society in the midst of the nations; they warn of impending judgment. But they also share a vision of hope beyond judgment—a hope based upon restoration of God's reign of righteousness and peace. Picking up the theme of the ancient promise to Abraham, the prophets perceive the blessing of God's righteous reign reaching to all humanity through the faithfulness of his restored people. It is a vision of "the mountain of the Lord's house" being established in a new and highly visible way among the peoples of the earth and the nations being attracted by the gracious covenant relationships of righteousness, peace, and salvation which characterize God's people.

> In days to come
> > the mountain of the Lord's house
> shall be established as the highest of the mountains,
> > and shall be raised up above the hills.
> Peoples shall stream to it,
> > and many nations shall come and say:
> "Come, let us go up to the mountain of the Lord,
> > to the house of the God of Jacob;
> that he may teach us his ways
> > and that we may walk in his paths."
> For out of Zion shall go forth instruction,
> > and the word of the Lord from Jerusalem.
> He shall judge between many peoples,
> > and shall arbitrate between strong nations far away;
> they shall beat their swords into plowshares,
> > and their spears into pruning hooks;
> nation shall not lift up sword against nation,
> > neither shall they learn war any more;
> but they shall all sit under their own vines
> > and under their own fig trees,

and no one shall make them afraid;
for the mouth of the Lord of hosts has spoken.
(Mic. 4:1-4; cf. Isa. 2:1-4; Zech. 8:20, 22).

According to his vision, swords will be forged into plow-shares and spears into pruning hooks. The instruments of destruction will be converted into resources placed at the service of humanity's needs. Warfare will be renounced as a means for solving interpersonal and international conflicts. God himself will be the arbiter of differences and will work through his "servant, . . . [who] will faithfully bring forth justice . . . in the earth" (Isa. 42:1-4). In a kind of sabbatical or jubilee restoration, "they shall all sit under their own vines and under their own fig trees, and no one shall make them afraid" (Mic. 4:4). This freedom from fear will become reality in the context of the new social structure of the messianic people of God drawn from all peoples and nations of the earth.

Pictured here is the restoration of a people who walk in the paths of the Lord, among whom the provisions of God's gracious covenant are concretely realized. They will become the magnet which attracts the peoples of the earth. The essential vision of a holy people is anticipated in Abraham's call to absolute dependence on God for both existence and survival, and in the Exodus-Sinai experience calling for social relationships determined by covenant values of righteousness and peace. These features also characterize the prophetic vision of God's restored people. God's people are again perceived as a true contrast-society whose very character communicates divine blessing to others.

Jesus' Vision

The messianic movement initiated by Jesus cannot be understood apart from the OT vision of God's people as a contrast-society. Jesus' kingdom preaching, teaching, and activity all point toward the restoration of God's people. This restoration is for the people to carry out in a definitive way God's plan for a holy people in the midst of the nations. The messianic mission is aimed at the establishment of the eschatological people of God in which the social order of the reign of God will be lived. Jesus perceives the messianic community in terms of the prophetic vision of the "Lord's house . . . established as the highest of the mountains." He concretely describes this new people of God as "the light of the world. A city built on a hill . . . that [others] may see your good works and give glory to your Father in heaven" (Matt. 5:14-16).

This is the context in which we must understand Jesus' revolutionary calls for his followers to absolutely renounce violence (Matt. 5:39-48) and coercive domination (Mark 10:42-45). They are to practice nonresistant love toward violent people and be shaped by a vision of authority which derives entirely from service. This perspective of a contrast-community stands in sharp contrast to secular societies, which are marked by the will to coerce and to exercise control over others. Precisely this kind of nonresistant love can communicate most powerfully its missionary witness to a God who loves his enemies and seeks to save them (Matt. 5:3, 9, 16, 44-48).

In light of this OT background, the petition in Jesus' prayer, "Hallowed be your name," expresses the hope that God will restore a people truly different in holiness (Matt. 6:9). It implies the restoration of the true people of God so that his reign may shine forth and his name may stand in all of its glory before all people (cf. Ezek. 20:41, 44; 36:22-24; Lev. 20:26; Deut. 7:6-11; Lohfink: 14-17, 124).

Jesus speaks about kingdom righteousness (Matt. 5) and confidence in the providence of God (Matt. 6:19-33). Such teachings presuppose the contrast-community envisioned in the call of Abraham and in God's gracious Sinai covenant. They are also built on the sabbatical and jubilee provisions. These OT promises all take on concrete form in the re-creation of the people of God. In this messianic event, God's reign is being reestablished. A new and different people of God is appearing in the midst of the nations, a people in which God's glory shines forth for the blessing of all peoples (Mic. 4:1-4; Matt. 5:14-16).

The concrete social form of the messianic community gathered by Jesus is already anticipated in the OT vision of God's people. They are to be a contrast-society set in the midst of the nations as a sign of God's saving purpose for all peoples. Jesus' great commission is based on this restored messianic community.

The Apostolic Community

The restored messianic community is the vision which determines the self-understanding of the apostolic communities in the NT. They see themselves essentially in contrast to contemporary Judaism as well as to paganism. This is the context of their life and mission.

The "once and now" pattern has been proposed as one of the categories for the church's self-understanding as a contrast-society in the midst of the rest of society (Lohfink: 125). This category is especially common in the NT epistles.[3] An example of this vision appears in Ephesians: "For *once* you were darkness, but *now* in the Lord you are light. Live as children of light" (Eph. 5:8). Darkness and light are figures for the two contrasting spheres—life as pagans, and life in the church. "In the Lord" or "in Christ" are not references to a purely mystical or spiritualized sphere; instead, they mean life within the realm of Christ's rule, the church.

The two contrasting spheres are sometimes described by long catalogues of vices and virtues (cf. Col. 3:8-14), which need not be understood primarily in terms of an individualistic ethic. Rather, they describe two contrasting social orders. Pagan society as a whole has a long list of insoluble problems; in contrast, God's new community supersedes old lines of social separation (Col. 3:10-11).

The contrast between the two humanities—the old and the

new—is another image used to underscore the essential nature of the church as God's substantially different countersociety (Eph. 2:15; 4:24; Col. 3:9-11). The image of the new creation communicates the same reality (2 Cor. 5:17; et al.). The contrast between the "present evil age" (Gal. 1:4) and "the age to come" (Heb. 6:5; cf. Eph. 2:7) is not merely a reference to salvation in a distant future. Whoever participates in the realm of Christ's rule is delivered from the present evil age. The Christian community realizes that it needs no longer to live in the bondage of evil nor according to the false structures of pagan society.

Jesus' prayer in John 17 reflects the contrast-society vision of God's people and their mission, which we have already noted in the OT. Jesus says about his followers, "They do not belong to the world, just as I do not belong to the world" (John 17:16). He surely implies that with himself something completely new has entered history, something which human society cannot produce on its own. Jesus Christ is uniquely the one in whom the holiness and glory of the Father shine forth in the world. He sanctifies his community so it can live concretely in his holiness and be sharply distinguished from the rest of society. The contrast-society lives in the midst of societies where the deceitfulness of evil has perpetuated degrading social forms. Christ's community serves to make this deception manifest and therefore becomes the object of the world's persecution (John 15:18-20).

The sanctification of the disciples of Jesus is described in this context in which the distance between the disciple-community and the world is set forth (John 17:17, 19). This is a prime example of the way in which the basic lines of the OT vision of the nature of God's contrast-society are continued in the NT. The sanctification of the messianic community is the biblical way of formulating the concept of the people of God as a divine contrast-society in the world.

Jesus held this OT background to be so fundamental for determining the character and describing the mission of the messianic community. It also gives meaning to one of the major self-designations which early Christians applied to themselves, "the saints." Originally the term appears to have been the self-designation of the earliest community in Jerusalem (cf. Rom. 15:25-26, 31; 1 Cor. 16:1; 2 Cor. 8:4; 9:1, 12). Later it was adopted by all communities, including those of predominantly Gentile origin. And for Paul, "saints" was a synonym for "church."[4] The term continued to be used as a real self-designation for Christians until the time of the Montanist crisis around the middle of the second century (Lohfink: 130).

The early church understood itself to be the holy people of God's own possession, a people whose pattern of life differed essentially from that of the rest of the world. This is the self-consciousness which stands behind 1 Peter 2:9-10.

> You are a chosen race, a royal priesthood, a holy nation, God's own people, in order that you may proclaim the mighty acts of him who called you out of darkness into his marvelous light.
> Once you were not a people,
>   but now you are God's people;
> once you had not received mercy,
>   but now you have received mercy.

This text also shows how vital the OT vision is for the early church's self-understanding (cf. Exod. 19:6). It shows clearly that the primary concern in the biblical vision is not merely the private holiness of individuals, important as this may be. The fundamental thrust of the passage is that the people of God (as a people) give witness to his saving purpose for all humanity. The unambiguous identity of the early church is the prime ingredient in the fulfillment of its mission. This contrast-society is both the context in which God's mercy is experienced and the instrument of God's mission to the peoples of the earth.

3

Church and Mission: The Constantinian Legacy

This vision of the identity and mission of the people of God is rooted in the very beginnings of their peoplehood in Abraham and the Exodus and again in the Messiah himself. Yet it faded once more, just as it had under the monarchy in Israel's history. The church's self-understanding as God's contrast-society and the idea of being God's sign among the nations undoubtedly faded gradually, especially from about the middle of the second century onward. However, the so-called "Constantinian turn" marks a profound break between what the primitive messianic community had been and what the Christian church was to become in relation to its basic sense of identity and role.

The Constantinian turn was, to a certain degree, already anticipated in ancient Israel's clamor for "a king to govern us, like

other nations" (1 Sam. 8:5). According to the biblical view, the
people of God mean something different from the national political structure. This, however, does not mean that peoplehood
under God is a purely spiritual and invisible reality. Israel is chosen by God to be his holy people; this calls for integrity of life in
all its spiritual and social dimensions. But with the advent of the
monarchy, this essential identity of the people of God tended to
become confused with national political structures in Israel. The
essentially charismatic nature of the life of God's people (deriv-
ing directly from the gifts of God's grace) was relegated to the
religious sphere of Israel's life. The functions of prophets as well
as priests were subordinated to the monarchy.

David was a prototype not only of the expected Messiah. He
consolidated political power in Israel and organized the "religious" aspects of Israel's life in the interests of the common welfare in Israel; in so doing, he also anticipated Constantine. This is
the context in which the prophets of Israel gather up the ancient
Abrahamic and Sinaitic vision of God's people as a contrast-
society for the blessing of the nations. They offer that vision as
their message of hope for the coming era of the messianic restoration of God's righteous reign.

The Constantinian turn is not limited to the period of the
reign of the Roman emperor Constantine the Great (306-337).
The process began long before Constantine became emperor
and continued long after. The Montanist crisis arose shortly after
the middle of the second century. In it we note signs that the
church no longer understood itself as essentially God's missionary community, his contrast-society set in the midst of the people of the earth, witnessing to his mighty acts. The church's authority no longer depended on the vital presence of the Spirit of
Christ in its midst, nor on the authority of its life in the world. In
its struggle with heterodoxy, the church gradually came to institutionalize its authority in the form of episcopacy, creed, and
canon. To be God's people now was coming to mean submission
to the bishop of Rome (and to other bishops who were in com-

munion with him), to subscribe to the contents of the Apostles' Creed, and to recognize authority only in those books of the NT which were generally coming to be recognized as canonical.[1]

In this Constantinian shift, the church moved in a relatively short time from its status as a persecuted minority to a majority which persecuted the dissidents within its ranks. Imperial edicts issued in 311 and 313 granted toleration to the Christian church in its life and worship and restored places of worship which had been confiscated in earlier persecutions (Bettenson: 15-16).

In 313 the Christian clergy were completely freed from public duties to dedicate themselves exclusively to their religious functions, "for it seems that when they render the greatest homage to Divinity, then the greatest benefits befall the commonwealth" (Bettenson: 17-18). Sunday was officially declared to be a day of rest in all cities of the empire in 321 (Bettenson: 18-19; Eusebius 10.7). Finally, edicts of Theodosius in 380 and 381 established the orthodoxy of Catholic Christians in communion with the bishops of Rome and Alexandria, forbidding all other expressions of faith (Bettenson: 22).

This shift represents a really fundamental change in the church's understanding of its self-identity and role. Some of these changes become especially noticeable in the writings of Augustine (354-430), who lived in the period immediately following Constantine. In his *City of God,* Augustine retained the language of the contrast vision of the people of God which we have noted in both Testaments as well as in the earliest centuries of the Christian church.

Augustine says the city of God is created from above, while the earthly city creates its own gods (18.54). In the city of God, true love reigns as it seeks the welfare of others; self-love dominates the earthly city (14.13, 28). The city of God is characterized by true peace; the earthly city is marked by conflict and warfare, or at best, the fragile peace established by war (15.4, 17). The city of God is characterized by humility, mutuality, and obedience (14.28); the earthly city lusts after domination (1; 4.6; 14.28).

However, Augustine did not identify the city of God with the visible community of the Messiah, the pilgrim church on earth, which in the NT is contrasted with non-Christian society. For purposes of contrast, Augustine held that the true church is the heavenly and eschatological city of God. But meanwhile the city of God and the earthly city are so irresolvably mixed that the pilgrim church cannot really be contrasted with pagan society. The city of the saints is heavenly. Although they are citizens on earth, they are essentially aliens awaiting the future coming of the kingdom (15.1). So the real location of the city of God is in a transcendent realm.

Augustine's vision is formally similar to the one expressed in Philippians 3:20-21. Yet the existence of a concrete contrast-society, so fundamental in the biblical experience, is notably absent from his view. Rather than thinking the gathering of a people of God as a community of witness, Augustine views the process as a transcendent gathering of those who are rescued from this world for life in the next (2.18).

Augustine's vision of the church is a mixed multitude in which evil and good are intermingled in confusion. Key images in the NT served for the church's self-understanding as God's apostolic contrast-community in the midst of the world. Now Augustine applied them to the people of God in the world to come (18.49).[2] The inevitable effects of the Constantinian shift on the church resulted in turning it away from the biblical vision of God's people as his missionary community. No longer was it a contrast-society witnessing faithfully to God's saving purpose for all humanity. In Augustine, the realization of this vision is postponed into the future. The church's mission is reduced to preparing individuals for participation in that future.

Only after the Constantinian turn did the church begin to project into the future the vision of messianic peace which the pre-exilic prophets had proclaimed (Isa. 2:1-4; Mic. 4:1-4). Justin Martyr (c. 150) had rejected both the futuristic and the individualistic alternatives which the church later came to adopt. He in-

sisted that the vision was being fulfilled concretely in the life of
the Christian community of his own time. Believers had renounced all instruments of warfare and were beating swords
into plowshares and spears into tools for the cultivation of the
land (*Dialogue* 110).

As the Constantinian shift made itself increasingly felt, the
church's sense of holiness was gradually transformed. *Saints* had
once been the self-designation of all Christians and especially of
the community of the people of God itself. Now it became a term
to describe representative individuals in the church—martyrs,
ascetics, and priests. The NT's call to holiness was not entirely
overlooked. It was simply narrowed consistently to refer to the
private holiness of individual Christians or to particular groups
such as priests or the religious orders. Thus the deformed and
selective memory of the church allowed it to forget the really
fundamental biblical vision of the people of God as a holy nation, a concrete community of contrast in the midst of all other
peoples.

This innovation in the understanding of holiness was also a
part of the Augustinian heritage. In light of the nature of the
church which emerged from the Constantinian shift, Augustine
interpreted the parable of the wheat and the weeds as applying
to the church. But Jesus and the early church had said the field
with wheat and weeds is the world (Matt. 13:38). In Augustine's
view, the church is holy, not because of the effective holiness of
its members, but because it is destined to be perfected in holiness at the end of time (Gonzalez: 49).[3] This contradicts the biblical view of God's people with holiness which makes them an
effective sign of God's saving purpose within history.

Another element of this Augustinian heritage is the individualism which has plagued the church throughout its history. That
individualism has all but obscured the biblical vision of the
church and its role in much of Protestantism. This is illustrated
in Augustine's dialogue with Reason, following what certainly
must be one of the most eloquent prayers of the ancient church.

Augustine: I have made my prayer to God.
Reason: What then do you wish now?
Augustine: All that I have mentioned in my prayer.
Reason: Briefly summarize it.
Augustine: I wish to know God and the soul.
Reason: Nothing more?
Augustine: Nothing whatever. (*Soliloquies* 2.7)

This highly individualized mode of spirituality, so foreign to the biblical world of thought and practice, has become one of the hallmarks of Constantinian Christianity.

Such individualization is an almost inevitable consequence of viewing the reign of God as essentially transcendent. The loss of the biblical vision of God's people as a contrast-community has not been limited to Roman Catholicism. It has been equally characteristic of Constantinian Protestantism.

Adolph Harnack was one of the principal exponents of modern liberalism of the late-nineteenth and early-twentieth centuries. He also described the essence of Christianity as an individual and internal reality which is essentially a matter "of God and the soul, of the soul and its God" (Lohfink: 2). The church, for Harnack, was essentially invisible since it "remained for him a spiritual community, a society within human hearts (*societas in cordibus*), which could not be identified with any of the concrete churches of his day (Lohfink: 3).

Furthermore, the concrete forms which holiness takes in the Christian community were transferred to the inner realm of "the right intention of the individual" (Lohfink: 2). Therefore, what the church no longer is in fact (due to the Constantinian shift) it becomes by virtue of the good intentions of its members. This view decisively undercuts the biblical vision of a contrast-people whose life is concretely formed by the values of God's covenant righteousness.

This individualistic vision of the church and salvation characterized liberal theology of the period. However, it has by no means been limited to liberalism. It is ironic that this view has since come to characterize much of conservative evangelical thought and practice, shaping both the life and mission of the church. These fruits of Constantinianism (implicit, as well as real) continue to determine the church's view of salvation, the church's ministries, the images upon which we draw for the church's self-understanding, and the forms which the church's life and mission take.

Thus evangelistic strategies are oriented by the implicit Constantinianism which continues to characterize large sectors of modern Protestantism. With appeals to biblical language, evangelists perpetuate the otherworldly and individualistic elements of the Augustinian heritage. In reality, these appeals bypass the biblical paradigm of the people of God as a witnessing contrast-community.

Perhaps the image which most aptly describes the mentality and the evangelistic practices of much of modern Christianity is that of the giant supermarket in which "everyone moves around with a cart and picks out what he likes and needs" (Lohfink: 4). In this context, the message and practices of the church are carefully packaged and priced to fit the demands of the consumers. Such a church provides for the needs of individuals conveniently and economically, allowing them to remain comfortable in their anonymity, which in the biblical vision means being lost.

The Church in Mission

The establishment of the monarchy in Israel frustrated the primitive biblical intention of a distinctive people which would serve as God's instrument of blessing to all humankind. So also the Constantinian turn in the fourth century cut short the NT vision of the new people of God as an apostolic contrast-society in the midst of the world. Israel's prophets picked up the saving vision which the monarchy had rendered ineffective and restated it as their message of hope for the future. That future was initially realized in the advent of the Messiah and the emergence of a new messianic community of witness. As we have seen, howev-

er, this fresh vision of peoplehood and mission was later nulli-
fied again in the Constantinian synthesis of church and society.

In Judaism, the heritage of the monarchy led to an effective
separation of holy peoplehood and missionary activity. This, at
least in part, was the situation which Jesus denounced so ener-
getically (Matt. 23:13-15). With the coming of the Constantinian
shift, the life of the church was also effectively separated from its
mission. Rather than being a "city set on a hill," the church became an ark of salvation and a field filled with wheat and weeds,
awaiting the consummation of all things.

Mission was no longer perceived as the essential role of a
charismatic contrast-society. Instead, it became the task of soli-
tary monks and the religious orders who exercised the apostolic
function in place of the church. Only within the sectarian
groups, such as the Waldensians of the eleventh and twelfth centuries and the sixteenth-century Anabaptists, do we find those
who broke the grip of Constantinianism and were able to join
church and mission with an integrity similar to that which
marked the messianic community of the NT.

With the advent of Constantinian Protestantism, church life
remained divorced from mission. Within Protestantism there
was practically no sense of mission. Furthermore, in rejecting
monasticism, Protestants had eliminated the missionary orders
in their midst. This was the vacuum in Protestantism which Pietism sought to fill about a century and a half later. But the new
missionary structures of Pietism, like the missionary orders
within Roman Catholicism, were set up on the fringes of the
church, thus effectively perpetuating the Constantinian separation of church and mission.

Although the formal demise of Constantinianism is generally
recognized, the ecclesiological and missiological aspects of its
heritage have not disappeared. Until this very day, orthodox
Christians hold the church to be fully God's holy people. Yet
they are certainly not anywhere near the contrast-society of witness to God's saving glory, envisioned in both OT and NT. On

the other hand, mission continues to be carried out by para-church or independent agencies and individuals with apparently no felt need for the holy contrast-community of witness for which all the peoples of the earth yearn.

The thesis of this book is that the church can be authentically the church according to the biblical vision only as it indeed becomes God's contrast-society of witness. Likewise, mission which is effective witness to the restoration of God's saving rule over humankind can be carried out biblically only as it is rooted in God's contrast-community. If we are to grasp anew this biblical vision, we need to overcome the tragic results of the monarchical and Constantinian shifts, which we have noted. We can do this in a radical return to the biblical images of God's contrast-community—the church in mission.

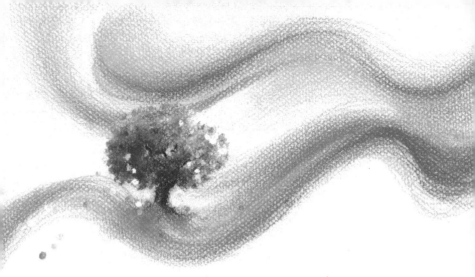

Biblical Images of the Church in Mission

Pilgrimage Images

4

The Way

If we take Luke's historical and theological reporting serious-ly, "the Way" must have been one of the Christian community's earliest self-designations. In the book of Acts are several in-stances where the term "way" (*hodos*) is used in an absolute sense as a designation for the Christian community (9:2; 18:25-26 ["of the Lord," "of God"]; 19:9, 23; 22:4; 24:14, 22). The New Revised Standard Version consistently translates the term as "the Way" or "this Way."

However, the significance of the Way as an image for the ear-ly church's self-understanding of its nature and mission is by no means limited to these explicit references. In the NT there is a broad base of figurative references to the Way which illuminate the meaning of the term as a metaphor used in the primitive church's self-understanding.

All four of the Gospels begin with a reference to Isaiah 40:3: "A voice cries: 'In the wilderness prepare the *way* of the Lord, make straight in the desert a highway for our God' " (cf. Matt. 3:3; 11:10; Mark 1:2-3; Luke 1:76; 3:4-5; 7:27; John 1:23; empha-sis added). In every case the Gospel writers understand the voice to be that of John the Baptist, who has come to prepare the way for the Messiah and the salvation which he is bringing.

A wide variety of texts from all strands of the NT tradition—

from Matthew to Revelation—refer to Jesus' messianic salvation as "the way of God," "the way of peace," "the way of salvation," "the right way."[1]

In the synoptic Gospels, "the way to Jerusalem" furnishes the primary setting for instructing the disciples in Jesus' understanding of the role of vicarious suffering and servanthood in his own messianic mission as well as in that of his disciples. Incidentally, in the book of Acts "on the way" is also where Saul the persecutor meets Jesus, whom he persecuted (Acts 9:17, 27; 26:13).

Jesus taught about the two ways (Matt. 7:13-14). His own messianic self-understanding claimed himself as "the way" (John 14:4-6). The NT understands Jesus as the "new and living way" (Heb. 9:8-14; 10:19-25). All these strands are essential to grasp the meaning of this metaphor in the primitive community's self-understanding.

The figurative use of "to walk" is common in the ethical sections of Paul's writings. It also appears strongly in the Catholic Epistles (attributed to James, Peter, John, and Jude).[2] Such walking becomes more intelligible in light of this biblical vision of the Christian community as "the Way."

There are direct allusions to the *way* as an image of the messianic community's self-understanding, as well as indirect ways in which the figure is employed in the NT. Thus we are confronted with an important image for understanding the nature and mission of the church.

An Essential Image of Ecclesiological Self-Understanding

The Way was taken over early by the primitive Christian community and used as an image to express its self-understanding as the new people of the Messiah. In six or seven separate episodes related in the book of Acts, we find an unmistakable identification of the community of believers with the Way (Minear, 1960:148-152).

In Acts 9:1-2 those "who belonged to the Way" are clearly

identified with "the disciples of the Lord." In Acts 18:25-26, Luke says Apollos "had been instructed in the Way of the Lord" but "knew only the baptism of John." On hearing him in Ephesus, Priscilla and Aquila "explained the Way of God to him more accurately." Acts 19:8-9 refers to Paul's presentation of the message of the kingdom of God—a message resisted by those who "spoke evil of the Way." This confrontation led to the withdrawal of the disciples, those of the Way, from the synagogue. Acts 19:23 refers to a public upheaval instigated by the guild of silversmiths because their economic interests had become jeopardized by the life and message of the people of the Way. The reference to the Way in Acts 22:4 comes in the context of Paul's defense before the Jerusalem mob. He admitted that he had once "persecuted this Way up to the point of death."

The remaining references to "the Way" are found in the narrative of Paul's defense before Felix against charges of representatives of the Jerusalem hierarchy. Paul insisted that the movement which they called "the sect of the Nazarenes" was more properly named "the Way" (Acts 24:5, 14). At the conclusion of the hearing, Felix is described as being "rather well informed about the Way" (24:22).

Here the terms "sect" and "Way" call for further clarification (Schlier: 180-181). The term translated "sect" (*hairesis*) referred in ancient Hellenistic society to a voluntary group characterized by a common lifestyle and teaching. In ancient Greece the name was applied to philosophical schools, and in Judaism the term was applied to religious groups such as the Essenes, Sadducees, and Pharisees. This is the general sense in which the term is used in the NT. There are references to "the sect/party (*hairesis*) of the Sadducees" and to "the sect/party (*hairesis*) of the Pharisees" (Acts 5:17 and 15:5, NRSV/RSV; cf. 26:5). Opponents of the movement, as well as Jews in general, tended to view the primitive Christian community in the same light, calling them a "*hairesis*" (24:5, 14; 28:22).

Paul rejected the implication that the primitive Christian

community was a sect or party (*hairesis*) in the same sense that the name could be applied to Essenes, Sadducees, and Pharisees, or to philosophical schools. Yet the fact that "the Way" was called *hairesis* by others testifies to its nature as a voluntarily constituted community characterized by a particular conduct and message. In later NT usage of the term (1 Cor. 1:19; Gal. 5:20; 2 Pet. 2:1), *hairesis* carries the meaning of divisive actions and destructive ideas. Its use as a term for heterodoxy is a post-NT development in the Christian church (Schlier). Here our concern is to show that "the Way" is an early (perhaps the earliest) name by which the disciples referred to themselves in the emerging Christian community.

OT Background of the Way Image

The source of this metaphor for the church is found in the OT usage of the image. God's character (Deut. 32:4; Ezek. 18:25) as well as his purposes and will for humanity, are described by means of this image (Michaelis: 42-96). In the OT passages, *hodos* means "walk," "conduct," or "manner of life." The parallelism in Exodus 18:20 makes this meaning clear: "teach them the statutes and instructions and make known to them the way they are to go and the things they are to do."

But more often and more significantly, *hodos* means God's will for his people. "The way (or ways) of God (or the Lord)," refers to the course which God himself takes, to his acts, his dealings, and his purposes. Humans walk in the ways of the Lord inasmuch as they are the ways which he has commanded (Jer. 7:23; Deut. 5:32-33). *Hodos* is practically synonymous with commandment. In this sense, the way of the Lord, which is also his intention for his people, is sometimes referred to as the "good way" (Jer. 6:16), the "way of righteousness" (Prov. 8:20), the "way that is blameless" (Ps. 101:2, 6), the "way everlasting" (Ps. 139:24). This sharply contrasts with "the way of the wicked" (Ps. 1:6; Prov. 4:19).

God's character and purpose are the norm for the ways taken

by his people. In the OT the ways of the Lord are not conceived of as ways *to* God or *to* heaven, as though the goal sought determines the way taken. Instead, the character and gracious commandment of God stands at the beginning of the way of his covenant people. In contrast, ancient extrabiblical writings, both Jewish and pagan (as well as extracanonical Christian writings) use the metaphor more as a goal, a path *to* virtue or reward, or a way *to* God.

NT Background of the Way Image
The Way of the Lord—a New Exodus

It was surely no mere coincidence that the early Christians understood the nature of their life and mission as a messianic people by means of the "way" image. The roots of this ecclesiological self-understanding are readily discernible in the NT, especially in the Gospels.

Pre-exilic prophets refer frequently to the exodus from Egypt as the basis for their call to repentance and renewal among God's people (Hos. 11:1-5; Isa. 11:15-16). The prophets of the exile built their message of hope on the same motif. The prophetic voice announces the way by which Yahweh will lead his people back through the desert in a new exodus. And, as he had done at an earlier time, God will again intervene to save his people (Jer. 16:14-15; 31:2; Isa. 46:3-4; 63:9). The first exodus, characterized by the mighty saving acts of Yahweh, is a type and a pledge of a new exodus from Babylonian captivity back to Jerusalem. The days of the exodus from Egypt and the Mosaic covenant, time of Yahweh's mighty saving acts, are about to occur again. Therefore, "in the wilderness prepare the way of the Lord" (Isa. 40:3).

John the Baptist chose a desert site for his preaching so that the people had to *go out* to him (Mark 1:4-5). Thus in the context of Israel's exodus tradition, he announced a new messianic era. In the writings of Israel's prophets, the way of the desert is symbolic of a new beginning, repentance, and the final gathering of

God's people (cf. Hos. 2:14-23).

The evangelists all have this text refer to Jesus rather than to Yahweh. The focal point of their story is the way of Jesus, just as in the OT the focus was on the way of God, on his character, his purpose, his words, his saving acts. John the Baptist announces "the way of the Lord." The coming of the Messiah means a new exodus and a new covenant. Jesus is the way (John 14:6; Heb. 10:20). Quite understandably, the primitive Christian community called itself simply "the Way."

The Way to Jerusalem

In the synoptic Gospels, "the way to Jerusalem" appears to be one of the organizing themes for telling the story of Jesus' life and mission. Walking on "the way" furnishes a primary setting for Jesus to instruct his followers in the meaning and realities of discipleship. Following Jesus was a physical fact in the life of the disciples. However, the primitive church surely saw more in this way than a literal journey to the city of Jerusalem.

"On the way" we read Peter's messianic confession; Jesus' interpretation of the meaning of his own suffering, rejection, and death; Peter's resistance to the idea and Jesus' rebuke (Mark 8:27-33 and par.). Peter's resistance and Jesus' warning reflected the experience of many of Jesus' followers in the early church. To take up one's cross and follow Jesus was to take the way to Jerusalem with Jesus and his disciples (Mark 8:34-38 and par.).

"On the way" Jesus had occasion to teach the meaning of true greatness from the perspective of the kingdom of God (Mark 9:33-37 and par.). And "going into the way" furnished the occasion to teach his followers about the danger of possessions (see Greek of Mark 10:17-31 and par.).

"On the road going up to Jerusalem" Jesus warned his disciples for a third time of the suffering that his messiahship involved (Mark 10:32-40 and par.). The early church well understood that accompanying Jesus in the way was to drink from his cup and to be baptized with his baptism.

Paul said, "In my flesh I am completing what is lacking in Christ's afflictions." Thus he reflects the early church's vision of life in the way. The disciple way is also the way of suffering for others.

The Parable of the Two Ways

In both Matthew (7:13-14) and Luke (13:23-24), Jesus concludes summaries of the substance of discipleship with an invitation to enter the "narrow gate" and to take the "hard road." The metaphor of the two ways was familiar in the ancient world in both Judaism and Hellenism. However, the roots of Jesus' usage of this parable are certainly to be found in the Law and the Prophets of the OT. "See, I have set before you today life and prosperity, death and adversity. If you obey the commandments of the Lord your God . . . by . . . walking in his ways, and observing his commandments, . . . then you shall live" (Deut. 30:15-16). "You must follow exactly the path that the Lord your God has commanded you, so that you may live" (Deut. 5:33). "Thus says the Lord: See, I am setting before you the way of life and the way of death" (Jer. 21:8).

The narrow way, which Jesus himself has entered and to which he invites his disciples, is not so much a way *to* life as a way *of* life. This way of Jesus is the goal (Michaelis: 71). The metaphor of the ways is a summons to discipleship, to the way of the Lord, which in the OT was the way of Yahweh and now is identified with the way of Jesus, God's Messiah.

The evangelists place Jesus' metaphor of the ways in the context of the Sermon on the Mount (Matt. 5–7; as well as Luke's Sermon on the Plain, Luke 6:17-49). Thus they express the primitive Christian conviction that "the way of the Lord" is not a vague spirituality to which would-be disciples can be invited unconditionally. The way of Yahweh was the way of his commandments. So also the way of Jesus is concretely the way of his words and deeds, of his life and his death and his resurrection, the way oriented by his living Spirit. The community's experience of life in the narrow way of Jesus contributed substantially to their self-understanding.

"I Am the Way"

Jesus' words "I am the way" are recorded in the Gospel of John (14:6). The letter to the Hebrews refers to Jesus as "the new and living way" (10:20; cf. 9:8). These texts make a solid contribution to our understanding of the meaning of the way as one of the primitive community's earliest self-designations. The disciple community recognized in Jesus "the true and living way." Jesus himself claimed to be the authentic way of access to God (John 14:7). This way was open to Jesus' disciples precisely because they knew the way he was taking (14:4).

Thomas, surely speaking on behalf of the disciple community, protested their lack of knowledge. They did not know where he was going because the way to the Father is the way of the cross. Although they had accompanied Jesus all along the "way to Jerusalem," they still could not perceive the meaning of the way of the cross. By laying down his life for them (John 13:37-38), he showed "the way where I am going." Although they did not follow Jesus then, they would follow Jesus after he had gone (14:2-3).

In brief, the way which Jesus declared himself to be was his love-expressing, life-giving death. To know this way is to know Jesus, to know the Father, and to follow Jesus in obedience to his new commandment: "Just as I have loved you, you also should love one another" (John 13:34; cf. 14:15).

In John's Gospel the image of the way carries fundamental meaning which is both christological and ecclesiological. The image illuminates the meaning of Jesus' life and death and points to the nature and mission of the church as the "community of the passion of the Father's love expressed supremely by Jesus the Way" (Minear, 1960:150).[3]

"The New and Living Way"

The epistle to the Hebrews (9:8-14; 10:19-25) reflects a similar view. In Jesus' obedience unto death, he manifests himself most clearly as the way. He has opened to us a "new and living way." Christians have generally tended to interpret these passages in terms of the priesthood of all believers and to accent universal access to the throne of grace. Yet here, too, the martyr way of suffering witness is in view. In the light of Jesus' way-opening death (Heb. 10:19-20), believers are exhorted to "hold fast to the confession of our hope without wavering," a possibility precisely because of Jesus' own faithfulness to the end (10:24). What is explicit in John 14 is implied here. The way opened up to us by Jesus is the martyr way of unwavering witness.

Walking in the Way

Fully consistent with the use of the "way" image for the self-designation of the NT community is the widespread use of "to walk" (*peripateō*) in the ethical exhortations of the NT.[4] Believers are counseled to "walk in love, as Christ has loved us and gave himself up for us" (Eph. 5:2, RSV); "to walk just as he walked" (1 John 2:6); and to "lead lives [Greek: to walk] worthy of the Lord" (Col. 1:10). These instructions take on fuller meaning when we remember that the messianic community referred to itself with this earliest image as "those of the way." They meant the way most fully and clearly revealed by Jesus, the Way.

The Radical Way

The context in which the image of the way is employed in the NT is conflict of one type or another. And in every case, "the Way" is contrasted with the Jewish community from which its members had first emerged. To call themselves the Way was to claim the status of being the community in which the way of God was truly to be found. But, as Jesus, the Way, had shown, authentic witness to this fact could be given only through vicarious suffering.

The "way" image for understanding the nature and mission of the church was apparently most useful within the Jewish matrix of the messianic movement. The community apparently found other images more useful in Greek and Roman contexts. The use of this image is continued in the writings of the post-apostolic Fathers at the end of the first century and the beginning of the second century (1 Clement 36.1). However, the freshness and authenticity which characterizes the use of the image in the NT is missing. Although the metaphor of the two ways is found in both the Didache (1–6) and the Epistle of Barnabas (18–20), it is used in a much more moralistic way. Missing is the radicality which the way of the cross taken by Jesus gave to the image in the NT.

The way is an image which communicated powerfully in a church in conflict with evil powers, in a church which lives under the sign of the cross, in a martyr church of suffering witness. When these are lost, the image, too, loses its appealing power.

5

Sojourners

In the NT we find an important series of images for the church drawn from political and economic spheres. Prominent among these is the family of terms generally translated "stranger" or "to sojourn."[1] Other terms included in this configuration include those translated "exiles" or "pilgrims,"[2] "foreign" or "foreigner,"[3] "the dispersion,"[4] and "citizens."[5]

In the Greek-speaking world of the first century, sojourners (*paroikos*) were resident aliens. Although they lived together with citizens under the protection of a common authority, they could claim no civil rights. They were foreigners or refugees whose existence was at best precarious. *Paroikos* or the related verb *paroikeō* appears in conjunction with *parepidēmos* in Hebrews 11:9-13 ("living in tents" as "foreigners") and 1 Peter 2:11 ("as aliens and exiles").

This term *parepidēmos* for "exile" or "pilgrim" carried the idea of temporary residence alongside citizens. These are transitory foreigners or refugees. Taken together, such terms underscore both the precarious and provisional nature of the community of faith in its existence and mission in the midst of the "kingdoms of this world," among whom they are "scattered" (in "the Dispersion," *diaspora*, 1 Pet. 1:1) and "foreigners" (*xenoi*).

The NT pictures the church as exiles, sojourners, and strangers (1 Pet. 1:1; 2:11; Heb. 11:13). The Christian community is made up of sojourning strangers (1 Pet. 2:11; 4:1-6) in the midst of the kingdom of darkness, whose values are derived from "human passions." Stated positively, the community whose citizenship is in the kingdom of God gives testimony to the fact that its relationship to the prevailing system is one of sojourn and exile (Heb. 11:9-16). Their pilgrimage is evidence that they are already citizens of another kingdom. The epistle to the Hebrews depicts the church as the community of faith living "as in a foreign land" (11:9). Like their prototype, Abraham, the community of faith by its very nature is composed of tent dwellers (Minear, 1960:61-62).

OT Roots of the Sojourners Image

The key to the NT understanding of this image lies in its OT background rather than in the secular Greek usage of the term. In the OT, Abraham especially is described as a sojourner in Egypt (Gen. 12:10), in Canaan (Gen. 17:8), in Gerar (Gen. 20:1), in the land of the Philistines (Gen. 21:34), among the Hittites (Gen. 23:4), and in Hebron (Gen. 35:27). The life of Isaac, Jacob, and the sons of Jacob in Canaan and in Egypt is similarly described.

This alien sojourner status, so freely confessed by Abraham and experienced by the patriarchs in general, did not come to an end when the land of promise became a possession. The patriarchs in their condition of sojourner are accepted as a type or paradigm in whom God's people see their own true nature reflected. Israel is to confess, "A wandering Aramean [Jacob] was my ancestor" (Deut. 26:5). Throughout Abraham's years of wandering, his status as sojourner was a sign of his faith and obedience toward God. It is also a model of the modesty which God's people must always reflect as they live under his gracious covenant promises. This is the sense in which Abraham is regarded as a sojourner in Hebrews 11:8-16. Such a sojourner status characterized the NT community (Schmidt, 1967:846).

In the Psalms, the idea of the sojourn of God's people is intertwined with the possession of the Promised Land. In the context of a recital of God's mighty saving acts in Psalm 105, Israel is described as sojourners:

> "To you I will give the land of Canaan
>   as your portion for an inheritance."
> When they were few in number,
>   of little account, and strangers in it,
> wandering from nation to nation,
>   from one kingdom to another people,
> he allowed no one to oppress them;
>   he rebuked kings on their account,
> saying, "Touch not my anointed ones;
>   do my prophets no harm." (Ps. 105:11-15)

The sojourn in Canaan is likewise described as dwelling in tents (Ps. 78:55; 61:4; 15:1). This parallelism in the last two texts suggests that sojourning is not merely a matter of alien residence in a strictly literal sense; it means dwelling with God. And this is possible only for the righteous. However, in the background lies the thought that to dwell with God is to regard one's life on earth as a sojourn (Schmidt, 1967:843-844).

David, Israel's representative king, described Israel as it stood before God. "For we are aliens and transients before you, as were all our ancestors; our days on the earth are like a shadow" (1 Chron. 29:15). What is true of Israel is also true of each Israelite, personally: "For I am your passing guest, an alien, like all my forebears" (Ps. 39:12b). God's sojourning people see themselves as the objects of his grace: "I live as an alien in the land; do not hide your commandments from me" (Ps. 119:19).

Israel's self-understanding as a band of sojourners had definite ethical implications as well as spiritual ones. "The land shall not be sold in perpetuity, for the land is mine; with me you are but aliens and tenants" (Lev. 25:23). Even though politically Israel had become an independent nation, both morally and spiritually Israel understood its identity in terms of a community of sojourners in relation to God, by whose will and mercy alone they lived.

The Sojourner Image in the NT

The *paroikos* (sojourner) family of terms is used as a figurative description of the people of God seven times in the NT. In all of these NT references to the image, there is an accompanying OT reference or allusion. The roots of this image for the self-understanding of the church are firmly based in the old covenant people of God.

In Stephen's recital of salvation history, he recalled that Abraham's "descendants would be resident aliens (*paroikoi*) in a country belonging to others" (Acts 7:6; cf. Gen. 15:13). In the same recital, he declared that "Moses . . . became a resident alien (*paroikos*) in the land of Midian" (Acts 7:29; cf. Exod. 2:15). In one of Paul's recitals of the story of God's saving acts, he remembered that "the God of this people Israel chose our ancestors and made the people great during their stay (*paroikia*) in the land of Egypt" (Acts 13:17; cf. Exod. 6:1, 6). Apparently the sojourning character of God's people was viewed as no mere coincidence in the history of salvation.

Another especially important NT passage in which *paroikos* appears is Hebrews 11:9-13. The impact of the idea of the sojourning of God's people is further reinforced in this passage by the use of a series of related terms: "a foreign land" (*allotrian*) (11:9), "strangers" (*xenoi*) (11:13), and "exiles" (*parepidēmoi*) (11:13). Abraham is listed among the heroes of faith on the basis of his faith manifested in his obedience to God's call to become a sojourner (11:8-9; cf. Gen. 23:4; 26:3). Behind this expression of faith lay his motive: "he looked forward to the city that has foundations, whose architect and builder is God" (11:10).

Interpreters usually understand this passage as referring to heaven: "Because he will one day be a citizen of the heavenly city, he is a resident alien on earth" (Schmidt, 1967:851). However, fulfillment of the awaited promise need not be postponed beyond the end of historical time line as we know it. Hebrews 11:39-40 suggests that the NT community saw itself as already recipient of the promise in at least an anticipatory way. According to Hebrews 6:12, believers "inherit the promises" now (present tense). Although they did continue to await a final fulfillment of God's promises, the messianic community recognized that God's reign had come into their midst. Furthermore, this reality simply intensified their self-understanding as sojourners rather than making that continuing stance unnecessary.

First Peter 2:9-11 is another key passage for grasping the self-understanding of the NT community. Four key images applied to the people of God in the OT are used in verse 9 to describe the messianic community of the new covenant. In this context Peter naturally calls the apostolic community "aliens" (*paroikoi*) and "exiles" (*parepidēmoi*), in tune with the confessions of the patriarchs, the prophets, and the psalmists (alluding to Ps. 39:12), and with NT recitals of the story of salvation. Here, however, the contrast is not between the earthly and the heavenly cities but between the kingdom of darkness and the kingdom inaugurated by the Messiah. Just as in the case of the patriarchs, the status of sojourner in the world leads to an alternate conduct.

The call to holiness and to exile or sojourning (*paroikia*) in 1 Peter 1:17 is based squarely on the nature of God himself and his kingdom, in contrast to the fallen world. The primary dualism here appears to be between two kingdoms, the reign of fallen flesh and the reign of God, rather than between two worlds, this world and the next.

Ephesians 2:19 says, "So then you are no longer strangers and aliens, but you are citizens with the saints and also members of the household of God." At first glance the verse may appear to be a contradiction to 1 Peter 1:17 and 2:11. However, this is not the case because different spheres of estrangement are in view. Gentile Christians are no longer strangers to the commonwealth of Israel (Eph. 2:12, 19). God's new people of promise include those who were outsiders, who were not a people. So, in reality, this passage points to a realignment of the spheres of estrangement and belonging. While they are no longer aliens in relation to God's family, precisely for this reason they become sojourners in relation to the kingdom of disobedience.

It is remarkable how the NT community could apply two antithetical images, both drawn from the sphere of politics, to itself—citizens and aliens. Citizenship was understood with reference to God and his people, and sojourning was understood with reference to the world. The Christian community are "citizens with the saints and also members of the household of God" (Eph. 2:19). The "commonwealth of Israel" from which they were once alienated (Eph. 2:12) has become the new family of God into which erstwhile aliens are incorporated.

The citizenship metaphor is used in the NT for the same kind of ethical encouragement as the sojourner image. In the heart of an ethical section of his letter to the Philippians, Paul reminds his readers that "our citizenship (*politeuma*) is in heaven, and it is from there that we are expecting a Savior, the Lord Jesus Christ" (3:20). In another context Paul counsels his readers, "Only, live your life in a manner (*politeuomai*) worthy of the gospel of Christ" (Phil. 1:27). In a concrete sense, the future of God's promise determined the present in the life and witness of the primitive community.

The early church reflected this reality as they confessed, "For here we have no lasting city, but we are looking for the city that is to come" (Heb. 13:14). To belong to the church meant that one's citizenship was no longer on earth (in an earthly city). It was rather in heaven (in the kingdom of God). Although God's reign had come into their midst, they still awaited it in its fullness. This understanding of citizenship was significant in the church during the first and second centuries. However, from the third century onward, it increasingly lost its appeal and power as an image (Schmidt, 1967:852, n. 65).

Another political image, the dispersion, is closely related to the sojourner figure in 1 Peter 1:1 and James 1:1. The dispersion of Israel throughout the world of the first century becomes in these passages an image for the church's self-understanding: "Peter, an apostle of Jesus Christ, To the exiles (*parepidēmois*) of the Dispersion (*diaspora*) in Pontus, Galatia, Cappadocia, Asia, and Bithynia, who have been chosen and destined by God the Father" (1 Pet. 1:1-2).

For his part, James applies the image "the twelve tribes in the Dispersion" to the Christian community to whom his letter is directed (James 1:1). "The twelve tribes" is evidently used here also as an image for the Christian church in the same way as other terms applied to Israel came to be applied to the messianic community (cf. Matt. 19:28; Luke 22:30; Gal. 6:16). Likewise, the word *diaspora* was used as a technical term for the scattering of Jews among the nations (cf. LXX, Deut. 28:25; 30:4). This was particularly so following the Babylonian captivity (Judith 5:19; 2 Macc. 1:27; John 7:35). Now it is borrowed to express the self-understanding of the primitive Christian community (Schmidt, 1964:102-104).

The image of the *diaspora*, as applied to the primitive Christian community, is likely more than a mere reference to believers being geographically scattered among the nations of the first-century world. The *diaspora* image reflects, rather, the self-understanding of the NT church. As such, it serves as a complement to the other terms in this configuration of metaphors—sojourners, aliens, exiles, and strangers.

Jesus as Sojourner

This sojourner piety of the primitive Christian community is based on the experience of the people of God in the OT. But it receives fresh impetus in the community's memory of the sojourning nature of Jesus' own mission. Both Matthew (8:20) and Luke (9:58) report Jesus' words, "Foxes have holes, and birds of the air have nests; but the Son of Man has nowhere to lay his head." In both cases the context is Jesus' call to discipleship among his followers. While the term *sojourner* itself is not used, it is clear that Jesus saw his own status as one of sojourning, and the early Christian community understood its vocation along similar lines. In Matthew 25:35, Jesus identifies himself with the stranger (*xenos*) whom his authentic disciples welcomed.

In the fourth Gospel, Jesus' sojourning carries consequences for his disciples. We read that "he came to what was his own, and his own people did not accept him. . . . And the Word became flesh and lived [*eskēnōsen,* pitched his tent, dwelt] among us, and we have seen his glory, the glory as of a father's only son, full of grace and truth" (John 1:11, 14). Later, two of John's disciples overheard him refer to Jesus as "the Lamb of God," and followed him. They asked Jesus, "Rabbi, . . . where are you staying (*meneis*)?" Jesus replied, "Come and see." So "they came and saw where he was staying (*menei*); and stayed (*emeinan*) with him that day" (1:38-39). John's language here evokes the image of one who dwells in tents in a foreign land.

In John 14:2 we find a similar vision. "In my Father's house (*oikia*) there are many dwelling places (*monai*). . . . I go to prepare a place (*topon*) for you." Some read this text as envisioning "mansions" of the kind in which the rich and powerful dwell; but such interpretations find their hermeneutic keys in other kinds of images.

Revelation 21:3 provides a clue to understanding the incarnation in terms of the sojourner image. "See, the home (*skēnē*) of God is among mortals. He will dwell (*skēnōsei*) with them as their God; they will be his peoples (*laoi*), and God himself will be with them." In its worship the suffering and sojourning community gathered and shepherded by the Messiah celebrated the way in which the "Lamb . . . who is seated on the throne will shelter [*skēnōsei,* literally, "spread his tabernacle over"] them" (Rev. 7:14-15). This community of sojourners was finding shelter in God's tabernacle, just as did God's people of old.

The prophetic conflict with institutionalized faith reaches its climax in Jesus and in the sojourning of the NT community.

Facing disaster and exile, the prophets insisted that God's people could not appeal to the land in defense of the status quo, nor to the temple, nor to their own national theologies, nor to Yahweh himself. In Ezekiel's vision, Yahweh is driven from his sanctuary (8:6), and the elders say he "has forsaken the land" (8:12). Finally, "the glory of the Lord ascended from the middle of the city" (11:23). Jeremiah, also using sojourner imagery, cries, "O hope of Israel, its savior in time of trouble, why should you be like a stranger in the land, like a traveler turning aside for the night?" (Jer. 14:8).

This is the prophetic critique which Jesus and the primitive community took up. Jesus is condemned for being unawed by the temple's splendor and insisting that the destruction of the temple that is "made with hands" will certainly come to pass. Furthermore, the loss will not be substantial because the God of Israel dwells in a temple "not made with hands" (Mark 14:58). On several occasions Jesus apparently mentioned the destruction of the temple and the misuse of its courts to keep the nations from worshiping there (Mark 11:15-17 et par.; 14:58 et par.; John 2:19). The various allusions to the theme in the Gospels make one think that there must have been some basis for the accusations of Jesus' enemies, even though these were twisted by prejudice and misinterpreted.

Stephen, following his recital of salvation history, including references to the sojourning of God's people (Acts 7:6, 29), was stoned for, among other things, insisting that "the Most High does not dwell in houses made with hands" (7:48, NRSV note). The formula "made with hands" was in the OT commonly applied to idols (Isa. 2:18; 10:11; Lev. 26:30) and, in the Septuagint version of Isaiah 16:12, even to the temple itself. Stephen's criticism of the temple, epitome of the Jewish religious institution, must have been especially offensive to his hearers.

Paul also insisted that the "Lord of heaven and earth does not live in shrines made by human hands " (Acts 17:24). This critique of the temple reaches its climax in the NT in the epistle to the Hebrews: "For Christ did not enter a sanctuary made by human hands, . . . but he entered into heaven itself" (Heb. 9:24).

As this group of images has reminded us, the NT sees the church as essentially the sojourning people of God. They are aliens among the fallen kingdoms of this world and citizens of a city of God's own making.

The Sojourner Image in the Early Church

In the second century the church continued to consider itself as a community of sojourners. The Epistle to Diognetus, probably written by the apologist Quadratus around A.D. 125, uses the sojourner image powerfully to describe the life and mission of the Christian community.

> They reside in their respective countries, but only as aliens. They take part in everything as citizens and put up with everything as foreigners. Every foreign land is their home, and every home a foreign land. They marry like all others and beget children; but they do not expose their offspring. Their board they spread for all, but not their bed. They find themselves *in the flesh*, but do not live *according to the flesh*.
>
> They spend their days on earth, but hold citizenship in heaven. They obey the established laws, but in their private lives they rise above the laws. They love all men, but are persecuted by all. They are unknown, yet are condemned; they are put to death, but it is life that they receive. *They are poor, and enrich many*; destitute of everything, they abound in everything. They are dishonored, and in their dishonor find their glory. They are calumniated, and are vindicated. *They are reviled, and they bless*; they are insulted and render honor. Doing good, they are penalized as evildoers; when penalized, they rejoice because they are quickened into life. The Jews make war on them as foreigners, the Greeks persecute them; and those who hate them are at a loss to explain their hatred. (Quadratus? 139)

The community's sojourner status determines its conduct in all areas of its life and mission. To be a community of sojourners meant living against the current of dominant social values in their affirmation of life, their defense of women, and their solidarity with the poor and outcasts in society.

Before the close of the first century, we find the sojourner image being applied to local Christian assemblies. In the prologue of 1 Clement we read: "The church of God which sojourns at Rome, to the church of God sojourning at Corinth" (Clement: 229). By the middle of the second century, we find this usage of the sojourner image on the increase. Polycarp greets the Philippian congregation as "the Church of God sojourning in Philippi" (Polycarp: 283). In the prologue to the Martyrdom of Polycarp, we read: "The Church of God which sojourns in Smyrna, to the Church of God which sojourns in Philomelium, and to all the sojournings of the Holy Catholic Church in every place" (Smyrna: 313).

What has served as an image for the self-understanding of the life and mission of the church in the NT has now become a technical term to refer to a local congregation. Out of this background, the Greek word *paroikos* (foreigner, exile) is the root of the Latin word *parochia* and the English word *parish*, which emerge as designations for a local church! Following the Constantinian shift, the meaning of the term came to be distorted beyond recognition. Rather than being sojourners and aliens in either a literal or figurative sense, "parishioners" in the established churches are generally the opposite. They are settled people who *belong* in both the secular and the ecclesiastical societies. Even in the free churches, most parishioners are anything but sojourners and aliens in their society.[6]

The Sojourner Message of Hope

The implications of the sojourner image for the mission of the people of God are taken for granted in both Testaments. Abraham, prototype of the biblical sojourner, is also representative of God's salvific intention that "in you all the families of the earth shall be blessed" (Gen. 12:3). Jesus was the authentic sojourner from whom the messianic community drew its sense of identity as well as its vision of God's mission in the world. For Peter, the alien status of God's people is essential to both their life and their mission in the world (1 Pet. 2:9-11).

The gospel of the kingdom can be shared authentically only by citizens of that kingdom. This means that the world will assign to them the status of sojourners and aliens, an identity which they joyfully accept. It takes a community alien to the worldly system of domination and evil to be able to communicate in it a truly saving gospel. As citizens of the city "coming down out of heaven from God" (Rev. 21:10), only that community of Jesus has a message of true hope.

6

The Poor

The image of the poor includes a configuration of interrelated metaphors and terms. When taken as a whole in its biblical context, it becomes a major category in the self-understanding of the church in the NT. The poor appear as the special objects of God's concern in the OT, and in the NT they are the special objects of the messianic mission. This apparent favor of God for the poor is being recognized more and more by biblical scholars. However, Christians have not so widely recognized the missiological coordinate of this fact: "the poor" is an image for the early Christian community's self-understanding.

In a number of NT texts, there is an implicit identification of the poor with the messianic community. In the Lukan version of the Beatitudes, we read, "Blessed are you who are poor, for yours is the kingdom of God" (Luke 6:20). Biblical scholars recognize that the Sermon on the Mount (as well as the Sermon on the Plain) is addressed to the disciple community and reflects the ethics and the self-understanding of that earliest Christian community.

The image of the poor, as applied to the primitive church, is not strictly limited to the use of the term *ptōkos* (poor). The biblical concept of poorness includes a family of terms generally translated as "humble," "lowly," "base" (*tapeinos*, et al.), "meek" and "meekness" (*praus*, et al.). The "gentle and humble" Jesus invited his followers and disciples to take his yoke upon them. This meant they were to imitate him as his followers and disciples. Frequently believers apply this in the area of personal piety. Much less frequently have they viewed *poor* or *humble* as an important image for ecclesiological self-understanding.

In Romans 15:26 the term "poor" may well be a synonym for the "saints" and a designation for the early Christian community in Jerusalem.[1] In James "the poor in the world" form the community of God's election (2:5). The community is formed of "lowly (*tapeinos*)" brothers and sisters (1:9). The humble are the beneficiaries of God's grace (4:6). And the community is characterized by the meekness of its members (1:9; 3:13).

This image for the early church's self-understanding was decidedly counterculture in the Greco-Roman setting surrounding primitive Christianity. The poor, the meek, and the humble, as images for the church, were no more attractive in the first century milieu than they are in the modern world. People saw poverty as an unmitigated misfortune and disgrace. The very idea that the poor are under special divine protection was alien to Greek thought. In social conflicts the poor did not dare to invoke the help of the gods (Hauck: 887).

A similar thing can be said about Greek attitudes toward humility and meekness. Briefly stated, in the Greek and Roman world, these were considered as vices rather than virtues. Aristotle, for example, insisted that the foremost of the human virtues was "largeness of spirit (*megalopsychia*)," a kind of proud and haughty spirit which would not accept the insults of others; and a sense of personal honor and of one's own rights.

The Greeks generally used *tapeinos* in a negative and disparaging sense, meaning lowly, servile, petty. They could not imagine that a person would intentionally humble oneself. Yet the Greeks understood that one might be humbled in a situation beyond one's control. The quality often translated as "humility" (*tapeinophrosune*, literally: humble-mindedness) was recommended half a dozen times by Paul and Peter in the NT. For the Greeks it meant weakness, vile character, and timidity (Grundmann: 1-26).

The biblical image of poverty or humility as an essential element of the primitive church's self-understanding ran counter to the predominant cultural values which the church of the first-century faced in its mission.

OT Roots of the Image

Due undoubtedly to the different concept of humanity which characterized Hebrew thought, the OT takes a much more positive attitude toward traits of humility and meekness. For the Hebrews, the people of God live in relation to Yahweh and as objects of his gracious covenant. Therefore, the only adequate response is obedient submission, humility, and meekness.

This vision is developed especially in Isaiah. The promised messianic reign of peace is God's gift to the humble, the meek, and the poor; to those whose only option is to trust God for his salvation. These people are set in contrast to the haughty, the violent, the rich, and the proud (Isa. 2). The messianic reign is described as righteousness among the poor and equity for the meek and humble (11:4). The people of God are the poor and afflicted who find their refuge in Zion (14:32). The city of God is the place of protection for his people, the poor and the lowly (25:4). In the prophetic vision of Second Isaiah, this view is further developed. God's humble and afflicted people experience his mercy and compassion (49:13). God promises a covenant of peace to the humble and lowly (54:10-11). God's messianic salvation will be the legacy of the humble (66:2; Grundmann: 10).

The Hebrew equivalent of *ptōkos* primarily expresses a relationship rather than social distress. Conditions require dependence on Yahweh and also on the community. The antonym of poorness is violence rather than wealth (Bammel: 888). In fact, the term *poor* carries moral and spiritual significance and bears kinship with humility and meekness (Ps. 18:27). The poor were those in Israel whose only alternative was to trust Yahweh for their survival, in the context of the community of the covenant.

One observes two complementary strands of thought in the OT attitude toward the poor. First of all, the poor are portrayed as special objects of Yahweh's concern; therefore, they should be the objects of Israel's concern. Yahweh, unlike the Greek gods, is Protector of the poor, and his people are guided by a whole series of provisions designed to alleviate human suffering. In the second place, the prophets, in their energetic denunciation of the injustices of the wealthy and the powerful, tend to equate the poor with the people of God. The people who were delivered out of Egypt by Yahweh's mighty saving acts were a poor people, whose only source of hope was to trust Yahweh for deliverance and sustenance (Amos 2:10ff.; Exod. 22:21; 23:9). The poetic parallelism of Isaiah 3:15 identifies "the poor" with "my people" (cf. Isa. 10:2; 14:32).

This vision of the people of God as the poor is stated explicitly in Zephaniah 3:11b-12:

> I will remove from your midst your proudly exultant ones,
>   and you shall no longer be haughty in my holy mountain.
> For I will leave in the midst of you
>   a people humble and lowly.
> They shall seek refuge in the name of the Lord.

The same vision is also reflected in Isaiah 29:19: "The meek shall obtain fresh joy in the Lord, and the neediest people (RSV: the poor) shall exult in the Holy One of Israel." In Psalm 37 the meek, the poor, and the righteous are upheld by God against the wicked, the haughty, and the violent. Following the experience of exile, the prophetic vision for the future of God's poor and afflicted people was stated in terms of freedom from want, from oppression, and from the fear of violence (Isa. 54:11-17).

During the intertestamental period, social cleavages arose due to distress caused by wars. An ethos of poverty developed which stood in sharp contrast to the more wealthy elements of

Jewish society. The lot of the poor of the land (*'am ha'arets*) became nearly intolerable. In rabbinic circles there was some ideal-
ization of the poor, but this did nothing to alleviate their misery.
Their best source of hope was the voluntary practice of philan-
thropy. First-century Judaism took for granted the economic and
social distinctions which divided the people into classes. The
postexilic tendency to take a negative attitude toward the poor
prevailed, and poverty was seen at best as a misfortune, but
more usually as a curse. This is the socioeconomic environment
in which the NT finds its setting (Bammel: 899-902).

The Poor—Object of the Messianic Mission

Primary texts for our understanding of the NT vision of the
poor as objects of messianic salvation are Luke 4:18 and 7:22-23,
together with its parallel in Matthew 11:5-6.

> The Spirit of the Lord is upon me,
>   because he has anointed me
>   to bring good news to the poor.
> He has sent me to proclaim release to the captives
>   and recovery of sight to the blind,
>   to let the oppressed go free,
> to proclaim the year of the Lord's favor. (Luke 4:18-19)

This text, a free quotation from Isaiah 61:1-2, is used by Luke
to introduce Jesus' messianic ministry. It therefore offers a key to
understanding the nature of that mission. In view of the parallelism which characterizes Hebrew poetry, we may take lines 3–6
to be parallel. Gospel healing and liberation come to the poor,
who are here described as captives, blind, and oppressed.

Six signs of messianic salvation are enumerated in Matthew
11:5: "The blind receive their sight, the lame walk, lepers are
cleansed, the deaf hear, the dead are raised, and the poor have
good news brought to them." But the accent clearly falls on the
last phrase, not merely because it concludes the series of quotations, but because it, of all the signs of salvation cited, is the only

one which proved to be a scandal (11:6). The offering of God's salvation to the poor was the really scandalous element in the mission of Jesus. That the poor are declared blessed (Matt. 5:3; Luke 6:20) was offensive in first-century Judaism, especially to the religious establishment. So Jesus declared that those who do not take offense in him (and his mission to the poor) will also be blessed (Matt. 11:6).

Who are these poor who are the express objects of Christ's saving mission? We may surely assume that they include the poor who in the OT were special objects of Yahweh's saving concern. Among them were those effectively needy in an economic sense, those without inheritance in Israel, who thereby were bereft of their means of economic support. The category also included those called humble, weak, afflicted, meek, and lowly. Strangers, widows, and orphans were also objects of Yahweh's special concern in ancient Israel. They included all those whose only hope was to trust God both for providence and protection, for salvation in the fullest sense.

It comes as no surprise, then, to find a similar understanding of the poor shared by Jesus and reflected in the Gospels. The poor surely included those who literally suffered from economic need. Some families in Israel had lost their inheritance, and many in precarious economic situations had been forced to sell their services to the wealthy. To them, the proclamation of the "year of the Lord's favor" was certainly good news (Luke 4:18; the year of Jubilee, Lev. 25; Yoder, 1994:60-75). However, it was apparently bad news for some of the synagogue-goers in Nazareth (Luke 4:28-29).

We take our clue from the scandal caused by the poor being brought into God's kingdom by the gospel. The poor included those whom Jesus' adversaries called "tax collectors," "prostitutes," and "sinners" (Matt. 11:19; 21:31-32). These were counted among the poor, not simply because they notoriously broke God's laws, but because respectable members of the community pointed the finger at them and public opinion closed all doors of hope to them. The poor also included those whose professions made it impossible for them to keep the Jewish ritual laws. Such were tanners, shepherds, money changers, and tax collectors.

The category of the poor also included those who in the NT are called "the little ones" (Matt. 10:42; 18:10, 14; Mark 9:42); "the least of these" (Matt. 25:40, 45); "infants" (Matt. 11:25); the "stranger," the "naked," the "sick," and those "in prison" (Matt. 25:31-46). "Poor" is also a key term for the Gentile world, outsiders to whom Christ's mission is also directed (as with an OT widow and leper in Luke 4:24-27).

The Lukan version of Jesus' parable of the great banquet (14:15-24) is generally interpreted as a picture of the eschatological messianic banquet. In Jewish expectation for the end of human history, that celebration would mark the culmination of the restoration of God's saving reign. According to the parable, this is the place where the poor and the outcasts will finally find fellowship in God's house. The three invitations issued in the parable apparently are allegorical references to the various groups to whom the messianic message is directed.

First, Judaism is represented in its religious and political leaders. They reject the invitation to participate in the messianic kingdom due to its deep involvement in temporal affairs: self-serving power, wealth, and pleasure (cf. Luke 8:14).

The second invitation apparently refers to the messianic mission described in the Gospels. It is directed to "the poor, the crippled, the blind, and the lame" (14:21). This is the motif which runs throughout the Gospel reports of Jesus' ministry (Luke 4:18-21; 7:22; 14:13; Matt. 15:30-31; cf. John 5:3). Jesus ministers to the poor, the outcasts, and those who, according to official Judaism, are outside the realm of salvation. These are the ones who gladly hear Jesus and receive the good news with unbounded joy.

The third invitation is issued to those along "the roads and lanes" (Luke 14:23). These who are outside the city are the Gentiles, also objects of Jesus' compassion and the subsequent apostolic mission (cf. Luke 4:24, 27).

"The poor, the crippled, the blind, and the lame" (Luke 14:21) are the outcasts within Judaism. They included not only the poor in an economic sense but also others who were, according to official Judaism, outside the pale of salvation and bereft of all social and spiritual hope. Their only hope for salvation was to trust in the compassionate providence of God, beyond the scope of the official system.

In addition to Judaism's own outsiders, "the poor" is also a key term for the Gentile world, the outsiders to whom Christ's mission is ultimately directed (Luke 4:24-27; 24:47). This appears to be the main point of the instructions to the host and the parable of the great banquet in Luke 14:12-24. In both cases, "the poor, the crippled, the lame, and the blind" (14:13, 21) and the outsiders (14:23) will finally be the guests in the eschatological messianic banquet. They will find fellowship in the Father's house.

The category of the poor included all those economically, socially, culturally, and religiously disadvantaged people. Such persons were held in contempt by the powerful, the wealthy, and the recognized religious elements of society. In the opinion of the moral majority, the poor included all those whose ignorance of religious matters and lack of moral seriousness closed for them the way to salvation. But Jesus offered rest to those who were "weary" and "carrying heavy burdens" (Matt. 11:28).

For Jesus, then, the category of the poor includes the same wide range of human suffering, weakness, hopelessness, and lostness as it did in the prophetic vision of the OT. The poor are the needy, the hungry and thirsty, the naked and the stranger, the sick and imprisoned, those who mourn, the heavy laden, the last, the least, the lost, the sinners (see Jeremias, 1971:108-113).

In contrast to Luke's Gospel, the term *ptōkos* does not appear in Acts. However, this does not mean that Jesus' vision of messianic mission did not persist in the early community. On the contrary, "the poor" of the banquet invitation of Luke 14, the

Gentiles, are the prime objects of the apostolic mission. The early church also took seriously its mission to the economically poor as well as the social and religious outcasts. The continuation of the common meals which the disciples had experienced with Jesus contributed to erasing social and economic distinctions (Acts 4:32-34). The responsibility of the twelve—and later of the seven—for table service (*diakonein*), its ministry to the widows, and the individual instances of sharing of property—these all point to a community that went far beyond the synagogue in its concrete concern for the poor (Bammel: 912).

Paul, in the mission to the Gentiles, continued the messianic mission to the poor, as interpreted by Luke (4:18-25; 14:15-24). In the spirit of Jesus' ministry, "the poor have good news brought to them" (Luke 7:22). But Paul and his co-workers did not reach out only to Gentiles, as representatives of the broad category of the poor. To judge by texts such as 1 Corinthians 1:27 and 2 Corinthians 8:2, Paul and his colleagues in mission did direct their message to the economically, socially, culturally, and religiously disadvantaged, in the authentic tradition of Jesus.

The Poor—A Mark of the Messianic Community

There is an implicit identification of God's people with the poor in a few of the prophetic passages in the OT. This vision is intensified in the NT description of the Messiah and his community. Jesus himself is described as being poor. In the infancy stories, particularly in Luke, God's concern for the poor and the identification of Jesus with them is underscored.[2] The Gospels present Jesus as "friend of tax collectors and sinners" as well as being effectively poor with no fixed dwelling (Luke 7:34; 9:58).

This is the tradition to which Paul appeals in 2 Corinthians 8:9. "For you know the generous act of our Lord Jesus Christ, that though he was rich, yet for your sakes he became poor, so that by his poverty you might become rich." While the term "rich" in this passage must be interpreted metaphorically, there is no reason to believe that Jesus' poverty was not understood literally in the early church. Likewise, the passage in Philippians 2:6-8 celebrates Jesus' willingness to empty and humble himself. This is not based so much on speculation about the two natures of Christ (divine and human) as it is on the fact that Jesus had lived among them as a poor person.

In both Matthew (5:1-12) and Luke (6:20-26), the Beatitudes begin with the poor. This is undoubtedly the fundamental beatitude which describes the messianic community. The following Beatitudes elaborate on this basic characteristic. In the biblical usage of the term, the afflicted, the hungry, the meek, the persecuted are all included in the category of the poor. Rather than taking the Beatitudes as eight independent characteristics of the community, we should understand that the messianic community which inherits the kingdom is essentially poor. The nature and mission of this community of the poor is then developed in the Beatitudes.

In both Matthew and Luke, the messianic community is identified as "the poor." This is especially clear in the Lukan version, "Blessed are *you* who are poor." Jesus' followers in the original setting of the words, and the contemporary community to which Luke's Gospel is addressed—both are identified as "the poor." The same is true of Matthew's version. Jesus' teachings in the Sermon on the Mount are directed to his disciples (Matt. 5:1-2), and secondarily, they are addressed to the Christian community in which the first Gospel was read.

The differences in the Lukan and Matthean versions of this beatitude are frequently pointed out. In Luke, the reference is apparently to the poor in the sense of the economically needy. In Matthew, the reference is to the wider biblical meaning: the humble, the poor before God. Jesus used Isaiah 61:1-2 to identify his messianic mission as giving good news to the poor. He therefore understood the term to include "the afflicted," "the brokenhearted," and "the captives." Jesus understood "the poor" in its broad and inclusive biblical sense. He most certainly did not refer exclusively to the economically dispossessed, nor did he spiritualize the term to include only the humble. We may account for the differences between the two versions which have come to us in this way: Matthew was writing to a community faced with the Pharisaic temptation to spiritual pride, while Luke addressed a community suffering from oppression. Both reflect faithfully different aspects of the full intention of Jesus (Jeremias, 1971:112-113).

Matthew 11:28-30 indicates not only that Jesus was "gentle and humble" but also that this characterized the community gathered by him. In Matthew's Gospel, Jesus invites all who "are weary and are carrying heavy burdens" to come to him. This comes at the conclusion of several paragraphs elaborating his understanding of messianic mission as giving good news to the poor (11:5). These "poor" include those who try to take the kingdom of heaven by violence and force (11:12; Jeremias, 1971:111-112); "tax collectors and sinners" (11:19); the Gentiles of "Tyre and Sidon" (11:22); the "infants" (11:25); and finally the weary and the burdened (11:28). This chapter suggests that the Gospel is addressed to a community of the poor.

The term "the poor" as found in Galatians 2:10 and Romans 15:26 may well have been a designation for the Christian community in Jerusalem (Bammel: 909).[3] The coincidence of drought, crop failures, and a sabbatical year caused widespread scarcity in Judea from A.D. 47 to 49 (Jeremias, 1969:142-143). Yet this hardly accounts for the designation of the saints in Jerusalem as "the poor" at the time of the writing of the epistle to the Romans some ten years later. It is likely that "the poor" may have been one of the self-designations of the earliest Christian community of Jerusalem (Bammel: 909).

James 2:5 describes the poor as objects of God's election in a way strongly reminiscent of the first beatitude. The poor are heirs of the kingdom. To describe the Christian community, James uses other terms from the spectrum of the biblical meaning of the term "poor." *Tapeinos* (in one or another of its forms) appears four times in James. God's grace is given to the humble

(4:6). Twice meekness is encouraged as the appropriate stance for God's people. The book of James seems to reflect a community in which the characteristic qualities of poverty, meekness, and humility are beginning to give way. The rich and the powerful are beginning to seek entrance into the church (Bammel: 911).

Ptōkos is by no means the only term to designate the church as "the poor." The *tapeinos* family of terms, generally translated "lowly," "humble," or "humility," is used approximately thirty times in the NT. And the *praus* family, translated as "meek" or "meekness," appears some fifteen times. Together with *ptōkos*, all of these terms refer to "the poor" in its comprehensive biblical sense. They furnish us with really substantial evidence that the early Christian community understood itself to be "the community of the poor." Indeed, the terms for both poverty and humility can be traced back to the same Hebrew root and concept (Bammel: 910, n. 237).

Taking their cue from Jesus himself, the apostolic writers urged the community to take seriously its essential nature as "the community of the poor." They could do this by ordering their relationships in terms of humility and meekness. Paul referred to himself personally "as poor" (2 Cor. 6:10) and "humble" (Acts 20:18). He called for the same attitudes and actions in the communities which he planted in his mission. In Philippians 2:3-8, Paul identifies humility as a characteristic of the community and explicitly appeals to Jesus Christ as the model to be followed. In Ephesians 4:1-2, humility and meekness are essential characteristics of the Christian community responding to the very nature of its calling.

The apostolic appeals for humility, based on both the example and the teachings of Jesus, carry a sense of urgency. They have to do with the very nature of the community's self-understanding (1 Pet. 5:5-6; James 4:6,10; Phil. 2:3-8; Eph. 4:1-2).

Implications for the Church's Mission

This image of the church as poor carries implications for our understanding of the mission of the church. Jesus' missionary charge to the twelve (Matt. 10) and his description of his own messianic mission (11:5-6) match each other. They can be summed up as preaching good news to the poor. This was the mission that Jesus charged his followers to carry out. The good news is the message that "the kingdom of heaven is at hand" (10:7). This is expressly called "gospel" (9:35). The poor, in the case of the disciples' mission, are "the lost sheep of the house of Israel" (10:6), the sick, the dead, the lepers, the demon possessed (10:8). All such people are called the poor in the Gospels. The mission of Jesus was to the poor (Matt. 11:5; cf. 9:18-33), and this is the same mission with which the disciples were charged.

The church *as poor* and the church giving good news *to the poor* are two fundamental coordinates of the Christian mission. Wherever the church is seduced by temptations to power, prestige, and property, it cannot communicate the gospel of the kingdom with integrity. This is so because the full-orbed message of the gospel has been obscured. Therefore, the poor do not perceive the gospel of the kingdom in the message that is communicated.

Recent theology and missiology have been speaking forcefully about the church's option for the poor. The church must opt for the poor if it is to be faithful to its Lord. However, the image of the poor as an essential component of the church's own identity reminds us that the option *for* the poor can be made with integrity only by a church *of* the poor.

This was what the prophets had in mind when they called on Israel to "return to the desert." This is what occurred in the incarnation (2 Cor. 8:9; Phil. 2). Jesus called the original messianic community to this (Matt. 16:24-25; 19:21, 27). This is what the church of the first century understood (Luke 6:20-22). This has also been understood generally in radical renewal movements throughout Christian history.[4]

In the absence of an authentic identity as "the poor," the church has sought to "opt for the poor." But its missionary endeavors have resulted in the communication of a mutilated gospel. Until the church "as poor" brings good news "to the poor," its missionary enterprise will be an empty caricature of what Jesus intended.

Biblical Images of the Church in Mission

New-Order Images

7

The Kingdom of God

The kingdom of God is an important image for understanding the biblical vision of God's saving activity. It appears first of all in the vocation of Israel, then in the redemptive mission of his Messiah, and finally in the life and mission of the messianic community, the church. While the term "kingdom" is found in all parts of the NT, it plays a dominant role in the synoptic Gospels.[1]

According to the unanimous testimony of the four Gospels, Jesus came announcing the kingdom of God. His mission as the Messiah of God in the world was fundamentally this: to proclaim the kingdom of God and God's righteousness. Through the presence of Jesus in their midst, people were able to catch a glimpse of the kingdom of God with a clarity they had never before experienced (see Driver, 1993b:65-69).

Although Jesus' messianic mission consisted essentially in "proclaiming the kingdom of God," the precise meaning of the term is nowhere defined in the NT.[2] But it is apparent that Jesus' hearers were familiar with the concept. Even though the phrase "kingdom of God" appears rarely in the OT, the idea of Yahweh's kingship permeated all of life in ancient Israel.

In the Bible, the kingdom of God is a primary image for understanding God's saving strategy and for grasping the nature and mission of the church. However, for a number of reasons, this image has been widely neglected and misunderstood by the church as it sought to understand God's purposes in its own life and mission. Biblical scholars have correctly observed that Jesus came proclaiming the kingdom of God. However, many concluded that what appeared instead was the church, and its mission consists of proclaiming Christ. At best, this is a dangerous half-truth: to proclaim the Messiah is to preach the kingdom in which God's Anointed One is Lord. A dilemma appears in this articulation of the vision; the confusion undoubtedly reflects more the Constantinian legacy present in the church than it does a lack of clarity and integrity in the vision and strategy of Jesus.

In traditional Catholicism, the kingdom of God came to be practically identified, somewhat triumphalistically, with the Holy Catholic Church, established in the Roman Empire. This robbed the image of its power to inspire the people of God to a more biblical faithfulness in its commitment to God's mission in the world.

In the Protestant tradition was a tendency to bypass the Gospels and to begin with a "salvation by faith alone" reading of Paul's writings. This has contributed to a somewhat individualistic understanding of salvation and a view of the true church as largely invisible. Such a perspective robbed the kingdom metaphor of its vitality and its power to inspire the imagination of God's people. In this context, the kingdom-of-God image was either neglected or largely recast into inwardly spiritual and futuristic terms.

However, in the course of the twentieth century, we have witnessed in some sectors of the church a notable revival of interest in the kingdom image. Johann Christoph Blumhardt (1805-1880) and Christoph Friedrich Blumhardt (1842-1919) caught a remarkably biblical vision of the kingdom of God. This happened in the course of their pastoral ministries and theological reflection during the last half of the nineteenth century and the early years of the twentieth century in southwestern Germany.

The elder Blumhardt struggled with demon possession in the congregation of which he was pastor. He came to understand that because "Jesus is Victor," the kingdom of God has become a real possibility for the church's life here and now. The reality of the kingdom was perceived to be equally relevant to the inner sphere or the personal dimensions of spiritual warfare, and to the concrete socioeconomic structures of the day. The insights and convictions which grew out of this overarching concern for the cause of the kingdom were carried forward by others. Among them were Eberhard Arnold and the Society of Brothers, and the leaders of the Confessing Church in Germany in the early 1930s. In the name of the Messiah whom they confessed as Lord, they resisted the totalitarian and nationalistic claims of the state.

Drawing on this Blumhardtian legacy, Christians have gradually been discerning the demonic dimensions of social structures. Through their experiences in World War II, European Christians were able to perceive the essentially demonic nature of the institutional structures of their social and political life. Earlier they had thought those institutions were Christianized. A more radical reading of the NT gospel of the kingdom provided them with a key for responding to the challenges of the anti-Christian kingdoms of their time, secular as well as religious.

In recent decades we have again witnessed a resurgence in interest in the biblical image of the kingdom of God. There are several reasons for this revival. One is the persecution and suffering to which many Christians have been subjected in our time. The reign of God transcends human expectations. Thus it constitutes a key ingredient in the hope which sustains suffering Christians, particularly in areas of conflict in our world. Conditions of political and economic oppression and privation have confronted many Christians in Latin America. They have studied Jesus' proclamation of the kingdom, God's new order of justice, peace, liberation, and covenant community. There they found a relevant key for understanding God's Word and will for their life and mission as the people of God (Catholic: 27).[3]

God's reign has also furnished such oppressed believers with hope that sustains them in the midst of persecution. The book of Revelation, for example, powerfully portrays God's kingdom as his alternative to the kingdoms of this world. It is eagerly read by these brothers and sisters. It provides them with encouragement in their pilgrimage and spiritual strength to resist the evil powers which oppress them.

During the final decades of the twentieth century, Christians rarely ask, "Is there life *after* death?" Instead, they ask, "Is there life *before* death?" In a world plagued by the realities of human misery, oppression, and suffering, Christians are finding in the Bible a message of justice, peace, liberation, and reconciliation. In the biblical motif of the kingdom of God, we find summed up God's saving intention for a new humanity within a restored creation. This is characterized by healed relationships with the Creator, as well as with fellow humans and the rest of the created order. The biblical view of the kingdom of God offers a framework in which to understand more wholistically the nature and mission of a transformed and transforming messianic community.

The Kingdom of God in the Old Testament

Far from being a mere abstraction or figure of speech, God's righteous reign was a reality in the experience of ancient Israel. In fact, Psalms 145 and 146 are concrete examples of the way God's people celebrated God's kingship in their corporate worship. Psalm 145 begins, "I will extol you, my God and *King*." Psalm 146 comes to a close with the confident declaration that "the Lord will *reign* forever." In Psalm 145:11-13, the term "kingdom" occurs four times, praising God for "your kingdom," "your dominion."

Someone has aptly said that worship is the most subversive

activity in which the people of God can engage. We praise God as King and confess that God alone "will reign forever." That is to deny, at least implicitly, the absolute loyalty that worldly sovereigns generally claim for themselves. Of course, God's kingdom is quite different from the kingdoms of this world, but not in the way in which many Christians in our time imagine.[4] One of the dimensions of this difference is to be found in the warning articulated in Psalm 146:3: "Do not put your trust in princes."

God's reign is really envisioned as the saving alternative to the fallen structures of human government. As a whole host of biblical texts remind us, true security and well-being are to be found by nonviolently trusting in God. We should not seek our security in the prowess of military preparedness. Since the time of Constantine, the church has tended to gloss over the fundamental differences between the kingdom of God and the fallen kingdoms of this world. Believers have viewed the fallen powers more as allies than as competing alternatives.

According to this psalm (and many more biblical texts), the kingdom of God does not *supplement* the exercise of civil authority, as Augustine and many Christians have since imagined. Instead, it claims to *supplant* the exercise of that kind of political power which is based on the capacity to coerce compliance.

To understand the kingdom of God and its dynamics, we must remember that God formed Israel as his people. In doing so, God freed them from Egypt, not merely from their Egyptian taskmasters. The exodus meant being liberated from that system which depends on the exercise of coercive power, of which Egypt was the principal representative of the period. Historically, the alternative to Egypt was the reign of God, graciously constituted at Sinai.

In the NT, the alternative to Rome (under the code name of Babylon, in Rev. 17–18) is the faithful and suffering messianic community, whose true citizenship is in the kingdom of heaven.

Psalms 145–146 underscore the fundamental nature of God's reign. It is characterized by the concrete practice of those righteous relationships that correspond to life as ordered by God's gracious covenant. The kingdom of God is seen most clearly in the way in which the Lord shows his merciful providence toward the weak and oppressed. Principal attributes of divine kingship are mercy, goodness, faithfulness, and providence.

God is absolutely faithful in keeping his gracious covenant promise. He "executes justice for the oppressed, . . . gives food to the hungry, . . . sets the prisoners free, . . . opens the eyes of the blind, . . . lifts up those who are bowed down, . . . loves the righteous, . . . watches over the strangers, . . . upholds the orphan and the widow, but the way of the wicked he brings to ruin" (Ps. 146:7-9; cf. 145:13c-20; 72:10b-14).

The vision of the kingdom that we find in these psalms appears time after time in the Psalter, as well as in other parts of the OT. "The Lord works vindication and justice for all who are oppressed" (Ps. 103:6). "He satisfies the thirsty, and the hungry he fills with good things" (Ps. 107:9). "He leads out the prisoners to prosperity" (Ps. 68:6; cf. Isa. 42:7). The Lord "executes justice for the orphan and the widow, and . . . loves the strangers, providing them food and clothing" (Deut. 10:18; cf. Exod. 22:21-22). These, then, are the essential characteristics by which we can recognize the kingdom of God. God's reign takes these concrete social forms.

Psalm 146 is a part of a collection of great psalms with which ancient Israel regularly celebrated its identity as the people of God. They have been called the Hallel Psalms because they all begin with the phrase "Praise the Lord." These psalms were recited by the Jewish people during the great religious festivals in which the people of God commemorated their spiritual identity. These included the Feast of Hanukkah, Passover, Unleavened Bread, Pentecost, and Tabernacles.

In later Judaism, Psalms 146–150 apparently became a part of the daily morning prayers offered in the synagogue. Psalm 146 sums up so remarkably the biblical vision of the concrete forms that God's kingdom takes in the midst of his people; it came to be a part of Israel's official liturgy.

Yet this vision of God's reign is not limited to the Psalms. Following Israel's return from exile, the prophetic vision of a messianic restoration of God's righteous reign included the anointing of God's Servant "to bring good news to the oppressed, . . . to bind up the brokenhearted, . . . to proclaim liberty to the captives, and release to the prisoners" (Isa. 61:1).

Jesus Revealed the Kingdom Most Fully

When we come to the NT, we should not be surprised to discover that these are precisely the same signs that characterized Jesus' activity as God's Anointed. He was commissioned by God to restore his gracious reign among his people, as well as to the ends of the earth. No one in Israel imagined that there could be a Messiah without a kingdom! To confess that Jesus is the Messiah means declaring that God's reign has appeared. According to Matthew's Gospel, Jesus began his messianic ministry "proclaiming the good news of the kingdom and curing every disease and every sickness among the people" (Matt. 4:23).

According to the NT, the power of the new order was already operative in Jesus. Everything he said and did was related to the coming of God's kingdom. Jesus' exorcisms are prime examples of the way in which the reign of God was being inaugurated. In his messianic mission, Jesus had assailed and overcome the evil one. "But if it is by the Spirit of God that I cast out demons, then the kingdom of God has come to you. Or how can one enter a strong man's house and plunder his property, without first tying up the strong man? Then indeed the house can be plundered" (Matt. 12:28-29; cf. Luke 11:20-22).[5]

The imagery of Jesus' struggle against the tempter and the wild beasts in the wilderness furnishes us with a vision of the "second Adam." This new Adam has begun to reverse the effects of the disobedience of the first Adam (Rom. 5:12-21). In effect, the mission of Jesus has been to reverse the consequences of evil in the world: disease, demon possession, the hostility of nature, social and religious and ethnic rivalries, hunger, economic exploitation, empty religiosity, alienation, and death. The conflict which characterized Jesus' ministry was, in reality, the struggle of the new order to displace the era of sin and death. Therefore, all who trust in their wealth, power, and prestige for their security react violently because the values of the new order threaten their false sources of security (Driver, 1993a:92-93).

John the Baptist sent his disciples to Jesus with a query concerning the coming of the Messiah and the establishing of God's kingdom in their midst. Jesus' response echoed the ancient biblical vision of God's righteous reign found in the Psalms and the prophets: "Go and tell John what you hear and see: the blind receive their sight, the lame walk, the lepers are cleansed, the deaf hear, the dead are raised, and the poor have good news brought to them'" (Matt. 11:4-5).

These, according to Jesus, are conclusive signs of the presence of the kingdom. The righteous reign of God becomes manifest in the gracious, saving, provident ways in which God is at work among the poor, the oppressed and the suffering. God does this work through his Messiah and later through the messianic community. This is the vision that marked Jesus' ministry.

Suppose Israel had taken seriously the message of its prophets and its own liturgical tradition. Then it would have been able to recognize the kingdom of God when it came into their midst in the person and ministry of Jesus of Nazareth. The kingdom expectations of the Jewish people in general included the vindication of the righteous—the existing religious and political institutions. This was to happen through the destruction of Israel's oppressors, the enemies of the Jewish nation.

Therefore, Judaism was not able to recognize the kingdom when it did appear in their midst. The message continually recited in their religious festivals reminded them of the concrete social forms which the reign of God takes in the midst of this people. But that message had fallen on deaf ears.

Here is an example of the uncanny capability of religion,

when institutionalized, to domesticate the faith of a people. The message of God's reign had earlier been a powerful instrument for the liberating salvation of God's people. But the religious institutions had now been transformed into instruments for the preservation of the economic, social, and political status quo.

Israel was able to celebrate the concrete social forms of God's kingdom in their worship liturgy. Yet at the same time, Israel remained blind to it when it appeared in their midst. That should call Christians to reflect seriously. We may be rigorously religious and unquestionably orthodox. In spite of all that, we may still be unable to recognize the most elemental signs of the kingdom of God when they appear before our eyes on the stage of history.

This is exactly what happened to many first-century Jews. It happened precisely to those who were the most scrupulously religious, the most intellectually enlightened, the most well-to-do economically, and the most powerful politically. On the other hand, there were the tax collectors, lepers, those who because of their occupations were considered unclean (tanners and shepherds), Galileans and Samaritans, Gentiles, prostitutes, the poor and disinherited, women and orphans, the humble and "the little ones." These social pariahs of Judaism crowded around Jesus, clamoring to enter the kingdom that their leaders had rejected (Matt. 21:31-32: cf. 11:12).

If we have the courage to be honest about the implications of this Jewish experience for the church of our own time, we will be able to recognize that the same thing has been happening to us. God's kingdom has come into our midst, and we risk missing it because we are concerning ourselves with another kind of kingdom.

As the ancient psalm reminds us, the kingdom of God is in our midst when the Lord brings justice for the oppressed, food for the hungry, freedom for prisoners, sight for the blind, relief for those bowed down, love for the righteous, care for the strangers, and help for the orphan and widow (Ps. 146:7-9).

The challenge before us is to apply these kingdom criteria to the difficult questions with which we are confronted. We need to discern with clarity the signs which characterize God's kingdom, with its upside-down values. God invites us to courageously submit, with absolute loyalty and obedience, to his reign.

The vision which guided Jesus in his messianic mission was inspired by the ancient biblical message contained in the liberating activity of God in the exodus and at Sinai, and articulated by the prophets and the psalmists. It was the biblical vision of the kingdom of God. This is the same mission Jesus entrusted to his followers in the messianic community. "As you go, proclaim the good news, 'The kingdom of heaven has come near.' Cure the sick, raise the dead, cleanse the lepers, cast out demons. You received without payment; give without payment" (Matt. 10:7-8).

Like Jesus, the community of the Messiah has been commissioned to live out the reality of the presence of the kingdom in the world, thereby fulfilling the commission it has received. This is the community which anticipates the kingdom; it is a sign of the kingdom; and it fulfills its mission in the service of the kingdom.

Such a vision of God's reign should orient all our evangelizing deeds and words. In this way the spiritual power that characterizes God's kingdom, present in the mission of Jesus, will also characterize the church's evangelization.

Kingdom, Church, and Mission

Pentecost is essential to a biblical understanding of kingdom, church, and mission. Pentecost is often interpreted in a largely individualistic way, in terms of personal holiness and/or charismatic experience. These personal aspects of Pentecost are certainly not to be disparaged. However, it is noteworthy that the book of Acts sets Pentecost in a kingdom context. In this context, the church and its missionary role are best understood (Driver, 1993a:101-102).

"After his suffering [Jesus] presented himself alive to [the apostles], . . . appearing to them during forty days and speaking about the kingdom of God. . . . He ordered them not to leave Jerusalem, but to wait there for the promise of the Father. . . . 'You will be baptized with the Holy Spirit' " (Acts 1:3-5). In response to the disciples' question about the restoration of the kingdom to Israel, Jesus replied, "You will receive power when the Holy Spirit has come upon you; and you will be my witnesses in Jerusalem, in all Judea and Samaria, and to the ends of the earth" (1:8).

The words about the Holy Spirit coming upon them are a clear echo of the way the angel Gabriel announced the birth of Jesus to Mary: "The Holy Spirit will come upon you, and the power of the Most High will overshadow you" (Luke 1:35). Here Jesus addresses the disciples, who in the power of the same Spirit have been made into a new body, the church, "a new creation" in Christ (2 Cor. 5:17). At the heart of the Pentecost experience is the creation of a new body—the body of Christ, the community of the kingdom.

The disciples at first were mistakenly nationalistic about the coming kingdom (Acts 1:6). But Jesus points them to the true response to kingdom expectation: the creation of a community commissioned with the task of witnessing, in the power of the Spirit, to the kingdom and to its Lord, King Jesus (Acts 1:8).

The church, of itself, is not the kingdom. It is, rather, the messianic community in the service of the kingdom. It witnesses to the kingdom. In its life and values, it anticipates the kingdom. It is the community charged with continuing the messianic mission in the same Spirit and strategy that characterized Jesus' mission. It is the community in which the signs of the kingdom are most clearly evident.

We must resist the temptation to identify the church with the kingdom of God. In traditional Catholicism, established in the Holy Roman Empire, the church pretended (somewhat triumphalistically) to be the kingdom, even when the signs envisioned by the Psalms and the prophets and recovered by Jesus were missing. In this way the image of the kingdom of God lost its power to inspire God's people, and the church's witness to the world lost its credibility.

We must also resist the temptation to clearly separate the kingdom and the church, as some Protestant interpretations, such as dispensationalism, have done. According to this tradition, the kingdom of God, as Jesus proclaimed it, was one thing, and still remains strictly future; the church, when it arose, was totally another thing, a stopgap provision while waiting for the kingdom.

The church must be defined by its relation to the kingdom. Rather than separating church and mission, as Constantinian Protestantism has done, the role of the church is defined as mission, full-orbed witness to God's kingdom in the power of his Spirit. The church is commissioned to continue the messianic mission of Jesus. Like Jesus, we proclaim the kingdom of God by deed and word. Like Jesus, we dedicate ourselves to those activities which correspond to God's kingdom. Authentic signs of the kingdom should be evident in the church. And together with Jesus, we fervently pray, "Your kingdom come. Your will be done, on earth as it is in heaven" (Matt. 6:10).

8

New Creation

The new creation, with the configuration of images which it represents, is one of the principal images by which the early church understood its nature and mission. However, as the church gradually moved away from its roots in the NT, ironically, the future increasingly receded into the distance. The eschatological vision, characterized by God's promise of restored creation, gradually lost its power to attract. This, in turn, led to the fading of the dynamic vision of mission which the new creation inspired.

Especially from the fourth century onward, the new creation image has all but ceased to stir the imagination of the church. The image has come to be interpreted in largely futuristic terms, thereby losing its power to reflect the church's true identity and to illuminate in a full-orbed way its role as participant in God's mission in the world.

However, the new creation is a powerful metaphor for understanding the NT vision of the church's identity and role. The image helps us understand the church's mission in the world. The church as the new creation stands between what God has already done in the past, and what God will certainly renew and complete. He will fulfill his purpose by creative intervention as salvation history moves onward toward its final outcome.

The church stands in the chain of God's creative acts: the creation of the ordered universe and humanity, the creation of a people which bears the Lord's name through the call of Abraham, and clearly in the Exodus-Sinai experience. Thus the church is "a kind of first fruits of [God's] creatures" (James 1:18). The church is a new creation and a new humanity, "the new Jerusalem, coming down out of heaven from God" (Rev. 21:2; cf. 3:12; Gal. 4:26). It anticipates the time when God will finish "making all things new" (Rev. 21:5). This configuration of images points eloquently to the church's unique mission as God's sign of the future.

Creation and New Creation in the Old Testament

The ancient Hebrews were less concerned with the formal details of creation than were the other peoples of the Ancient Near East. This does not mean that the OT is relatively unconcerned with the idea of God's creative work. It means, rather, that creation is set in the context of their wholistic vision of God's saving activity. The OT conceives of creation as the beginning of salvation history. This means that creation is viewed as the first among Yahweh's saving acts.

According to the OT narrative, creation is effected by God's word-acts (Gen. 1-2; Pss. 104-105). Even though creation is the first of God's great saving acts, there is a sense in which God's creative work continues with his ongoing activity in nature in behalf of his people, as well as in his saving and provident interest in their history (Pss. 104-105). All the aspects of God's intervention in nature as well as in the events of history are integral parts of God's saving will (McKensie: 1,293-1,294).

The prophets of Israel spoke of a new creation—of "new heavens and a new earth" (Isa. 65:17; 66:22). Elaborating further on the theme of the new creation, they speak of God doing "a new thing" (Jer. 31:22), of the creation of "a new heart" and "a new spirit" (Ezek. 11:19; 36:26), and of "a new covenant" (Jer. 31:31). God's new creative activity is described by means of a number of images. The desert, arid and inhospitable toward humankind, will become "a fruitful field" (Isa. 32:15; 35:1-2, 6b, 7a; 41:18-20). The fertility of the land, the gift of God's providence, will become superabundant (Ezek. 36:6-12; Joel 3:18; Amos 9:13). Uncertainties of inclement seasons and the darkness of night shall be overcome (Zech. 14:7). So will the violence that characterizes human relationships, as well as the animal kingdom (Mic. 4:1-4; Isa. 2:1-4; 11:6-9; 65:25).

The prophets look beyond the current situation characterized by broken covenant relationships and the corresponding expressions of God's wounded covenant love, his jealous wrath. They envision a new creation characterized by the pouring out of God's Spirit upon his people, who will dwell together in justice, righteousness, and peace (Isa. 32:15-18; McKensie: 1,294). According to the prophetic vision, God's new creative activity is restoring his people to covenant blessedness within salvation history (Isa. 40:28-31; 41:20; 42:5-9; 43:18-19; 51:9-11).

No matter how dark the present and the immediate future seemed, the prophetic hope was expressed by the image of a new creation. God, the original Creator, is also the eschatological Creator. The first creation will come to its fruition in the creation of the new heaven and the new earth. This is not an enchanted sphere of utopian fantasy. Instead, the new creation is viewed as the completion of God's intention for original creation. In the OT, both creations are integral parts of the history of salvation. They are both gifts of God's saving providence (Eichrodt: 106-107). This is the promise that is picked up in the NT: "We wait for new heavens and a new earth, where righteousness is at home" (2 Pet. 3:13). It is "a new heaven and a new earth, . . . the new Jerusalem, coming down out of heaven from God" (Rev. 21:1-2; cf. 3:12). The hope of God's people that he will "make all things new" is solidly rooted in the faith of the OT.

New Creation in the New Testament: The Gospels

The new creation motif in the NT is not limited to a future period of fulfillment beyond history. The messianic era initiated by Jesus is described from its beginning by the new creation image. The new creation points to the goal of God's saving activity and was a vital part of early Christian hope; it is also reflected in the life of Christians upon this earth because in Christ, it has literally come into the present. Although English versions do not generally make this fact clear, in reality, Jesus "created (*epoiēsen*) the twelve" in a new messianic community (Mark 3:14-16a). The twelve symbolize the new people of God, restored anew by the creative act of God's Messiah. Literally, "in Christ there is a new creation" (2 Cor. 5:17).

In the birth narratives found in the synoptic Gospels, God is the one who intervenes in the history of his people. The Holy Spirit, active in creation, is the agent who initiates this new creation (Matt. 1:20; Luke 1:35). Luke refers to the manner in which Jesus was given a physical body with the following words, directed to Mary, "The Holy Spirit will come upon you." Later, in anticipation of Pentecost, the same words are used to describe the creation of a witnessing community—the new body of Christ (Acts 1:8). The Pentecostal experience of the Holy Spirit is primarily the creation of a new people. It is God's Spirit who creates the new order (Joel 2:28-29).

Only in the Spirit of God is it possible to break down national and social barriers, group interests, caste systems, and the domination of one sex over the other. The creative work of God's Spirit has immediate social consequences. The community of the Spirit is a new social reality. The church, empowered by the creative Spirit of God, is the firstfruits of a new creation with cosmic dimensions. Apostolic reflection on the church as a new creation was anchored directly in the messianic mission of Jesus and indirectly in the OT.

According to the NT, wherever the Spirit of God is at work, there God is active in a new creation. In the synoptic Gospels, Jesus healed and expelled demons in the power of the Spirit. These were sure signs of the inbreaking kingdom—God's new acts of creation. The activity of the Spirit in the presence and work of Christ means that God's new world has arrived earlier than expected (Luke 11:20; Matt. 12:28; Foerster: 1034).[1]

But the presence of God's reign was not limited to its power in humans. The NT also shares the prophets' vision of the material world as the setting of God's new creation. The renewing of creation was also manifest in the calming of the chaotic sea, in the filling of empty wine vats, and in the abundant provision of rations for all (Matt. 8:23-27; John 2:3-8; Matt. 14:13-21 and parallels). The redemptive power of Jesus manifests itself in the renewal of all creation, humanity as well as nature. In the mission of Jesus, the eschatological vision of the new creation was already unfolding.

The parables of the new cloth and the new wine point to a newness which cannot be mixed with the old or contained in it. These parables point to the essential newness of the age which has come in Christ. The context of these parables in all three Synoptics (Matt. 9:16-17; Mark 2:21-22; Luke 5:36-39) refers to the Jewish custom of fasting. They therefore probably allude to the fact that the kingdom being brought by Jesus calls for far more than a few adjustments in Jewish piety. There surely is a deeper implication. A radical newness has come in Jesus which first-century Judaism had not been able to appreciate fully. There is a newness in both the form and the substance of Jesus' messianic mission which can best be described as making God's original creation new.

The Gospel of John also understands the mission of Jesus in terms of a new creation (Vawter: 417-418, 424-431). The allusion to God's original creation in John's prologue (John 1:1-5) sets the stage for the new creation of the Messiah (1:19—2:11). Just as God created originally through his Word, Jesus is the creative Word, active in a new creation (1:1, 14). As in the original creation, the new creation of the Messiah is set in a seven-day span of time (1:29, 35, 39-42, 43; 2:1).[2] This seven-day period of new creation culminates in the manifestation of Jesus' glory and the creation of a new community of believing disciples (2:11).

This is the image which is picked up and widely used in a series of Pauline texts (Rom. 8:19-23; 2 Cor. 5:17; Gal. 6:15; Eph. 2:10-16; Col. 1:15-20). Closely related to the new-creation image are the images of firstfruits (Rom. 6:4-6; 1 Cor. 15:20-23; Eph. 4:13; James 1:18), new humanity (Eph. 2:15; 4:22-24; Col. 3:9-11), and the last Adam (Rom. 5:12-21; 1 Cor. 15:20-22, 44-50).

New Creation in the New Testament: Paul's Writings

"For neither circumcision nor uncircumcision is anything; but a new creation is everything! As for those who will follow this rule—peace be upon them, and mercy, and upon the Israel of God" (Gal. 6:15-16). In the new messianic era, the renewal of creation for which the prophets of Israel hoped has begun under the impulse of the Spirit of God. The ritual which in the past separated Jews from Gentiles has been superseded in this new creation.

The newness of creation is not merely the result of discontinuing this outward formality; it grows out of the dynamic intervention of the Spirit, God's gift of the messianic era. The context in Galatians makes this clear. To live in God's new order is to "walk by the Spirit," to be "led by the Spirit," to produce "the fruit of the Spirit," to "live by the Spirit," and to "be guided by the Spirit" (Gal. 5:16, 18, 22-23, 25). Using another metaphor, "If you sow to the Spirit, you will reap eternal life from the Spirit," the harvest of God's new creation (Gal. 6:8).[3]

The new creation is infinitely more than individuals becoming "new creatures," important as this reality may be in personal experience. The reference in the following verse to "the Israel of God" points to the essentially corporate sense of the term. "The Israel of God," here a parallel of the phrase, "a new creation," is the new people of God gathered in the Messiah. "If you belong to Christ, then you are Abraham's offspring, heirs according to the promise" (Gal. 3:29). God once created a people for himself in the call of Abraham (Gen. 12:1-3) and in the Exodus-Sinai event (Isa. 43:15-21). Likewise, the messianic community is a new creation, the new Israel of God. According to this Pauline vision, the church is the locus of God's new creative activity to which the prophets of Israel aspired.

Another key text for understanding the Pauline view of the new creation image for the church is 2 Corinthians 5:17: "So if anyone is in Christ, there is a new creation: everything old has passed away; see, everything has become new!" (NRSV). However, most English translations follow the Revised Standard Version and interpret the new creation as an image of what happens to the individual who comes to Christ, rather than applying it to the church: "If any one is in Christ, he is a new creation" (RSV).

The translation of this verse in *The Living Bible* is an even more striking example of the way in which modern Protestant Christians approach the task of biblical interpretation with presuppositions of Western individualism and a preoccupation with personal guilt: "When someone becomes a Christian, he becomes a brand new person inside. He is not the same anymore. A new life has begun!" This has become a classic text for describing a widely held Protestant view of personal conversion. The biblical view of the essentially corporate nature of the new creation image has been displaced.

This translation does not have a real basis in the text itself (Yoder, 1980:129-133). First of all, the pronoun "he" is not in the original text. When it is supplied in the interests of a smoother reading, the meaning of the text is changed. The new creation becomes an image for the individual who is in Christ, rather than for the church.

Second, the noun *ktisis* generally refers to creation or to the act of creation. Nowhere in the NT is it used to refer to individuals as such. When this noun is used to denote people, the reference is to categories of people or to human institutions.

Furthermore, the context of the verse indicates that Paul has in mind a new social order. He no longer evaluates people according to carnal criteria or by the world's values (2 Cor. 5:16; cf. Gal. 6:15). The ethnic identities of Jews or Gentiles have become unimportant. What really matters is the new peoplehood which they share in Christ.

A more accurate translation of 2 Corinthians 5:17 is given in the New Revised Standard Version or The New English Bible and might read as follows: "So when anyone is in Christ, there is a new creation; the old order has lost its force, the new one has been created." Christ is the instrument through whom this new social reality comes into being (2 Cor. 5:18).

This interpretation of 2 Corinthians 5:17 is supported by all of the parallel passages in the NT. Galatians 6:15, the only other place where the term "new creation" (*kainē ktisis*) appears in the NT, refers to superseding Jew-Gentile differences in a new creation. In another parallel (Eph. 2:15), to reconcile Jews and Gentiles is to create a new humanity. Ephesians 4:24 exhorts believers, "Clothe yourselves with the new self [humanity], created according to the likeness of God." This climaxes the apostle's call to unity (Eph. 4:1-16). Here, too, this new creation is characterized by mutuality (Eph. 4:25, 28-29, 32). Finally, the parallel passage in Colossians 3:9-11 also speaks of the "new self" being renewed after the image of its Creator. Thus all those divisive social distinctions which plague humanity are superseded in Christ.

In the early Christian hymn in Colossians 1:15-20, Jesus is praised as the personification of God's creative presence. Christ is viewed not only as the pattern for creation but also as the goal toward which creation moves.[4] "He is . . . the firstborn of all creation; for in him all things in heaven and on earth were created— . . . all things have been created through him and for him." The biblical conviction that God's purpose is to renew creation is rooted in the prophetic tradition of ancient Israel. It is picked up in the Gospel reports of Jesus' messianic activity, and incorporated in the faith and worship of the believing community.

In the two parallel stanzas of the hymn, Christ is confessed to be supreme over the created order, "the firstborn of all creation" (Col. 1:15-17), and Lord of the new creation, the church, "the firstborn from the dead" (1:18-20). "The firstborn of all creation" can refer to Christ as preexistent Lord (cf. 1:17). But in its biblical usage, "firstborn" is a title of honor (cf. Exod. 4:22; Ps. 89:27). Rather than merely assigning to Christ priority in time, the principal thrust of the term in this confession surely points to his supremacy.

"For in him all things . . . were created" (Col. 1:16) expresses the conviction that Christ is the unifying center for the restoration of harmony in the universe. In Christ "all things in heaven and on earth were created, things visible and invisible." This points concretely to the cosmic character of the reconciling work of Christ, including the physical and spiritual realms of matter and beings, as well as the social order.

Christ "is before all things, and in him all things hold together" (Col. 1:17). Here is a dynamic expression of the unrestricted dominion over the created order by the One to whom the church is subject in its mission to the world (Reicke: 687). This phrase climaxes the first stanza, which celebrates the cosmic dimensions of new creation in Christ. The church confesses that in Christ the entire created order finds its real meaning and coherence. Such faith provides a powerful overarching motivation for the church's mission in the world.

The second stanza of the hymn highlights the reality of the new creation. Christ "is the head of the body, the church; he is the beginning, the firstborn from the dead" (Col. 1:18). In Paul's writings "head" carries the idea of source of life and growth as well as source of authority. As "beginning," Christ is the foundation of the new and redeemed humanity, the church, "a new creation" (cf. Gal. 6:15; 2 Cor. 5:17). The phrase, "firstborn from the dead," establishes a parallelism with the first stanza ("firstborn of all creation," Col. 1:15). The risen Christ is supreme in God's new creation, anticipated as such in the church, and to be realized universally as supreme.

For in Christ "all the fullness of God was pleased to dwell" (Col. 1:19). Jesus is the fullest expression of God's creating and re-creating purpose. This climactic expression is reserved for the second stanza, which refers to the church. The Christian congregation in Colossae was only about seven years old and was small in number, a group which could squeeze together into the house of one of the members. To this church, Paul says, in effect, "The restoring activity of God is seen most fully in Christ. And this he shares with his body, the church. And this new creation which has already begun in the church will finally extend to the whole universe." Amazing! This is not a mere affirmation of divine immanence. It is the confession that the cosmic dimensions of God's new creation are already beginning in Christ and in the church. The messianic mission of Christ and his community points toward a whole new creation.

The early Christian community clearly perceived a close relationship between Christology and the symbolic character of its witness. The true nature of Christ shines forth with clarity only when the church makes visible the messianic alternative of the new creation which has come about in the world. The Christology of the primitive church's confessions is far from being the largely speculative activity which has characterized much of the later church's theology. Instead, it spoke most directly to the question of the identity and role of the church itself.

The church is the place where, in a new act of creation, God has inaugurated a reconciled community. However, the community of the new creation can also become a sign to the evil world of the world's downfall (Phil. 1:27-28). So in reality, the church is both a sign of salvation and a sign of judgment, depending on how the world responds to the symbolic testimony of God's people. These missionary consequences of the community of the new creation are intelligible only in the light of the OT motif of God's people as a sign which attracts the nations.

The Firstfruits of New Creation

Firstfruits is an image drawn from the OT and employed in several ways in the NT. It enriches even more the biblical understanding of the church as a new creation. James 1:18 shows this convergence of metaphors. "In fulfillment of his [the Father of lights'] own purpose he gave us birth by the word of truth, so that we would become a kind of first fruits of his creatures." This text implies that the church is not simply and finally the new creation. It is only the first installment of God's new act of creation.

The image of firstfruits is drawn from the cultic practices of ancient Israel. The offering of firstfruits was from an early part of the oncoming grain harvest. It was a testimony of gratitude for God's prodigal generosity as well as a symbol of offering the whole harvest, which was about to be gathered. In addition, it furnished the occasion for God's people to recall with thanksgiving the mighty acts of God. The Lord, beginning with "a wandering Aramean," had created Israel into a "great nation, mighty and populous, . . . and gave [them] . . . a land flowing with milk and honey" (Deut. 26:5-9).

Although the image of firstfruits is employed only eight times by three NT writers, it adds an important dimension to our understanding of the NT idea of the church as a new creation (Rom. 8:23; 11:16; 16:5; 1 Cor. 15:20, 23; 16:15; James 1:18; Rev. 14:4). The image is used in the NT in essentially four ways. (1) Christ in his resurrection is the firstfruits of the dead (1 Cor. 15:20-23). (2) The Spirit is the firstfruits or pledge of the full-orbed familihood (adoption of sons and daughters) and peoplehood (Gentiles and Jews) which characterize God's new creation (Rom. 8:23; 11:16; cf. 2 Cor. 1:22; 5:5). (3) The first believers in a given geographical area are firstfruits; they represent the promise and power of the gospel in the whole area (Rom. 16:5; 1 Cor. 16:15). (4) The church is God's firstfruits from among humankind (James 1:18; Rev. 14:4).

In Romans 8:18-25, Paul affirms the participation of both humanity and the natural universe in the benefits of Christ's saving work.[5] According to the biblical vision, the cosmos itself suffers the consequences of humanity's sin (Gen. 3:17). Human rebellion not only broke the relationship of communion with God but also introduced disorder and violence in all creation. The universe, created for humanity, also shares in humanity's destiny. Cursed, due to human sin, it shares in the violence and disorder which characterize humanity. Humans are destined to glory, as a result of the work of Christ; so also the rest of the universe is destined to redemption.

Cosmic restoration is linked to humanity's restoration in Christ. Restored humanity will live in peace among themselves and with God in a world which has also been transformed by his Spirit. Because of the death and resurrection of Christ, the suffering and pain in which both humanity and creation participate are no longer the unbearable agonies of death. In reality, they have become the birthing pains which announce the arrival of the new era. God's people confidently affirm this hope, thanks to the guarantee of God's Spirit.

As well as being the first installment of the harvest, the firstfruits were also a pledge of the final delivery of the whole. As firstfruits, the Spirit of Christ in the midst of God's people is an anticipation of final salvation, not only of redeemed humanity but also of restored creation. The presence of the Spirit in the church anticipates cosmic restoration as well as personal and social salvation (2 Cor. 5:5). The Spirit of Christ is the key to the life of God's people here and now (Rom. 8:2, 4-5, 9, 11, 13-14, 16). The Spirit is also source and sign of hope for the future salvation of humanity and the cosmos.

The firstfruits image, although limited in its usage in the NT, is significant for our understanding of the church's identity and role. First of all, this image reflects a strong sense of the church's mission in the world. The church plays a strategic role in salvation history. In its life in the world, the church is characterized by a certain solidarity with the first creation and experiences the contradictions of its fallen condition (Rom. 8:22-23). But as the new community of the Spirit, the church is also a sign of hope (Rom. 8:24-25). The firstfruits of the new creation are found in the church. The church is "what [God] has made us, created in Christ Jesus for good works" which fulfill God's original purpose for humankind (Eph. 2:10).

The presence of the Spirit of Christ, "the beginning of God's creation," distinguishes the church as firstfruits of God's new creation (Rom. 8:14). As firstfruits, the church is the sign of hope which links fallen creation to the new creation. If the church is to be the living community of the Spirit, it must participate in God's mission in the world. As firstfruits, the church is the saving link between the Creator and all of his creatures, between fallen creation and the restoration of the new creation.

As firstfruits of God's new creation, the church incarnates the "pull of the future." In a certain sense the life and mission of the church consists of realizing, in all of its dynamic potential, "the presence of the future." This is the real tension which should characterize the relationship between the church and the world. The two creations, the old creation which is fallen and the new creation restored in the image of its Maker, do not coexist on equal terms. God's purpose for the future is expressed in the new creation, not in the old. The fundamental "goodness" of God's original creation is confessed (1 Cor. 10:26; 1 Tim. 4:4; Rev. 4:11; 10:6). Yet the newness of creation in Christ receives the major accent in the NT (2 Cor. 5:17; et al.).

"The spirit of adoption" (Rom. 8:15) emancipates the church from bondage to decay (Rom. 8:20). These firstfruits of the harvest are destined to affect all creatures. The new creation, whose firstfruits are present in the church, spearheads a transformation which God intends for all creation. This is the context in which the church is commissioned to "proclaim the good news to the whole creation" (Mark 16:15; Col. 1:23). The church's participation in this universal mission is carried out with joyful and expectant confidence under the authority of the One who has promised to make "all things new" (Rev. 21:5).

9

New Humanity

The new creation and firstfruits metaphors converge in a number of NT passages with the image of the new humanity in the early church's self-understanding (Eph. 2:13-18; 4:22-24; Col. 3:9-11; Rom. 5:12-21; 6:4-6; 1 Cor. 15:20-22, 45-49). In the biblical vision, humanity and the created universe are interrelated. Humanity and creation alike have suffered the fatally disruptive consequences of humanity's disobedience. However, according to the early Christian confession, Jesus Christ, the "last Adam," is head of a new humanity as well as agent of creation's restoration. This was envisioned by the prophets of Israel during the crucial period before and after the exile. Their vision inspired Jesus in his messianic activity aimed at restoring God's covenant people. This restored messianic community is further described in Pauline writings by means of the image of a new humanity. In this vision, Jesus was the "last Adam" who characterized concretely the new humanity re-created in his image.

The Old Testament Background

The human setting in which Jesus was creating a new humanity, as described in the NT, was characterized by animosity and outright hatred. By the first century, Israel's misdirected struggle to maintain its own identity in the midst of the nations had evolved into policies of separation, isolation, intolerance, and outright hatred toward non-Jews. Gentiles reciprocated with similar attitudes toward the Jews. There was, however, another current which tended to soften this nationalistic spirit of intolerance and hatred. The book of Ruth was a reminder that a pious Moabitess was among the ancestors of king David (and Jesus). Also, the book of Jonah reminded readers of God's merciful disposition toward the most hated of Israel's enemies, and of their vocation to mission among the nations.

The background for understanding the NT view of a new humanity is found in the prophetic hope that the messianic era would be for the salvation of the nations. This prophetic vision inspired Jesus' own messianic self-understanding as well as that of the early Christian community. According to this view, Yahweh would reign over all humanity, and the people of God would fulfill a saving function at the center of his purposes. The prophets share this message through a variety of images (see Isa. 2:1-4; Mic. 4:1-4; Zech. 8:20-22; 14:6-11). It is the vision of "the mountain of the house of the Lord" being established in a new and visible way among the peoples of the earth. The nations would be attracted by covenant relationships of righteousness, peace, and salvation—which characterize God's people.

According to this vision, swords will be beaten into plowshares and spears into pruning hooks. The tools of destruction will become resources placed at the service of humanity's needs. Warfare will be renounced as a means for resolving conflicts. God himself will be the arbiter of differences and will work through his "servant," who "will faithfully bring forth justice . . . in the earth" (Isa. 42:1-4). In a kind of sabbatical or jubilee restoration, "they shall all sit under their own vines and under their own fig trees, and no one shall make them afraid" (Mic. 4:4). This freedom from fear will become reality in the context of a new social structure—the messianic people of God made up of all peoples and nations of the earth.

Such a messianic restoration of God's kingdom would be

marked by the ingathering of the nations. It offers a remarkable contrast to the exclusiveness and outright hostility of many Jew-Gentile relationships, especially following the exile. In addition to the prophetic texts already noted, the Servant Songs of Isaiah tell how the servant is anointed by the Spirit of God to "bring forth justice" to the nations and to offer "a covenant to the people, a light to the nations." This is so that God's "salvation may reach to the end of the earth" (Isa. 42:1, 6; 49:6). "Many nations shall join themselves to the Lord on that day, and shall be my people; and I will dwell in your midst" (Zech. 2:11). These prophetic references to God's saving purpose for all nations are among those from which Jesus drew for his messianic self-understanding.

The Messianic Mission of Jesus

The view that Luke 4:17-30 is a summary preview of Jesus' messianic mission is widely held by scholars. The quotation from Isaiah 61:1-2 shows that God's sabbatical and Jubilee provisions for establishing righteousness among his people are a paradigm for messianic salvation. In his Gospel Luke shows that Jesus did, indeed, carry out his mission of proclamation and service in line with this vision.

Jesus' references to the inclusion of Gentiles within the saving purposes of God (Luke 4:24-27) were too much for the synagogue participants in Nazareth to accept. They attempted to put him to death. This Lukan passage is a microcosm of Jesus' messianic mission: God's gracious offer of peace, righteousness, and salvation to all peoples, even at the cost of the life of the Messiah himself.

The Synoptic accounts of Jesus' messianic activity show that Luke's preview was right on target. Matthew (12:18-20) claims that Jesus' ministry to the needy was the fulfillment of Isaiah 42:1-4. Even more notably, he emphasized the fact that the messianic mission is for the Gentiles. The story of the wise men in Matthew's Gospel reflects the hope that the benefits of God's restored reign may reach to the nations. In the prophetic vision, the restoration of God's rule over Israel was an expression of his intention for all humanity. "Nations shall come to your light, and kings to the brightness of your dawn. . . . They shall bring gold and frankincense, and shall proclaim the praise of the Lord" (Isa. 60:3, 6b; cf. Ps. 72:10b-14).

Matthew's genealogical listing surely intends to present Jesus as a true son of God's people, as son of Abraham and son of David. Yet the names of the four Gentile women among Jesus' ancestors indicate a notable absence of the sense—widespread in first-century Judaism—of moral superiority and racial prejudice in the primitive messianic community.[1]

Even within Israel, Jesus' ministry was to the poor, the outcasts, those without hope, those for whom, according to the most highly respected religious conviction of the time, the door of salvation was closed. According to the official view, Jesus' messianic activity was so unpredictable that at one point, at least, the question was seriously raised as to whether Jesus might defect to the Gentiles (John 7:35). His concern for the Samaritans is amply reported in the Gospels.

In Mark's version of the temple cleansing, the Gentile motif is again prominent. God's house "shall be called a house of prayer for all the nations" (Mark 11:17; cf. Isa. 56:7). Both Mark (11:18) and Luke (19:47) report that this was the point at which "the chief priests, the scribes, and the leaders of the people kept looking for a way to kill him" (Luke 19:47). Jesus decisively intervened in favor of freeing the court of the Gentiles for the purpose for which it was intended—prayer. That action triggered the events that ended in his crucifixion.

According to all of the Gospels, Jesus began his mission inviting people to follow him as disciples and become part of the messianic community. The earliest disciples may well have been a homogeneous group of Galileans, but the community soon came to be characterized by its diversity. In the group were Judeans and Galileans, ex-Zealots and former collaborators with the established regime. In Jesus' traveling retinue, as he went "through cities and villages, proclaiming and bringing the good news of the kingdom," were both women and men (Luke 8:1-3). Jesus gathered together a community in which mutually antagonistic groups were reconciled to one another.

The rich and the poor, educated and uneducated, country people and city dwellers, men and women were all gathered together into a reconciled community. Both men and women belonged to Jesus' circle of disciples. From the beginning, it was Jesus' intention that this disciple group would represent the newly restored people of God. Jesus was calling all kinds of people to participate in the messianic community. Thus he showed that the new pattern of the kingdom is a social order in which there is no discrimination against women, or the poor, or the unsuccessful, or children. This is the vision that oriented relationships in the early church.

The Pauline vision outlined in Ephesians 2:13-18 is not merely figurative. According to the Gospels, Jesus literally laid down his life for the creation of a new humanity characterized by peace and righteousness. Gentiles as well as Jews could participate fully in that new humanity. The fact that Gentiles and Jews were soon incorporated together into a new people of God is amply documented in Acts and the Epistles. Such a logically unlikely thing occurred so quickly (Rom. 1:16; Col. 3:11) in the face of so much social and religious pressure to the contrary. This must certainly be attributed to the effect of the life, death, and resurrection of Jesus Christ and to the continuing presence of his Spirit within the community.

The Pauline Vision of the New humanity

Now in Christ Jesus you who once were far off have been brought near by the blood of Christ. For he is our peace; in his flesh he has made both groups into one and has broken down the dividing wall, that is, the hostility between us. He has abolished the law with its commandments and ordinances, that he might create in himself one new humanity in place of the two, thus making peace, and might reconcile both groups to God in one body through the cross, thus putting to death that hostility through it. So he came and proclaimed peace to you who were far off and peace to those who were near; for through him both of us have access in one Spirit to the Father.

(Eph. 2:13-18)

This text sums up Paul's reflection on the significance of the atoning work of Christ in the face of human relationships marred by domination and exploitation (Gal. 3:25-29; Col. 3:9-11) and alienation from God (Col. 1:13). It points to the creation of a new messianic community, the church, which is at the center of God's purpose for humanity as well as for all creation (Eph. 3:3-11; cf. Col. 1:13-14). This new creation—the new humanity—is characterized by peace, reconciliation, and common life in the Spirit of God (see Driver, 1986:213-229).

Ephesians 2:13-18 is held together by a series of phrases which describe through whom, how, and by what means the new humanity has been created. Peace has been made between Jews and Gentiles as well as with God. This peace is messianic. It is found exclusively "in Christ Jesus," "in his flesh," "in one body," "through him" (2:13-14, 16, 18). This fact is so fundamental that the early church came to see Jesus as the personification of peace: "he is our peace" (2:14).

Other phrases refer to the way in which Christ achieved this peace: "by the blood of Christ," "in his flesh," "through the cross" (Eph. 2:13-16). Still other phrases describe the means of achieving peace. He "made both groups into one," "has broken down the dividing wall [of] hostility," "abolished the law with its commandments and ordinances," to "create in himself one new humanity," and "came and proclaimed peace" (2:14-17).

This messianic community is, first of all, a social reality. Christ is praised in this passage but not primarily for the peace which he brings to individual souls, although this may well be an important side effect. The peace in view here is a social reality in the church. It is first of all peace among humankind, Jews and

Gentiles, and only then between God and humanity (Eph. 2:16-17; Barth: 262).

Traditionally, theories of the atonement have tended to concentrate on the removal of barriers between individuals and God. However, in this text the barrier removed by the death of Christ is the one which separated human groups from each other. This leads to the creation of a new humanity in which both together are reconciled to God (Eph. 2:14-16).

Both Peter and Paul refer to the substance of the good news which Jesus Christ brings as the "gospel of peace" (Acts 10:36; Rom. 10:15; Eph. 2:17; 6:15). Jesus, in his messianic proclamation and activity, reconciled outsiders and insiders. He created peace in the messianic community, reconciling the factions represented among the disciples. In the early church, to be in the messianic community was to be reconciled with others, thereby concretely experiencing peace.

Paul's understanding of peace has sometimes become obscured in the thought and practices of the church. The roots for understanding the meaning of peace, as used in this passage, are to be found in the OT. Shalom is a broad concept, essential to the biblical understanding of relationships among people and between people and God. According to the prophets, true peace reigned when righteousness prevailed, when people were treated with equality and respect, and when salvation flourished. This was happening in the social order determined by God through the gracious covenant which he had given to his people.

Above all, shalom characterized the messianic kingdom in which God's true intention for his people would be realized. One of the clearest expressions of this vision is found in Isaiah:

> How beautiful upon the mountains
> are the feet of the messenger
> who announces peace,
> who brings good news,
> who announces salvation,
> who says to Zion, "Your God reigns." (52:7)

Shalom is experienced in the realm of God's righteous reign, present in the person of the Messiah. This helps us to understand why the early church confessed that "he is our peace" (Eph. 2:14), identifying peace with Christ, the Creator of the new humanity.

A New Social Order of Peace

The formation of a new humanity characterized by peace is a new act of creation. The surprising and utterly scandalous element in this is the fact that it began on the cross. While the first creation began with nature and culminated in the formation of humankind, the new creation is beginning with the formation of a new humanity, the firstfruits of a restoration with cosmic dimensions (Rom. 8:18-22).

The concept of newness, especially when used with reference to creation, denotes in the Bible a culmination or final fruition of God's will and work (Barth: 309). Of the two Greek words for denoting newness, references to the new humanity and the new creation generally employ *kainos,*[2] which means qualitative newness in contrast to temporal innovation.[3] The term bears an unequivocal eschatological content and refers to the "new age" which has dawned in Christ with the creation of a new humanity (Behm: 449).

The fact that this "one new humanity" is created out of both Jews and Gentiles is underscored in Ephesians 2:14-16. However, this "new humanity" is not the reduction of Jews and Gentiles into a homogeneous race of a third kind. Rather, the church is composed of Jews and Gentiles reconciled to one another by Christ, who has died for both groups. The existence of this new humanity is based upon liberation from the mutual exclusiveness of nationalism, religious pride, and individualism. It is characterized by an altogether new kind of social behavior. This gracious work of demolition and construction has happened to both Jews and Gentiles. The implication of this creation of "one new humanity" out of the two is that neither of the two can enjoy salvation, peace, and life without the other. People need each other if they are to be saved at all (Barth: 311).

New humanity is not composed simply of groups of like-minded and compatible people. The NT shows that the reconciliation of erstwhile enemies gives way to the creation of "one new humanity" (Matt. 5:23-24, 43-48; Gal. 2:11-14; Rom. 5:6-10). This new humanity is new in a truly revolutionary way. It is a social reality totally dependent upon God for its existence. It is a community which loves and forgives just as God has done in Christ (Eph. 4:32—5:2). The creation of this new humanity, characterized by peace, is neither a coincidence nor a secondary result of the saving work of Christ. The creation of a new humanity in which personal, social, and economic hostilities are all overcome in reconciliation is a direct and primary result of the life, death, and resurrection of God's Messiah.

Disciples of Jesus and the New Humanity

The new humanity image was apparently used in the instruction of new disciples, preparing them for baptism and participation in the life of the early church.

> You have stripped off the old self [man, humanity] with its practices and have clothed yourselves with the new self, which is being renewed in knowledge according to the image of its creator. In that renewal there is no longer Greek and Jew, circumcised and uncircumcised, barbarian, Scythian, slave and free; but Christ is all and in all! (Col. 3:9b-11)

Ephesians 4:22-24 is a parallel.

> You were taught to put away your former way of life, your old self, corrupt and deluded by its lusts, and to be renewed in the spirit of your minds, and to clothe yourselves with the new self, created according to the likeness of God in true righteousness and holiness.

Romans 6:4-6 expresses a similar concept using the same image. "Our old self [man] was crucified with him so that" (6a) "we too might walk in newness of life" (4c). All three of these passages were apparently used in the instruction of new believers in the early Christian community.

While basic instruction in the early church surely carried implications for the personal discipleship of individual Christians, the primary thrust of the new humanity image here is corporate. The dominant concern of catechesis in the early church was not merely with strictly personal ethics, but with the kind of people they were becoming. To be a member of the messianic community, one needed to participate in a new humanity.

The essentially corporate nature of the new humanity is also underscored in Ephesians 4:13-14. "Maturity [a complete man]" and "the measure of the full stature of Christ" are contrasted with the instability of "children." Here the primary reference is to the messianic community; in it all of the gifts of grace which the risen Christ bestows upon his body contribute to the growth and completion of its common life as a new humanity.

There are a number of obvious implications in these passages for the significance of the new humanity image in the church's self-understanding. (1) Humankind is divided into two distinct social solidarities—the "old humanity," which is corrupted; and the "new humanity," re-created after the likeness of God. (2) The "new humanity" is characterized by a continual process of renewal "after the image of its Creator" in "true righteousness and holiness." (3) Both the "old humanity" and the "new humanity" refer to corporate realities, and to participate in one or the other is more than a mere matter of individual ethical choices. It is a question of incorporation into the social fabric of a new humanity. It is participation in a new social order of things, in contrast to the old order which is deceptive and transient.

(4) In the old regime, the divisive and destructive differences of race, nationality, culture, classes, and religion proved to be insuperable. In the new humanity, these differences are all over-

come, and the Spirit of Christ is all pervasive. (5) The "image of
its creator" determines the social structures which mark the new
humanity. According to the contexts of these passages, it is the
new way of Jesus which provides the concrete model for social
behavior in the new humanity. In fact, Jesus himself is the New
Man, the new humanity, the new Adam.

The Last Adam

The archetypal image of Representative Man is expressed in
terms of the first Adam and the last Adam (Rom. 5:12-21; 1 Cor.
15:20-22, 44-49). It also contributes to our understanding of the
biblical image of the new humanity.[4] But even more importantly
for our purposes, it helps us to understand the relationship of
the church (the new humanity) to Jesus Christ (the New Man).[5]

In the Gospels, Jesus referred to himself most often as Son of
Man. While this title does not appear in Paul's writings, he picks
up its meaning in a set of similar terms: "the one who was to
come," "the one man" in contrast to Adam, who is simply called
Adam or "one man" who trespassed (Rom. 5:12-21). In 1 Corinthians 15:45-49, Christ is called "the last Adam," "the second
man," and "the man of heaven"—in contrast to "the first man,
Adam." Just as Jesus had done with regard to the Son of Man
(Mark 10:45), Paul relates "the last Adam" motif to the Suffering
Servant of Yahweh, who brings "justification leading to eternal
life" (Rom. 5:12-21; Phil. 2:6-11; Jeremias, 1964:141-143).

Behind this Pauline use of terms lies the Hebrew idea of corporate personality, in which the life of a people—their corporate
personality—was focused representatively in their leader. This
was an important concept for the articulation of the self-understanding of God's people. As the "anointed of Yahweh," the king
became the bearer, in a representative way, of Israel's destiny
(Jer. 30:18-22). Among the chief characteristics of this person
were being chosen by God and rendering obedience to God's
purpose for his people.

The NT shows a close relationship between the obedience

and vicarious suffering of God's Anointed (Messiah) and the way in which the kingship of Christ is exercised. This is certainly not coincidence (cf. Phil. 2:5-11). "The Lamb will conquer them, for he is Lord of lords and King of kings, and those with him are called and chosen and faithful" (Rev. 17:14). "The Lamb, . . . clothed in a robe dipped with blood," conquers through his name, "The Word of God," symbolized by the sharp sword coming from his mouth (Rev. 19:9, 13-15; cf. Heb. 4:12). He is "King of kings and Lord of lords" (Rev. 19:16).

As God's Anointed, Jesus carries representatively the mission and destiny of God's people. The life and mission of his people is anticipated in the saving work of Christ. In his suffering and victory, Jesus carries the suffering and victory of God's people.

This solidarity includes death as well as life. Christ's representative role as the New Adam includes his vicarious death in absolute obedience to the Father, a death in which we too participate (Rom. 5:12-21). Jesus is also viewed as the New Adam from the perspective of the resurrection (1 Cor. 15:20-22, 45-49). He is the life-giving Spirit and the image to which redeemed humanity will eventually be conformed. In Pauline writings characterized by new creation and new humanity images (Eph. 2:15; 4:13, 22, 24; Col. 3:9), Christ is viewed as the Representative Person in whom the people of God find fullness (Eph. 4:13).

In Romans 5:12-21, Paul presupposes the biblical vision of corporate personality. This includes a solidarity with Adam in his fallen condition. But there is also a new solidarity of grace in which Christ is viewed as Representative Head of a new humanity characterized by "righteousness of life." Adam was representative of the Fall, of the old creation in which sin and death are universally shared. Jesus is the Son of Man in whom the age of fulfillment has dawned.

Concretely, Paul understands the work of Christ the Representative Man as obedience to the Father unto the point of death on our behalf. The representative character of Christ's work tells us something about the vicariousness of his death. Jesus' death was not instead of ours in the sense that Christians are thereby exempt from death. As the New Adam, Jesus' death and resurrection were representative, anticipating our dying and being raised with him (1 Thess. 4:14; 5:10; 2 Cor. 5:15; 4:10; Rom. 14:9).

The Pauline image of Christ as Representative Man in 1 Corinthians 15:20-22, 45-49 is focused on his resurrection through which he is bearer of the possibility of life for all. He is both "a life-giving spirit" (15:45) and the Representative Man to whose image new humanity is destined to become conformed (15:49). This transformation has already begun to take place because the Lord is in reality the creative Spirit active in our midst (2 Cor. 3:18; 4:10-12).

Neither Adam nor Jesus was simply a private individual. Each was also an "Adam," a representative human being. What each of them was, others in their train have become. The first were, by nature, essentially physical and earthly, merely living souls. But those who participate in the new age, just as the Last Adam, are spiritual and heaven-oriented, sharers in the power of a life-giving Spirit (1 Cor. 15:45; cf. John 6:63).

Thus when Paul speaks about Adam and Jesus Christ, he refers representatively to two humanities. Adam represents what humankind might have been but has become: humanity made for communion with God, but who has become a slave to self. Jesus represents a new kind of humanity: humanity which not only dies but lives again. Jesus' representative role includes the present of new humanity as well as its future. He represents what we are now and what we will become: the community in which God's saving mission of reconciliation is being carried out, anticipating the restored future of communion with God.

Paul also writes that Jesus "is the image (*eikōn*) of the invisible God . . . [and] head of the body, the church; he is the beginning, the firstborn from the dead" (Col. 1:15-18). This metaphor must have spoken powerfully to ordinary first-century Colossian Christians. Jesus is the living portrait of a God commonly held to be invisible and distant. But Jesus is not simply the image of God. He is also the image of humanity as God intended it to be. Jesus offers a vision of humanity created in God's image, which had been mostly forgotten since the Fall. The Colossian hymn invites us to look at Jesus. He not only shows us what God is like. He also gives us a picture of what we were intended to be. Here, in the person of the New Man, is humanity as God intended. In his utter faithfulness to the Father, even to the point of death, Jesus has shown us what restored humanity will be.

Jesus Christ, in contrast to the first Adam, is the true human, the real image of God. Jesus incarnated "the new self, created according to the likeness of God," which his disciples are expected to "put on" (Eph. 4:24; Col. 3:10). Obedient unto death in his messianic mission, Jesus represents what the new messianic people are called to be. Jesus the Messiah, the Last Adam or the New Man, is in absolute obedience to the Father and concretely determines the substance and the form of mission for the messianic community.

This implies that the new humanity is shaped by Jesus Christ, the New Man.[6] Jesus' way in the world is concretely the model for our way of being the new humanity. The popular messianic temptations which Jesus rejected were not mere historical curiosities for the apostolic community. The concrete forms of the Servant of Yahweh as Jesus lived them out are also the example for us. They were recounted so that new disciples of Jesus would know what incorporation into the new humanity means. In the church's life, as well as in its mission, there are no shortcuts to salvation. To live with Christ means first to die with him. It also means that mission will always be cruciform. That Christ died does not only mean that all have died, but that they must continue to work out the concrete consequences of dying with Christ. To accept Jesus as the Messiah is to be willing to share in his suffering. So in this sense, the sufferings of Christ are not a substitute for ours but a pattern to which we must be conformed (Hooker: 82).

It means, too, that concrete expressions of reconciliation are signs pointing to a new humanity. This does not necessarily imply that all multiracial groups participate in the new creation. The point of this image for the mission of the church is that peacemaking is on target. This means the reconciliation of erstwhile enemies with one another and with God through authentic experiences of forgiveness and love of the kind that God has shown us through Jesus Christ. When barriers of separation and enmity are collapsing, those are authentic signs of mission modeled by the New Man for the new humanity.

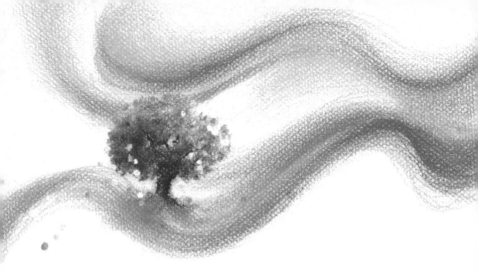

Biblical Images of the Church in Mission

Peoplehood Images

10

The People of God

Among the nearly one hundred images of the church which we find in the NT, the "people of God" is probably the earliest and certainly one of the most foundational for the church's self-understanding (Küng, 1967:119). The frequent references to this image in the NT show its importance.[1] The figure is used in fourteen of the NT writings. Other related images such as Israel, the twelve tribes, the circumcision, and the household of God are used in Galatians, Ephesians, Philippians, Colossians, 1 and 2 Thessalonians, and James. In only six of the NT books (1 and 2 Timothy, Philemon, and 1, 2, and 3 John) is the image missing.[2] So dominant a role does the image play in the ecclesiological self-understanding of the early Christian community that it is difficult to select a limited number of representative texts.[3]

To judge from its function in the NT, this image served primarily to identify the primitive Christian community as God's chosen people. In them the ancient covenant promises of salvation history find their ongoing fulfillment. Although these terms as such are not employed in the NT, it is clear that the disciples of Jesus understood themselves to be the *true* Israel and, before long, the *new* Israel (Küng, 1967:108).

In a sense not true of any of the other groups within first-century Judaism, the community of the Messiah believed that the promises of the old covenant had been fulfilled in their midst. God's reign had come. God's Spirit, gift of the new era, was among them. They lived in anticipation of the imminent consummation of God's reign. An authentic and new people of God, characterized by repentance (*metanoia*) and faith, had arisen in the midst of the old Israel. When these characteristics failed to flourish in "Israel according to the flesh" (1 Cor. 10:18, NRSV note), the messianic community quite naturally understood its identity and sense of mission in terms of the new and true Israel, as the "Israel of God" (Gal. 6:16). Those who once were not God's people are now, in fact, "children of the living God" (Rom. 9:26), "God's own people" (1 Pet. 2:9).

Our goal is to understand biblically the dimensions of meaning which this configuration of images carried in the NT community. Thus it is necessary to understand them as the early church did, in the context of their OT usage. The roots of the people-of-God image for the church's self-understanding are in the OT.

OT Roots of the People of God

The image of the people of God (*laos theou*) occurs more than two thousand times in the Septuagint, in contrast to its marked absence in pagan literature of the period. This prominence is surely due to the nature of the OT itself. It is essentially a salvation history of a people chosen by God as object and channel of divine blessing. In the biblical usage of the term, it carries a collective sense of community in which there is social and spiritual solidarity. By contrast, in both classic and popular Greek, the term is used primarily of people as a crowd or group of inhabitants. It refers especially to population in general as distinct from and subordinate to their rulers. When the plural form is used, it simply denotes the "number of individuals of whom the crowd is composed" (Strathmann, 1967a:30). In the Bible, however, the term refers to a specific people. It stresses both the social and spiritual unity of the people, as such, as well as the relationship of this people to their God.

The people-of-God image reflects the essence of Israel's self-understanding. The faith of Israel can be summed up in this statement: Yahweh is the God of Israel, and Israel is the people of Yahweh (Küng, 1967:117). The fact that Israel belongs to Yahweh is what gives meaning to the people-of-God image. This is the reality which underlies the mission of Moses:

> I am the Lord, and I will free you from the burdens of the Egyptians and deliver you from slavery to them. I will redeem you with an outstretched arm and with mighty acts of judgment. I will take you as my people, and I will be your God. (Exod. 6:6-7a)

This is the reality which characterizes the Sinaitic Covenant: "Now therefore, if you obey my voice and keep my covenant, you shall be my treasured possession out of all the peoples. Indeed, the whole earth is mine, but you shall be for me a priestly kingdom and a holy nation" (Exod. 19:5-6a). This is the context for the sabbatical and Jubilee provisions for ordering the life of God's people (Lev. 25). "I will maintain my covenant with you. . . . I will place my dwelling in your midst. . . . I will walk among you, and will be your God, and you shall be my people" (Lev. 26:9-12).

The theological implications of this fundamental relationship of peoplehood under God are further developed in Deuteronomy. The basis of Israel's peoplehood is the freely assumed saving initiative of Yahweh expressed in the election of his people: "For you are a people holy to the Lord your God; the Lord your God has chosen you out of all the peoples on earth to be his people, his treasured possession" (Deut. 7:6; cf. 4:37; 14:2). It was not due to Israel's power, moral, numerical, economic, or military, that God's people were the object of his gracious election. It was because of God's covenant love for the few, the weak, and the poor (Deut. 7:6-12; cf. 4:37).

Israel owed its existence to the electing, covenant-making, saving reign of God, to which it had freely committed itself (Exod. 19:8).[4] The life of God's people was determined by God's actions and character. Since God's love had called Israel into being, the nature of this relationship calls for his people to love God and to keep his commandments (Deut. 7:9). The Lord said, "You shall be holy, for I the Lord your God am holy" (Lev. 19:2). For the people of God, that is both a promise and an imperative. Concretely, the way of the God of Israel is distinctive; his people will be different. This holiness determines the character of Israel's worship.

As "a priestly kingdom" (Exod. 19:6), together with its representative priest, this people offers "spiritual sacrifices acceptable to God" (1 Pet. 2:5). Such offerings surpass the strictly cultic sphere. Biblical holiness is preeminently social holiness. The call to holiness among God's people is a call to act as God acts, to participate in the saving project of God himself. In practice, this means keeping the covenant (Exod. 19:5-6), keeping his commandments (Deut. 7:9; Lev. 20:7-8), caring for the aged (those who are no longer economically productive), and practicing justice toward bondservants (granting them Sabbath rest; Lev. 19:3). God's people are those who walk with God in his way of being and doing (Lev. 26:12). Israel is Yahweh's people only if it conducts itself accordingly (Deut. 28:9; Num. 15:40; Lev. 19:2).

The holiness of God's people does not depend on their ability to sanctify themselves either morally or with cultic rituals. They are holy by virtue of the fact that they are "a people holy to the Lord your God" (Deut. 7:6; Strathmann, 1967a:35). This does not mean that the holiness of God's people is a fiction (declared rather than real, only imputed). It is rather a constant reminder that the ultimate source of the holiness of God's people is God himself, to whom they owe their very being as well as the possibility of doing.

The promissory and imperative aspects of "you shall be holy, for I am holy" must always be held in tension by God's people. Meanwhile, they may be saved from the temptation to use their holiness as currency for trading on God's grace. The worship of God's people reminds us that the holiness of peoplehood is something to be received and celebrated in worship and life (Ps. 135; et al.) rather than simply a matter of wooden human endeavor.

Truly amazing is the belief that Yahweh is the God of Israel and that Israel is the people of God; this plays a predominant role throughout the OT. This vision of peoplehood under God in the context of covenant relationship unites the Pentateuch, the salvation story of the chroniclers, the worship of the Psalms, and the proclamation of the prophets. The basis of this relationship in the electing and sustaining covenant love of Yahweh is stated most forcefully in Deuteronomy. The liberating and covenant-making activity by which Yahweh has saved his people are, according to the prophetic vision, unique.

The source of this salvation is certainly not to be found in Israel itself. It is based exclusively in Yahweh who "set his heart on you and chose you" (Deut. 7:7; cf. 4:32-39; 7:6-11). The counterpart of God's redeeming activity is that Israel belongs to Yahweh. The fact of God's ownership underlies the prophetic calls to holiness and obedience.

Israel owed its life and existence to the free action of God in the history of his people. Peoplehood is based in the election, grace, love, and faithfulness of God. The Lord acted mercifully in calling the patriarch Abraham, in the liberation of his people from Egyptian slavery, in giving the covenant with its gracious provisions of law, and in sustaining and protecting his people in their ongoing life in the land of promise. The gracious action of God in the history of his people determines their identity. As object of God's election and instrument of his saving mission, Israel becomes the focus of creation, the center of the world and its history, God's own people (Titus 2:14).

God's covenant love was a powerful incentive to faithfulness and obedience in Israel. Yet God's people were also tempted to trade on God's promises, justifying the status quo of injustices on the grounds that God's covenant promises were eternal and the city of David was invincible (Mic. 3:11). In this arena the great prophets of the eighth and seventh centuries in Israel and Judah waged their battle in favor of making Israel's peoplehood real through faithful obedience to a faithful covenant God.[5]

The people may forsake God, turning their backs on the gracious promises of his covenant, and resorting to injustice and violence. Then they show that they are not God's people and that Yahweh of the covenant is not really their God (Hos. 1:9). Hosea's contemporary in the Southern Kingdom was no less categorical: "Hear the word of the Lord, you rulers of Sodom! Listen to the teaching of our God, you people of Gomorrah!" (Isa. 1:10). Even though they retained their cultic rituals, the absence of covenant righteousness in their social relationships showed that they were more akin to the worst of the pagan nations around them than to the people of God's own possession (Isa. 1:10-23).

However, denunciations of injustices and announcements of judgment are not the prophets' last word. Hosea follows his word of woe with a message of hope: "In the place where it was said to them, 'You are not my people,' it shall be said to them, 'Children of the living God' " (Hos. 1:10). And Isaiah reports a new word from the Lord: "Though your sins are like scarlet, they shall be like snow" (Isa. 1:18). Hope for the ongoing life of God's people lies in their willingness to repent, to return to the conditions of peoplehood under the gracious covenant of Yahweh.

When God's judgment finally swept over the Southern Kingdom, Jeremiah was in devastated Judah and Ezekiel was with the exiles in Babylon. Both struggled to keep authentic covenant faith alive among God's people. They were rooted in the foundation of Israel's peoplehood, the ancient exodus-Sinai faith. Thus they were able to see beyond the catastrophic dimensions of judgment and catch a glimpse of the future which the faithful covenant God had in store for his people:

> A new heart I will give you, and a new spirit I will put within you; and I will remove from your body the heart of stone and give you a heart of flesh. I will put my spirit within you, and make you follow my statutes and be careful to observe my ordinances. (Ezek. 36:26-27)

> The days are surely coming, says the Lord, when I will make a new covenant with the house of Israel and the house of Judah. It will not be like the covenant that I made with their ancestors when I took them by the hand to bring them out of the land of Egypt—a covenant that they broke. . . . But this is the covenant that I will make with the house of Israel: . . . I will put my law within them, and I will write it on their hearts; and I will be their God, and they shall be my people. (Jer. 31:31-33)

This prophetic vision of a renewed people provides the point of departure for their vision of mission in which peoplehood under God's gracious new covenant becomes universal in scope. The existence of a renewed people living under the covenant rule of God will be attractive to nations far and near. According to one image, God's people are as a mountain raised above the surrounding hills, to which the nations flow (Isa. 2:2-4; Mic. 4:1-4). In another image, life-giving water flows from Jerusalem to all nations (Ezek. 47:1-12; Zech. 14:6-9).

This view of the missionary character of God's people sweeps away all pretensions to exclusiveness or to privilege. God's people, together with his Messiah, are "a light to the nations" and God's instruments of "salvation . . . to the end of the earth" (Isa. 42:6; 49:6). Finally, peoplehood under the new covenant of the Messiah is anticipated in the prophetic note on which the OT comes to a close: "Sing and rejoice, O daughter of Zion! For lo, I will come and dwell in your midst, says the Lord. Many nations shall join themselves to the Lord on that day, and shall be my people" (Zech. 2:10-11a).

The early Christian community referred to itself as the "church (*ekklēsia*) of God" (cf. 1 Cor. 15:9; Gal. 1:13). Among contemporary Greeks *ekklēsia* meant a public assembly, the popular assembly of the political community. But the primary roots of the NT usage of this term are in the OT. The Septuagint used *ekklēsia* to translate *qahal*, the assembly of Yahweh's covenant people in his presence. In Deuteronomy 23:2-9, for example, *ekklēsia* means the true people of God, separated from unholiness and impurity. This is the context in which the earliest Christian community called itself the "church of God," God's chosen people, the true Israel.

The related concept of "the saints" was closely associated to the *ekklēsia* in the self-understanding of the earliest Christian community. This image had been used in conjunction with the idea of the people of God in the OT and referred specifically to the eschatological restoration of the people of God (Dan. 7). The messianic community saw itself as the holy people of God, being restored as part of God's coming reign. This sense of self-identity was still strong even after the Christian church broke out of its early Jewish matrix and became predominantly Gentile in its social composition. Thus it continued to understand itself essentially as God's holy people, the true Israel of God.

The People of God in the New Testament

In keeping with this prophetic vision of the people of God, the community gathered by faith in Jesus the Messiah increasingly understood itself to be the true Israel, the true people of God. The fact that Gentiles had entered into this peoplehood served to confirm the prophetic eschatological vision of the people of God. In fact, the ancient titles accorded to Israel, such as the people of God and other similar images, were far more fundamental to the early church's self-understanding than names of more recent coinage, such as "Christians."

In the NT, the term "people" (*laos*) is often used in the same sense as it was in the Septuagint. In many passages it simply means "nation." More importantly, it is applied specifically to Israel, as chosen by God to be his people, distinguishing them from "the nations." However, the NT moves beyond the Greek OT in that it frequently applies the title *laos* to the messianic community.[6] At the Jerusalem conference, James stated, "God first looked favorably on the Gentiles, to take from among them a people for his name" (Acts 15:14). This must have sounded shocking to Jewish ears. God's people and Gentiles were mutually exclusive terms in Judaism. However, it reflects the prophetic missionary vision of peoplehood that the early church received from Jesus.

The reference to "a people" in Acts 18:10 is equally amazing. Paul had separated himself from the synagogue in Corinth, where his message had been rejected. He dedicated his efforts to the Gentiles, who according to Judaism, were not God's people. At this point, Paul received a vision from the Lord confirming his mission and assuring him that "many in this city . . . are my people."

Similarly, Paul unites the Sinaitic promise (Lev. 26:12) and the prophetic vision of Ezekiel (37:27) and applies them to the Christian community in Corinth: "I will live in them and walk among them, and I will be their God, and they shall be my people" (2 Cor. 6:16). In the same vein, Paul quotes Hosea 2:23 and 1:10, texts in which the prophet refers to a repentant and restored Israel, to show that God's people include both Jews and Gentiles:

> He has called [us], not from the Jews only but also from the Gentiles[.] As indeed he says in Hosea, "Those who were not my people I will call 'my people,' and her who was not beloved I will call 'beloved.' " "And in the very place where it was said to them, 'You are not my people,' there they shall be called children of the living God." (Rom. 9:24-26)

The epistle to the Hebrews picks up Jeremiah's vision of the new covenant which God will make with "the house of Israel and the house of Judah" (Jer. 31:31-34). The writer applies that vision to the new people of the new covenant and relays God's message to the readers: "I will be their God, and they shall be my people" (Heb. 8:10-12). Both in explicit references as well as implicit inferences, the concept of the people of God is a dominant characteristic of the epistle to the Hebrews (Küng, 1967:122).

In the book of Revelation, the vision of the new heavens and the new earth is pictured in terms of Ezekiel 37:27: "See, the home of God is among mortals. He will dwell with them as their God; they will be his peoples, and God himself will be with them" (Rev. 21:3). Revelation applies the prophetic OT call to the people to go forth from Babylonian captivity in a new exodus of salvation (Isa. 48:20; Jer. 50:8; 51:45). The Revelator appeals to a new messianic people of God to dissociate itself from the complex and evil system of the fallen "Babylon" of the first century: "Come out of her, my people, so that you do take part in her sins, and so that you do not share in her plagues" (Rev. 18:4).

In Titus 2:14, the application of the OT title of the people of God to the Christian community is decisive. The psalmist declared that the Lord is the one "who will redeem Israel from all its iniquities" (Ps. 130:8). Titus applies this to the Messiah and to the Christian community, "Jesus Christ" is the one "who gave himself for us that he might redeem us from all iniquity." But even more pointedly, references to Israel as a people of God's own possession (Exod. 19:5-6.; Deut. 7:6; 14:2) are now applied to the Christian community, which is "a people of his own."

However, 1 Peter 2:9-10 draws together most forcefully the OT titles of peoplehood applied to Israel. It uses them to describe the nature and mission of the new messianic people of God. First Peter's four ancient titles of peoplehood, together with their corresponding adjectives of divine possession, all refer to Israel in the OT. In Isaiah 43:20c-21, Israel is called "my chosen people, the people whom I formed for myself so that they might declare my praise."

The three titles which follow in 1 Peter are all drawn from Exodus 19:5-6: "You shall be my treasured possession, . . . [and] you shall be for me a priestly kingdom and a holy nation" (cf. Isa. 43:21; Deut. 7:6; Mal. 3:17). As well as underscoring the collective dimensions of God's saving initiative, the text shows that the posture of God's people in the world is essentially missionary. "A royal priesthood" (1 Pet. 2:9) designates a people dedicated to the worship and service of God, their King. The conduct of this people in the midst of the nations must be such that it faithfully represents their God. "A holy nation" also points to a people whose identity is determined by its relationship to its God.

"God's own people" (1 Pet. 2:9) reflects a conviction which runs throughout the OT from Moses to the prophets and grounds the sense of belonging to the Lord. This is the conviction which also characterizes the new people of God and informs their understanding of their life and their mission. Just as Paul had done, Peter did not hesitate to apply the Hosea reference to renewed Israel to the predominantly Gentile messianic community. In this passage the prophetic vision of the missionary nature of peoplehood, which comes to its OT climax in Isaiah, finds its maximum NT expression. It is the essential vision of corporate witness which had come into the early church's practice through Jesus himself (cf. Matt. 5:13-16; et al.).

The biblical image of peoplehood tells us that to be without a people is to be without a God. To know God is to be a part of a people, God's people. Therefore, peoplehood is a part of the good news, as well as an essential instrument in its proclamation. Both Peter and Paul make this fact quite explicit. Peter states that those who are not a people have not received mercy. Conversely, to be God's people is to experience God's mercy (1 Pet. 2:10). Paul says that alienation from the commonwealth of Israel is to be "without God in the world" (Eph. 2:12). Conversely, relationship to the Father is found in the context of his people, in his family (Eph. 2:18-19).

Conclusion

In Israel's experience, it soon became clear that it was impossible to integrate into the biblical view of peoplehood both national and spiritual-ethical dimensions. For their part, the prophets saw that the second of these elements was the really essential one. Therefore, salvation would come to Israel the nation only through almost annihilating judgment.

What was foreseen in the OT became reality in the NT. In the church a fundamentally spiritual-ethical peoplehood is being realized through the reconciling work of Christ and the creative power and activity of his Spirit. This is the true people of God in which the fragmenting differences of race, sex, and economic and social conditions are all being overcome (Gal. 3:26-29). The faithfulness of God's people in the light of his promises is the hallmark of peoplehood in the early Christian community. This guides them in the debate with the synagogue over the question of who is the true people of God (Gal. 3:1-7; 3:8-9; 4:28; 6:16).

The same vision of true peoplehood characterizes the Corinthian letters. The apostasy and unfaithfulness of Israel serves as a negative example for warning the messianic people of God (1 Cor. 10:1-13). The veiled nature of revelation to the people of the OT stands in contrast to the clarity with which the community of the Spirit receives God's message (2 Cor. 3). The peoplehood of the messianic community is the condition which determines their life and mission. This relationship between essence and function is especially clear in 2 Corinthians 6:16-18: "They shall be my people" (16). Therefore, they should live as God's people (17) so that they may in truth be his people (18).

The transfer of the ancient title, the people of God, from Israel to the messianic community is foundational to its ecclesiological self-understanding. The remnant of the old Israel (according to the flesh) who believe can be grafted back onto God's olive tree, the elect people of God, the church (Rom. 9–11). Jesus understood that his mission was to fulfill the law and the prophets. Likewise, his community is the true people of God, the true Israel of God (Gal. 6:16), the true offspring of Abraham (Gal. 3:29), the true circumcision (Phil. 3:3), the true temple (1 Cor. 3:16), the true congregation (*ekklēsia*) of God. These references in the NT to other related metaphors simply strengthen the conviction that the early church's self-understanding was expressed most fundamentally in terms of peoplehood.[7]

The post-apostolic church continued to see itself as the "new people of God" in contrast to old Israel, or the first Israel (Epistle of Barnabas 7:5; 13:1). However, as the church moved away from its OT roots, its self-understanding as the people of God became dimmed. From around A.D. 150, Christian writers begin to use *laos* in the sense of the congregation assembled for worship and distinct from its leaders, giving rise to the distortion of this powerful peoplehood image and contributing to an unbiblical division of labor in the church—the laity (*laos*) and the clergy (Martyr, *Apology* 1.65).[8]

11

The Family of God

The "household of God" metaphor is employed, in its basic form, sparingly in the NT. However, together with its related metaphors, the family image constitutes one of the major biblical figures for understanding the nature and mission of the church. A leading biblical theologian of the past generation, Joachim Jeremias, has called this metaphor "Jesus' favorite image" for referring to the new people of God (1971:169). In Pauline thought, the family image occupies a primary role in his reflection on the nature and mission of the messianic community (Banks: 53-54).

The principal image in this configuration is "the household of God"[1] or "the household of faith."[2] But in addition to the six explicit references in the NT, there is a constellation of related expressions which point to the early Christian community as the family of God. These include Father, sons and daughters, brothers and sisters, slaves, servants, and stewards. But even more important in the early church's self-understanding as the family of God are the concrete familial forms which the early Christian groups took. This is especially clear in the frequent allusions to the house churches mentioned in Acts and Paul's epistles.[3] Jesus is the immediate source of the family image for the early church's understanding of its life and mission; indirectly, its roots are in the OT.

The Family Image in the Old Testament

The family image is employed in a variety of ways with reference to ancient Israel. The Hebrew term for family, usually translated "house," could apply to the entire nation, as "the house of Israel" (Isa. 5:7), or it could refer to a "household" living under one roof (Exod. 12:4). Related terms are variously translated as "tribe," "clan," "family," and "household." The meanings of these terms were somewhat fluid. There was apparently no biblical equivalent for the modern concept of the nuclear family, limited to spouses and their children.

In the OT, the term for family is used in an essentially social or political sense. In the call of Abraham, "all the families of the earth shall be blessed" (Gen. 12:3). According to the prophetic vision, "the vineyard of the Lord of hosts is the house of Israel" (Isa. 5:7). This usage of familial terms to refer to an entire people is fully compatible with the biblical understanding. This is so not merely because every individual was a member of a particular family unit. It is also true because the concept of family is basic to all social groupings and therefore essential for understanding the nature of the entire community.

Yahweh's saving relationship to Israel in the exodus-wilderness experience is vividly described in familial terms: "Thus says the Lord [to Pharaoh]: Israel is my firstborn son. I said to you, 'Let my son go that he may worship me.' But you refused to let him go; now I will kill your firstborn son" (Exod. 4:22-23). Moses later told the people, "In the wilderness, . . . you saw how the Lord your God carried you, just as one carries a child, all the way that you traveled until you reached this place" (Deut. 1:31).

In its better moments Israel confessed that Yahweh was the loving Father to whom they owed their very life and existence as a people: "When Israel was a child, I loved him, and out of Egypt I called my son" (Hos. 11:1). In the context of the covenant, Israel understood itself as brothers and sisters in the family of God (Jer. 31:31-34; cf. Deut. 15).

Israel's prophets used the family image to denounce the people's unfaithfulness and to call God's people back to the restoration of saving covenant relationships. Hosea (2), Ezekiel (16) and Isaiah (54:4-8) all envisioned the relationship of God and the people in terms of a marriage covenant between husband and wife. In this relationship Israel was the object of God's incomparable grace.

In Ezekiel's interpretation of the story, Judah's beginnings are pictured in the precarious existence of an abandoned newborn infant (16:4-6) who grows into beautiful womanhood (16:7) and is espoused by God in a marriage covenant. But the seductive temptations inherent to national prosperity and imperial power under their monarchs proved to be Judah's undoing (16:8-18). The unfaithfulness of God's people is denounced by the image of the wanton whoredom of an unfaithful wife, which surpasses even the degradation of a common prostitute (16:31-36). God's wrath, like the jealousy of a spurned spouse, is expressed in judgment upon his people, executed by Judah's earlier accomplices-in-evil now turned enemies (16:35-42). God's judgment takes the form of simply allowing the consequences of Israel's injustices and unfaithfulness to come crashing down on their own heads (16:43).

However, the wanton unfaithfulness of God's people is not the last word in this story. God, the ever-faithful spouse, remembers his covenanted love, and restored relationships arise again out of a new remembering of God's covenanted mercies (Ezek. 16:59-63). The salvation of God's people comes in the form of covenant relationships renewed "in righteousness and in justice, in steadfast love, and in mercy" (Hos. 2:16-19).

In the NT this husband-wife metaphor is picked up in Ephesians (5:23-32) to show the depth and the intimacy of the relationship between Christ (as husband) and the community of the New Covenant (as wife). In Revelation (19:6-9) the bride of the Lamb (19:7) stands in marked contrast to "Babylon, the great, mother of whores and of earth's abominations" (17:5). Here the marriage metaphor appears as a part of the primitive community's liturgy for celebrating the new covenant, characterized by the restoration of relationships among all peoples and with their God and the Lamb (Christ).[4]

In ancient Israel, everyone belonged to a family. This was a foundational element in their identity as persons. Therefore, the family was the point of departure for defining community. In biblical thought the family was tied inseparably to its father, and the story of the patriarch was the story of the family. Participation in this common history was far more important for defining the identity of the community than purely biological links to one of the ancestors. The patriarch is not merely an individual, nor is he the personification of the tribe. As fathers they take part in the ongoing life of the tribe, and death means being gathered unto the fathers. To be fully a person in ancient Israel, one needed to participate in a family whose story included a past of covenanted grace, a present of covenant faithfulness, and a future of covenant promise. In this grace story, each succeeding generation participates.

Family kinship is not based merely on blood relationships but more importantly on what might be called "common character." Family boundaries were flexible. Even in the absence of blood relationship, participation in the common values which characterize the family and assumption of its common story are signs of belonging to the family. Where this common character is lost, peoplehood is jeopardized, and the family becomes a "non-people" and perishes. Being a family means participating in a common tradition, sharing in a common character and a common destiny. This is the biblical vision of the "house of Israel" characterized by God's covenant promise and the faithfulness of the fathers, on which the NT understanding is rooted. "God's house," in which Moses had been a faithful servant, became God's house, over which Christ was faithful "as a son, and we are his house if we hold firm the confidence and . . . hope" (Heb. 3:1-6).

This OT background is essential for our understanding of the family image as it is used in the NT. In line with this vision, John the Baptist denounced the vain pretensions of the Pharisees and the Sadducees who came to him for baptism. John exposed the emptiness of their claim to "have Abraham as our ancestor" (Matt. 3:9). The casuistry of the Pharisees and the political intrigues and thirst for power on the part of the Sadducees set them in sharp contrast to the faith of Abraham. In view of this loss of Abrahamic character, biological continuity alone was an insufficient basis for claiming kinship. Instead, the household of God will include those who respond with the authentic fruits of repentance in obedience to the covenant faithfulness of God.

This understanding of family is further substantiated in the conversation of Jesus with the Jews recorded in John 8. The Jews claimed to be "descendants of Abraham" (8:33, 39). The response of Jesus went directly to the heart of the biblical meaning of family. "If you were Abraham's children, you would be doing what Abraham did" (8:39). The constitutive element in kinship is "common character" rather than biological continuity.

The Family Image in the New Testament

Although the roots of the family image applied to the church in the NT are to be found in the OT understanding of the relationship of God to his people, the immediate justification for its use in the NT is to be found in Jesus himself. In response to the widespread misunderstanding in contemporary Judaism, Jesus restored the radical biblical meaning of the term "family." He asked, " 'Who is my mother, and who are my brothers?' And pointing to his disciples, he said, 'Here are my mother and my brothers! For whoever does the will of my Father in heaven is my brother and sister and mother' " (Matt. 12:48-50).

In the Gospel of Mark we find a clear statement of what it means to participate in the "true family." Three alternatives to the true family are explicitly rejected in the Gospel: the biological family (Mark 3:20-21, 31-35), the religious family (3:22-30), and the geographic or political family (6:1-6). None of these families were able to recognize that God's saving alternative, his kingdom, was present in Jesus. Therefore, the radical conversion which would have prepared them for life in God's true family was not possible.

In contrast to these, there is a fourth alternative: the messianic community made up of disciples of Jesus who do the will of the Father (3:13-19, 34-35; 6:7-13). These literally "left all" to participate in God's family of the new order (Pikaza: 52-54; Mark 10:28-31). Paradoxically, in the new family of God's restored people, there are again brothers and sisters, mothers and children, but there are no fathers. Honorific titles are excluded in the new family of God. Patriarchal domination, together with its symbols, is displaced. In the new family there is but one Father, the One in heaven (Matt. 23:9). This new family is a sign of the arriving kingdom.

While the source of Jesus' use of the family image is undoubtedly his radical understanding of the OT, the contrast with contemporary Judaism is notable. Although the OT employed the Father image to understand Yahweh's liberating and saving activity toward Israel, this metaphor was largely neglected in Judaism. Brothers and sisters were vital terms to describe relationships among God's covenant people. In Judaism, they tended to become formal expressions for addressing fellow Jews. Pharisees had their "sons," and rabbis were occasionally described as "fathers." But the vital characteristic of covenant love in relationships was all but lost in an almost unilateral concern for the casuistry of law. In Judaism, biblical brotherhood and sisterhood became exclusively brotherhood. Jesus and the messianic community recovered a full-orbed vision of familihood in which sexual prejudices are overcome.

In marked contrast to his contemporaries, Jesus made the family image one of his favorites for understanding the character and mission of the messianic community. Jesus restored meaning to the family. He taught his followers to pray as he did to his Father, addressing him with almost shocking intimacy as "Abba" (Mark 14:36; Rom. 8:15; Gal. 4:6). In this family, hierarchies of supposed worth or personal honor are excluded. Those who are great are servants of all. Differences among members of this family are functional and contribute to the enrichment of the common life: "and you are all students [NRSV note: brothers]. . . . Nor are you to be called instructors, for you have one instructor, the Messiah" (Matt. 23:8-10).

The eschatological family is assigned priority over the purely biological family. Common life with Jesus took priority over previous ties. The disciples' community of life with Jesus was their community of destiny, in which they needed to be willing to suffer what Jesus suffered (10:38). In this family, God is Father (23:9). Jesus is Lord over the household, and its members are his disciples (10:25). Older women are mothers, while men and younger people are brothers and sisters (Mark 3:34). But at the same time, all are little children, even babes, in the family to whom the words of Jesus are directed (Matt. 11:25; Mark 10:24).

Life in the family of God is epitomized in its common meals. This communion is an anticipation of the great eschatological banquet of salvation. In its mission in the world, the messianic family reaches out to others as brothers and sisters (Matt. 25:40; Jeremias, 1971:169-170).

God as Father

The family image underscores the fundamental relationship of God as Father to his sons and daughters. But contrary to relationships in families which are essentially biological, participation in the family of God takes the form of freely assumed covenant relationships. Attitudes which characterize the relationship are of a personal order: love, devotion, commitment, and obedience, rather than those which characterize strictly biological families.

In contrast to other religions of the ancient Near East, the Bible does not describe sonship in terms of natural generation. However, our "birth" or "adoption" does respond solely to God's merciful initiative. To be a person is to participate in a family, to be integrated into a people. To the saving activity of God, as Father, we owe the possibility of being fully persons. By God's grace, those who were nobody can be fully persons. "In the very place where it was said to them, 'You are not my people,' there they shall be called 'children of the living God' " (Rom. 9:26).

Not only is God the Father of "the household of faith," but Jesus, as "the firstborn within a large family," is Lord over the household (Rom. 8:29). Contrary to what the church in its doctrinal tradition has often emphasized, the *quality* of sonship is assigned priority over the *rights* of sonship. The title given to Christ, "firstborn," is not so much a temporal description as it is an archetypal image. Jesus the "firstborn" is both supreme and unique in his obedience even "to the point of death" (Phil. 2:8). He is also the "firstborn within a large family" whose members are also called to obedience (Rom. 8:29; Col. 1:15). Jesus is concretely the measure and norm of our sonship. As sons and daughters of God, we are born of God into a new family, a new creation, in which we are "predestined to be conformed to the image of his Son" (Rom. 8:29).

In the "household of God" the Father's character is stamped upon the sons and daughters. The NT message is characterized by this vision, which is summed up in Ephesians 5:1: "Therefore be imitators of God, as beloved children." The concrete marks of this sonship constitute the very substance of kinship in the family of God and are listed in passages scattered throughout the NT. Children of God will be peacemakers, just as their Father (Matt. 5:9). They will forgive others just as God has forgiven in Christ (Eph. 4:32). They will love others just like God loves through

Christ, by giving themselves for others (Eph. 5:2). To love as God loves means seeking the welfare of enemies as well as friends (Matt. 5:43-48; 1 John 3:10-11).

"God is light," and "we walk in the light as he himself is in the light" (1 John 1:5, 7; Eph. 5:8; Rom. 13:12-14). The relationship of God's children to their Father is characterized by obedience (1 Pet. 1:14; Mark 3:35). God's children are made holy through the Messiah (Heb. 2:14). They are freed from all fears, including fear of death (Heb. 2:15). In the family of God, we literally survive as well as live, by confidently trusting in the absolute faithfulness of our Father (Gal. 3:26). As sons and daughters of God, we are called to continue the mission of God's Son in the world (John 17:18-23).[5]

Brothers and Sisters

Life in the household of God is not merely characterized by the Father-children relationship, basic as it may be. Since this family bears the stamp of God's character, the horizontal relationships of brothers and sisters in the family are also noteworthy and saving in their impact. The term "family of believers" or "brothers and sisters" (NRSV note: "brotherhood"; *adelphotēs*) appears only twice (1 Pet. 2:17; 5:9). Yet the idea of brother-sister relationships within God's family permeates the entire NT.

The term "brothers" (NRSV often: "brothers and sisters") is the most frequently used designation for Christians in the NT. It is employed some 250 times in the book of Acts and the epistles alone. In spite of its frequency and its occasional use in a more technical sense to refer to colleagues in mission (Gal. 1:2), Paul's use of the term is no mere formality. The term denotes the real relationship which unites believer-disciples in the household of faith (see, for example, Phil. 3:1; 4:1; 1 Cor. 15:58).

As an example of the concrete meaning of brotherhood in the NT, 1 Corinthians 8 can be cited. Paul writes movingly of the concern which stronger Christians should show toward the weak. This is so not merely because he is "the weak brother for whom Christ died" (8:11), but also because he is "my brother," and my responsibility toward "members" of my "family" is direct and concrete (8:13; see RSV; NRSV notes). In 1 John 3:16-17, the household of God is defined as the community of those who love like God loves and offer their lives for the brothers and sisters just as Jesus "laid down his life for us." This is concretely sharing goods and life with "a brother or sister in need."

As Paul reminded the Thessalonians, "love of the brothers and sisters" (*philadelphia*) in the household of God is a characteristic which is learned directly from the Father (1 Thess. 4:9). Only within the family in which God is Father do appeals like those found in Ephesians 4:32—5:2 make sense: "Be kind to one another, tenderhearted, forgiving one another, as God in Christ has forgiven you. Therefore be imitators of God, as beloved children, and live in love, as Christ loved us and gave himself up for us."

The frequency with which the terms "brothers and sisters" are employed in the NT certainly reflects the essential character of the community which uses this designation. In the community in which God's Spirit creates communion (*koinōnia*), family images are particularly useful for its self-understanding. Family images could challenge contemporary Judaism to recall the essential significance of family and to find true identity in the "household of God" being gathered by the Messiah. The image also communicated powerfully in first-century Greek and Roman society. There individuals were often displaced and drifting without being truly persons. It was a truly saving experience to become fully persons in the household of God, where life takes the form of communion. Brothers and sisters in the household of God developed mutual relationships of love and unselfish responsibility. This characterized the primitive Christian community.

The family metaphor, including the related images—Father, sons and daughters, brothers and sisters, servants and stewards —underscores the social character of salvation. In biblical perspective, individuals become persons in a full sense when they are persons-in-family. Participation in the household of God means becoming sons and daughters of our Father who is in heaven, and brothers and sisters of one another in the family of faith. Here people experience salvation in a full-orbed biblical sense. Autonomous individuals are not really whole persons. Neither are they saved persons in the biblical perspective. Salvation implies restoration of communion with both God and neighbor. The OT prophets referred to this reality as *shalom*. The apostles call this experience *koinōnia*. Both terms describe the concrete social form salvation takes. This is why the family image proved to be so useful for the self-understanding of the early church.

House Churches in the New Testament

The household or family played a fundamental role in the life and mission of the primitive messianic movement. This was the basic social unit made up of an extended family. It included husband and wife (and perhaps their elderly parents), children, slaves, servants, and even friends and acquaintances who joined themselves to the family unit for mutual benefit. These are probably the church units described in Acts 2:46. Members worshiped together, broke bread together in their common meals, received instruction in their common faith and life, and gave testimony to the gospel (Acts 5:42).

This "household" model of the church was continued in the apostolic mission that reached out beyond Jerusalem. The household of Cornelius in Caesarea was the first Christian community reported as established among the Gentiles (Acts 10:7, 24). In Philippi, Christian communities were established in the houses of Lydia and the jailer (Acts 16:15, 31-34). In Corinth, Christian communities included the households of Stephanas (1 Cor. 16:15) and Gaius (Acts 18:8; 1 Cor. 1:14-16; Rom. 16:23). Among the churches in Asia sending greetings to the communities in Corinth, we find "Aquila and Prisca, together with the church in their house" (1 Cor. 16:19).

Other house churches mentioned in the NT include the "household of Onesiphorus" (2 Tim. 1:16; 4:19); Philemon (Philem. 1-2); and "Nympha and the church in her house" (Col. 4:15). In Rome, there must have been at least five house churches at the time of the writing of the epistle: "Prisca and Aquila . . . and the church in their house" (Rom. 16:3-5); "those who belong to the family of Aristobulus" (16:10); "those in the Lord who belong to the family of Narcissus" (16:11); "Asyncritus, Phlegon, Hermes, Patrobas, Hermas, and the brothers and sisters who are with them" (16:14); "Philologus, Julia, Nereus and his sister, and Olympas, and all the saints who are with them" (16:15).

The significance of these early Christian house churches must not be underestimated. Paul himself established them and participated in them. This was the primary place where the sociological, racial, economic, and religious barriers, so entrenched in ancient society, were broken down and relativized. Barriers between Jews and Gentiles, free and slave, men and women, high and low, educated and uneducated—these all were destroyed in the new family. House churches were places where God's inbreaking new order was most apparent. They were signs of God's new order for humanity.

These early house churches were places where Christian familihood was realized most concretely. The communion of the Lord's table was not a mere symbol. It was also a reality. These fellowships were the center of the early church's worship, hospitality, and evangelization. The structure of this new "open family" transcended itself in its openness to others. It was an essential element in the mission of the early church.

The growth of the early church was notable. By the end of the second century, the church had spread throughout the entire Roman empire and even beyond its borders. This growth was not due to organized missionary activity. Robin Lane Fox comments that there are no signs of any mission directed by church authorities and, with the exception of Pantenus in India and one more, perhaps, we are not able to name a single Christian missionary active between Paul and Constantine (Fox: 282).

The secret of this evangelistic growth may be attributed largely to the existence of a different kind of people, "the household of God," whose presence in the empire took the form of house churches. These transforming communities were able to draw into their fellowship the pariahs and the outcasts of Greco-Roman society and effectively offer them salvation. It has been suggested that "the women's house" (the inner courtyard of the traditional household) was the place where the most effective evangelization took place.

It is difficult to determine whether the congregation was meeting in the home of one of its members, or whether the various extended family household units were themselves churches, or both. Yet it is clear that the household played an essential role, both in the church's self-understanding and in its mission. The family metaphor is vital for understanding the NT concept of the church.

Paralleling the household *context* of the community's gatherings, we also have household *language* to describe relationships among its members. It is possible that this correlation may have been accidental and that the primitive communities met in houses because they had nowhere else to meet. On the other hand, it is also possible that the early church's self-understanding, expressed in the family metaphor, blended quite naturally with their need for a place to assemble. In this event, house churches may have been the first choice of the early Christian communities.

In light of the family character of the Christian community, the homes of its members likely offered "the most conducive atmosphere in which they could give expression to the bond they had in common" (Banks: 60-61). It is interesting to note that the earliest Christian "meetinghouse," which has been discovered and identified, dates from the fourth decade of the third century.

It consisted essentially of an enlarged room attached to a family residence.

So it should come as no surprise to us that the family metaphor should be one of the primary images by means of which the early church understood its own nature and mission. The image of the household of God was especially appropriate due to its roots in the OT. There it described God's relationship to Israel and expressed the distinctive nature of family that bears the stamp of its Father's holy character. The household of God was also appropriate because the relationships symbolized by the family image were really experienced in the communion of the household of faith. In the messianic community, "family" ceased to be a mere metaphor and became a concrete spiritual and social reality.

Along with other changes that accompanied the Constantinian shift early in the fourth century, Christian congregations increasingly left their family matrix. What appeared was a new era of large temples, multitudinous meetings, eloquent and popular preachers whose sermons were applauded by their listeners. As the church in the Roman empire moved away from the *household context* of the primitive Christian community, the *household metaphor* also lost its power to stir the church's imagination. It then seemed expedient to use other images which were more akin to the current church realities.

12

The Shepherd and the Flock

The metaphor of the shepherd and the flock powerfully reflects the nature of the church in mission. It speaks, first of all, of the people of God who have been saved from oppression by evil powers, secular and religious, material and spiritual. It looks to the messianic restoration of God's people, offering hope to the hopeless and identity to the outcasts. It points to God's mission carried out in Christ: to the creation of a transformed and transforming community in which the true meaning of history finds its fulfillment.

The image of the shepherd and the flock is widely used in both Testaments. In the OT the reference is to the people of God, and in the NT the messianic community is described in this metaphor. The extensive use of these images in both Testaments indicates its importance for understanding the character and mission of God's people. The master image is that of shepherd-and-flock. Shepherd and sheep do not appear without the other being understood, at least by implication. In the OT, the shepherd is God himself or a shepherd appointed by God. In the NT, God is ultimately the Shepherd-Ruler of the flock, and Jesus

Christ is the chief shepherd. While others may also be shepherds, the flock is God's and is gathered by the Messiah.

Underlying the NT references to the pastoral image for the church's self-understanding is its extensive use in the OT. It is found in each of the major sections: the Pentateuch, the Psalms, and the Prophets. Before reflecting in depth on the NT usage of this metaphor and its role in the church's self-understanding, its OT roots must be reviewed.

Shepherd-and-Flock Imagery in the Old Testament

Yahweh is described as Shepherd of Israel in Genesis 48:15 and 49:24. While gods in the ancient Near East were given the title of shepherd, this was not the case in ancient Israel. Only rarely is God called by this title (Gen. 48:15; 49:24; Ps. 23:1; 80:1; cf. Ezek. 34:15; Isa. 40:11; Jer. 31:10). However, Yahweh's shepherding of Israel is celebrated in Hebrew piety (Jeremias, 1968:487-489). As shepherd, Yahweh leads "the people of Israel out of the land of Egypt."[1] God's saving activity in the exodus-wilderness experience filled the shepherd-flock metaphor with meaning. This is the salvation which God's people commemorate in the narration of their history and the celebration of their worship.

God is worshiped as the Shepherd who went "out before [his] people when [they] marched through the wilderness" (Ps. 68:7). He is the shepherd who guides his flock (Ps. 23:3), who leads it to well-watered pastures (Ps. 23:2; Jer. 50:19), who protects them with his staff (Ps. 23:4), who "gathers the outcasts of Israel" (Isa. 56:8).

The relationship between the shepherd-flock metaphor and the exodus-wilderness experience characterizes Israel's history. In Exodus and Deuteronomy, shepherd terms characterize the stories of the exodus ("to lead," "to guide," "to go before"). However, what is implicit in the shepherd language of the exodus becomes a vital metaphor in the Psalms (23:1-4; 28:9; 68:7; 74:1; 77:20; 78:52-53; 79:13; 80:1; 95:7; 100:3; 121:4). It is also a key image in the prophetic message of hope (Jer. 23:3; 31:10; 50:19; Ezek. 34:11-22; Isa. 40:10-11; 49:9-10; Mic. 4:6-8; 7:14).

Reciting the mighty saving acts of Yahweh in the exodus-Red Sea experience, the psalmist concludes: "You led your people like a flock by the hand of Moses and Aaron" (Ps. 77:11-20). In a similar rehearsal of salvation history, Psalm 78 sums up the exodus liberation and entrance into the Promised Land in terms of the shepherd-flock metaphor: "Then he led out his people like sheep, and guided them in the wilderness like a flock. He led them in safety, so that they were not afraid" (78:52-53a).

These experiences led Israel to invoke this image time after time in their prayers for renewal: "Give ear, O Shepherd of Israel, you who lead Joseph like a flock! . . . Come to save us! . . . Restore us, O God" (Ps. 80:1-3). The metaphor enriches Israel's corporate worship:

> O come, let us worship and bow down,
>   let us kneel before the Lord, our Maker!
> For he is our God,
>   and we are the people of his pasture,
>   and the sheep of his hand. (95:6-7; cf. 100:3)

In the ancient Near East, the title "shepherd" was applied to political and military leaders. However, the term is not applied as a royal title to rulers in Judah and Israel. On the contrary, the exilic prophets call the unfaithful leaders of God's people shepherds and announce impending judgment upon them. As a royal title, they reserve the term shepherd for an expected messianic "Son of David." Here we find a key to understanding the NT application of the term to Jesus. Rather than understanding it as a literal image of pastoral shepherding, attractive as this may be in the pastoral care of people in the church, it is, in reality, a title of messianic lordship.

Jeremiah announced judgment upon the unfaithful shepherds of God's flock, as well as promising restoration of a remnant from both Judah and Israel (Jer. 23:1-8; 31:10). God will set a messianic Shepherd over his flock who will rule with "justice and righteousness." The prophet looks forward to a new and greater exodus of salvation for God's people in which his covenant righteousness will prevail.

Similarly, Ezekiel prophesied against the shepherds of Israel, accusing them of self-serving ambition, exploitation, and violence (Ezek. 34:1-6). Therefore, God's judgment will come down upon them. God, who once redeemed his flock from Egypt, is now forced to rescue his sheep from the oppression of their own monarchs (34:7-10). Yahweh himself will gather together his scattered sheep, rescuing them from the lands in which they have been scattered in judgment, strengthening the weak, feeding them in justice, offering them the security of a "covenant of peace" in which fear is banished. "They shall know that I, the Lord their God, am with them, and that they, the house of Israel, are my people, says the Lord God. You are my sheep, the sheep of my pasture and I am your God, says the Lord God" (34:30-31). Jesus undoubtedly based his understanding of his own mission as well as that of his people on these passages (see John 10:1-18; Matt. 18:12-14; Luke 15:4-7).

In his message of hope following Babylonian exile, the prophet in Isaiah 40 picks up the same image used by Jeremiah and Ezekiel. God will again be Israel's shepherd. "He will feed his flock like a shepherd; he will gather the lambs in his arms, and carry them in his bosom, and gently lead the mother sheep" (Isa. 40:11). In the fourth Servant Song, the Servant of Yahweh gathers his scattered flock. The OT use of the shepherd-flock image comes to its climax in the vision of the one who will save the flock of God through his vicarious suffering (53:6).

Meanwhile, even after their return from exile, Judah's leaders continue to be false shepherds. In view of this, Zechariah promised that "the Lord their God will save them for they are the flock of his people." He will surely gather those who are scattered and oppressed, just as he had done in the exodus from Egypt and in the return from exile (Zech. 9:16; 10:2-12).

Shepherd-and-Flock Imagery in the New Testament

The image of the flock is used in seven NT passages.[2] The master image is that of shepherd-and-flock. Shepherd and flock do not appear in the NT without at least implying the other. If the metaphoric references to sheep[3] and shepherd[4] are added, we find that the shepherd-and-flock image occupies an important place in the NT. This group of images appears in eighteen different passages by seven writers. The appeal of this analogy is surely due to the fact that it is widely used in the OT. The image was well understood, particularly in the early Palestinian Christian community.

The prophetic vision of an eschatological gathering of the scattered sheep of Israel by its messianic shepherd (Ezek. 34) must have inspired Jesus' sense of mission. In Jesus, God was restoring his people. The shepherd-and-flock image points to the restoration of true peoplehood under God's reign. The twelve were commissioned to "go rather to the lost sheep of the house of Israel" (Matt. 10:6). Jesus understood that his own mission was first of all "to the lost sheep of the house of Israel" (Matt. 15:24). Early Jewish Christians confessed that God himself had come to his people through "the great shepherd of the sheep, by the blood of the eternal covenant" (Heb. 13:20).

In practically every instance, the flock is assumed to be God's (Acts 20:28; 1 Pet. 5:2). In this feature, the NT simply follows the OT tradition. God sent his Messiah as "the great shepherd of the sheep" (Heb. 13:20). Ultimately, it is God who is the Shepherd-Ruler of the flock. Jesus is the chief shepherd. There are under-shepherds who rule, not by dominating but by serving as examples, just as Jesus had done. But the flock remains God's possession (1 Pet. 5:2-4). Jesus gave words of comfort to his disciples: "Do not be afraid, little flock, for it is your Father's good pleasure to give you the kingdom" (Luke 12:32). The flock belongs to the Father.

Jesus' words of assurance in Luke 12:32 offer a valuable clue to the way in which the shepherd-flock image illuminated the self-understanding of the early Christian community. The first clue is found in the context in which the image is set. Jesus appeals to his followers to trust confidently in God's providence and in his invitation to assign highest priority to God's reign of justice and peace. This attitude characterizes the "little flock" (Luke 12:22-34). Matthew includes the same teachings in the summary with which he describes the messianic community (Matt. 5–7). In line with the prophetic vision (Jer. 23:1-8; Ezek. 34; Isa. 40:11; 53:6), the flock is identified as the restored remnant of God's people, those who dare to trust themselves to God's covenant faithfulness, as manifested supremely in God's Servant Messiah.

Furthermore, this little flock is, in a special sense, the community which anticipates the new age with its distinctive values and immense benefits. The encouragement to "fear not" is an assurance that the promised restoration of God's people has already begun in the messianic community. The term "little flock" is far more than a mere expression of affection. It surely means that Jesus saw the new community as the "flock" of Isaiah 40:11 and Ezekiel 34:12 in which divine restoration had already begun.

This is the flock which God had promised to gather. The outcasts of Israel, as well as foreigners, will be gathered together in God's flock, and God's house will become "a house of prayer for all peoples" (Isa. 56:6-8). Jesus understood that the inescapable task of the good shepherd includes bringing other sheep into the fold (John 10:16). It means compassion for sheep who have no shepherd (Mark 6:34; Matt. 9:36) and gathering those who are lost (Matt. 10:6; 15:24).

In line with Jesus' vision, the messianic community conceived of itself as the nucleus of this new order. Not long after the resurrection, Christians were tempted to identify the church with the kingdom of God (Acts 1:6). They were wrong, because the kingdom of God transcends all human institutions. Nevertheless, it is not enough to say that the messianic community is merely a herald of the future kingdom for which it waits. The church is the little flock which, by God's power, has been freed from the grip of the powers of this age so that it might participate in the age to come, already begun in Christ.

Celebrating Messianic Liberation: John 10:1-21

The parables in John 10 are the most important NT reference to the shepherd-flock image. John drew on the Jewish feasts for the organizing structure of his Gospel.[5] These liturgical festivals include three Passovers (2:13; 6:4; 11:55), an unnamed feast (5:1), the Feast of Booths (or Tabernacles; 7:2), and the Feast of Dedication (10:22). Since the metaphor of the shepherd and flock is found in John 10, the Feast of Booths and to some extent the Feast of Dedication provide contextual keys for understanding the meaning of this image in the church's self-understanding.

The Festival of Booths (John 7:2) was one of the three principal pilgrimage festivals in ancient Israel.[6] The booths constructed of branches undoubtedly reminded the Israelites of the shelters in which they stayed while gathering their harvests in the fall of the year. Yet more importantly, they also evoked the pilgrimage of Israel through the wilderness following the exodus of liberation from Egypt (Lev. 23:43).

The Feast of the Booths was likely the most popular of Israel's liturgical festivals (de Vaux: 94). In addition to sleeping and eating in the booth for seven days, there were other common activities which added color to the festival. The water libation ceremony each day was accompanied by the singing of the Hallel (Pss. 113–118), in which the pilgrims joined in the great cry, "Save us, we beseech you, O Lord" (Hebrew: *Hoshianna*; hosanna; Ps. 118:25; Mark 11:9-10 et par.). The second great common rite was the lighting of the huge torches in the temple court while the Levites chanted Psalms 120–134.

According to Deuteronomy 16, the three principal feasts were intended to serve as reminders of the mighty saving acts of

Yahweh in behalf of his people. It was a time for all Israelites to remember that they had been slaves in Egypt (Deut. 16:12). "Rejoice during your festival [of booths], you and your sons and your daughters, your male and female slaves, as well as the Levites, the strangers, the orphans, and the widows resident in your towns" (16:14).

The social dimensions of the feast are further emphasized in Deuteronomy 31:10-13. The Feast of Booths was occasion for instituting the sabbatical provisions of allowing the land to lie fallow, freeing indentured slaves, and canceling debts which could not be paid (cf. Exod. 21:1-11; Deut. 15:1-18). The incorporation of these sabbatical elements in the Feast of Booths added to its relevance in first-century Palestinian Judaism. The reading of the law of the covenant during the Feast of Booths (Deut. 31:11-13) added even more to this freedom festival.

Leviticus 23:39-43 gives the theological meaning of the festival. The use of booths is symbolic of Israel's wilderness wandering. The key for understanding the significance of the festival is stated quite simply: "That your generations may know that I made the people of Israel live in booths when I brought them out of the land of Egypt: I am the Lord your God" (Lev. 23:43).

Psalm 81 is representative of the liturgy used in the celebration of the Feast of Booths (de Vaux: 791; *Westminster:* 716; Murphy: 590). The jubilation of this most popular of Israel's festivals is expressed in the first lines. "Sing aloud to God our strength; shout for joy to the God of Jacob. Raise a song, sound the tambourine, the sweet lyre with the harp. Blow the trumpet at the new moon, at the full moon, on our festal day" (Ps. 81:1-3). This may well refer to the trumpet blast which signaled the year of Jubilee with its proclamation of liberty (Lev. 25:9-10).

Psalm 81:6-7a refers to liberation from Egyptian slavery: "I relieved your shoulder of the burden; your hands were freed from the basket. In distress you called, and I rescued you." In keeping with the historical motif of the Feast of Booths, there follows the reminder, "I am the Lord your God, who brought you up out of the land of Egypt" (Ps. 81:10). All of these motifs were symbolized in the Festival of the Booths.

Psalms 113–118 and 120–134 were also employed in the liturgies of the principal festivals, including the Feast of Booths. Their common elements include praise to Yahweh, sovereign over heaven and earth, who establishes justice, who liberates, preserves, and blesses the oppressed, the poor, and the needy. The mighty works of Yahweh on behalf of his people in the exodus and the forty years of wilderness sojourn are sure signs that he will bring his saving righteousness and peace to his people, and all nations will know that he alone is God.

The Feast of Dedication (John 10:22) dates from the recapture and subsequent purification and dedication of the temple by Judas Maccabeus in 165 B.C. Its resemblance to the Feast of Booths is deliberate. Celebrated on the twenty-fifth day of the ninth month and lasting nine days, it was an occasion for great rejoicing (1 Macc. 4:52-59). As in the Feast of Booths, the people celebrated with unbounded happiness their liberation from the oppressors and their freedom to worship in the place established by Yahweh. As in the Feast of Booths, the people carried green branches and palm shoots to show their joy while they recited the Hallel (Pss. 113-118). They also lit enormous lamps in the temple court, which gave the feast its other name, Festival of Lights (cf. John 8:12). These lamps, symbols of the law of the covenant, were later located in each house, assuring the festival's ongoing popularity after the destruction of the temple.

Just as the Festival of Booths provided the occasion to recall and celebrate freedom from Egypt in order to "serve Yahweh in the wilderness," so the Feast of Dedication offered an opportunity for the people to remember that just two months earlier they had been forced to seek shelter like wild animals in mountain hideouts and caverns due to the oppression of the Seleucids (2 Macc. 10:6-7). Jesus' parabolic description of the shepherd and flock in John 10 is framed within the context of these two festivals (John 7:2; 10:22).

By the first century, official Pharisaism tended to reduce the rich symbolism of both of these freedom festivals to a spiritualistic liturgy. God's promises were given a futuristic reference; thus they no longer spoke to contemporary forms of religious and social oppression. However, the symbolism of the Feast of Booths helped the messianic community of John's Gospel to understand the meaning of Christ and his liberating mission of righteousness and peace. In the Fourth Gospel, Jesus offers messianic liberation to God's flock as well as to "other sheep" not of the same fold (John 10:16; Zorrilla: 52-63).

The parables of the shepherd and flock are set in John 7:1—10:22, a passage framed by the twin festivals of Booths and Dedication. In John 7:1-9, Jesus' sphere of activity is "Galilee of the Gentiles" (Matt. 4:15) in contrast to Judea, headquarters of Jesus' enemies, leaders in Judaism. These leaders manage the public celebration of the Feast of Booths. Jesus and those with whom he is associated are there among the pilgrims from many countries. His presence and teaching at the feast challenges the Jewish leaders and their pretensions (7:10-24). The leaders' decision to kill Jesus (7:19, 30) will lead to a new exodus (cf. Luke 9:31, "departure"; Greek: *exodus*) in which unbelieving Jews will have no part. However, the people of the land and other outcasts, including the Gentiles, will participate in the new exodus which the feast symbolizes (John 7:25-36).

The water-pouring ritual was the occasion to point to Jesus (and to his Spirit) as the source of living water. For God's thirsty flock, Jesus is the Rock from whom they drink (Exod. 17:1-7; cf. 1 Cor. 10:4). For other outcasts such as the Samaritans, Jesus replaces Jacob's well (John 7:37-39; cf. 4:1-42). Jesus is the new Moses, the awaited prophet (7:40-44). Whoever is a friend of Jesus can expect to be accused by the authorities and to be despised as a Galilean (7:45-52).

In John 7:53—8:11, the scribes and Pharisees are pitted against Jesus. In this confrontation between Judaism's "defenders of the Law" and the One who is greater than the Law, the accused woman is set free, while her accusers are accused.

"I am the light of the world" (John 8:12; 9:5) probably reflects the festival practice of lighting the huge torches in the temple court; it points to Jesus as the one who guides in a new exodus-wilderness sojourn. This, of course, is more than Jewish officialdom was willing to accept. Three times during the Festival of Booths, Jesus referred to himself with an absolute "I AM" (8:24, 28, 58). Thus he further identified himself with his Father, the God of the exodus, and with the covenant given during the wilderness sojourn. Again Jesus was accused of being a Samaritan outcast and of being possessed by a demon. Jesus refuted the second charge but allowed the first to go unchallenged. The outcasts follow Jesus in the new exodus of liberation (8:36).

The blind man of John 9:1-41 is representative of Judaism's outcasts who are sought out by Jesus and led forth in the light. Jesus commanded the blind man to wash in the pool from which water was drawn for the Feast of Booths ritual, symbol of messianic blessing. This shows that henceforth Jesus is the source of all blessing. But the Pharisees, like the Egyptian oppressors in exodus, are destined to die in their guilt and blindness (9:39-41).

John 10:1-22 continues the same line of thought developed in chapters 7–9: Jesus incarnates the true spirit of the Feast of Booths by liberating the outcasts. The Jewish leaders, self-proclaimed custodians of the Law and its institutions, acted contrary to its spirit and sought to destroy the Liberator. This led to a division between the believing Jews and those who rejected his claims.

John 10:1-22 contains two main parabolic sections (10:1-5 and 7b-18) interspersed by clarifying commentary (10:6-7a and 19-22). The contrast in the first parable is between the shepherd and the stranger. The shepherd, who enters by the door, calls forth his sheep, leads them out, and goes before them. They follow him because they know his voice. The stranger climbs in by another way, but the sheep do not follow him. While these "strangers" may well be pseudo-messiahs, the epithet may equally be applied to Judaism's leaders. They were total strangers to the publicans and sinners, the poor, the Samaritans, and the little ones whom Jesus gathered into the kingdom.

The emphasis on the verbs "leads them out" (John 10:3, *exagei*) and "has brought out all his own" (10:4, *ekbalē*) is surely intentional. The first recalls the shepherding activity of Yahweh, who led his people out of Egypt in the exodus-wilderness experience. In the second instance, the verb is the same as the one translated "they drove him out" in John 9:34. There is a direct relationship between those whom the Jews cast out and the outcasts who are led forth by the Messiah.

The second section consists of a double parable: the door (John 10:7b-10) and the good shepherd (10:11-18). Jesus is the door of the sheep. This image is contained in the Hallel Psalms sung during the Feast of Booths. "This is the gate of the Lord; the righteous shall enter through it" (Ps. 118:20). Here again the contrast is between Jesus, the door, and the Jewish leaders identified as "thieves and bandits." Jesus offers salvation, freedom, sustenance, and abundant life. Jewish leadership, on the contrary, brings death and destruction.

Jesus, the Good Shepherd, "lays down his life for the sheep" (John 10:11-18). This image reflects the prophetic vision of the shepherd chosen by God to lead his people in the messianic era (Ezek. 34). In reality, this is a daring messianic claim, and it did not go unnoticed among Jesus' enemies (John 10:31-39). This image is anticipated in the OT. Yet the vision of the good shepherd's faithfulness to the point that he "lays down his life for the sheep" goes beyond the shepherd image found there and in subsequent Judaism (cf. John 15:13; 1 John 3:16). It is parallel to the vision of the Servant of Yahweh, whose vicarious suffering is of saving value (Isa. 52:13—53:12). In contrast to Jesus, the Good Shepherd, the Jewish leaders are hirelings who abandon the people to danger and destruction.

The relationship of the messianic shepherd to the Father, as well as to the sheep, is highly experiential. To know and to be known (John 10:14-15a), people must participate in the common life of God's flock. According to the biblical vision, God made himself known to his people preeminently through the saving experience of the exodus (Exod. 6:3-9). But the prophet lamented that Israel did not know God (Isa. 1:3). This image evokes the picture of a faithful messianic community, the flock of God, who knows its shepherd.

Jesus expressed concern for "other sheep that do not belong to this fold" but who will be incorporated into the messianic community (John 10:16). Then there will be one flock under the care of the Good Shepherd. This has been the object of speculation.[7] In light of the dependence of the shepherd-flock image on the OT, Isaiah 56:8 is especially pertinent. "Thus says the Lord God, who gathers the outcasts of Israel, I will gather others to them besides those already gathered." The messianic flock is made up of Israel's outcasts. According to the Gospel story, this was literally true (John 9:34). The woman taken in adultery and the blind man healed are representatives of this group known in the Gospels under a variety of names: the poor, the little ones, publicans, and sinners.

"His own people," who did not receive Jesus (John 1:11), are here replaced not only by his "own" sheep (10:14) but by "other sheep" as well (10:16). In addition to Judaism's outcasts, the Samaritans can be included in this category. In the prophetic vision of the shepherd and flock, the blessings of the messianic age will come upon both Judah and Israel (which includes the Samaritans; Jer. 23:6; Ezek. 34:23). This flock is made up of Judaism's outcasts and their erstwhile enemies, the Samaritans (as well as other Gentiles). Their unity will be a powerful witness in the messianic era (John 17:20-21).

The Samaritan participation in the flock of the Good Shepherd is further substantiated by the Jewish charge that Jesus might well be a Samaritan (8:48). Also, they recognize his willingness to teach among the Gentiles (7:35). Jesus had an open attitude toward the Samaritans (John 4; et al.), and so did the early Christian community (Acts 8; et al.). This stands in marked contrast to all other Jewish groups of that time. Paul's assertion that the church is fundamentally a community of reconciled enemies is solidly based on Jesus' own understanding of his mission: to gather together God's scattered flock in the messianic era of salvation.

God's restored flock owes its life to the shepherd's willingness to lay down his life for it. This was literally true of the community addressed by the Gospel of John. Jesus' insistence on gathering the outcasts and his claim to be their shepherd cost him his life. Outcasts and Samaritans are replacing unbelieving Jews in his flock. These believers are the sheep who follow Jesus in a new exodus.

The Feast of Booths offers a basic key to understanding the meaning of the shepherd-and-flock image in the Gospel of John. To be God's flock is to follow his Messiah in a new exodus of salvation. It is to come into the God's kingdom, which means to be saved and to be righteous, as the Hallel Psalm reminded pilgrims gathered for the festival (Ps. 118:20-21). It is to be gathered together among the world's outcasts and to be reconciled with all erstwhile enemies. This is the community which carried forward the messianic mission to Judaism's outcasts, to Samaritans, and to the Gentiles with remarkable integrity.

Yet the church, like Judaism's leaders, has often become preoccupied with maintaining its religious and doctrinal structures and has ceased to concretely live its exodus of liberation and its wilderness sojourn. Thus the vision of its essential nature becomes blurred and its mission to outcasts and former enemies is blunted. Rather than inspiring the church to mission, the shepherd-and-flock image is used pastorally to comfort individual members in their lethargy.

The shepherd-and-flock image also appears in the book of Revelation (7:9-17). Again, the key to understanding the image is the Feast of Booths. God's flock, which is now complete, comes from "every nation, from all tribes and peoples and languages" (7:9). The palms in their hands evoke the unbounded joy of the Festival of Booths, celebrating righteousness and victory. They joyfully cry, "Salvation belongs to our God who is seated on the throne, and to the Lamb" (7:10). This is the fulfilled counterpart of the Hallel cry, "Save us, we beseech you, O Lord" (Ps. 118:25).

The passage pictures the Lamb who "shepherds" (*poimanei*) God's flock. The power exercised by the Shepherd's "laying down his life" is underscored by this image. "The Lamb at the center of the throne will be their shepherd, and he will guide them to springs of the water of life" (Rev. 7:17). But this idyllic vision rests upon the fact that "they have washed their robes and made them white in the blood of the Lamb" (7:14). The blood of the shepherd makes white the robes of the flock.

Not only does the Lamb shepherd the flock, he will also "shepherd" the nations (Rev. 19:15). In this kingdom, the cross is the crown. The death of Jesus as the Good Shepherd and as the slaughtered Lamb completely permeated the common life of God's flock. Paul charged the Ephesian elders to "watch over yourselves and over all the flock, . . . to shepherd the church of God that he obtained with the blood of his own Son" (Acts 20:28). This fact determined the behavior of both sheep and shepherds (see Minear, 1960:86ff.). For this reason all shepherding among the flock of God must take the form of suffering servanthood (1 Pet. 5:1-5; et al.).

"The one who is seated on the throne will shelter [*skenōsei*, literally, "spread a tabernacle over"] them" (Rev. 7:15). And "the Lamb . . . will guide them to springs of the water of life" (7:17). These both are reminders of the Feast of Booths or Tabernacles. They celebrate the fact that the Messiah is the Shepherd who tabernacles (John 1:14, *eskēnōsen*) among them. He leads out God's flock in a new exodus of liberation which will culminate in the gathering of the nations.

Biblical Images of the Church in Mission

Images of Transformation

13

Salt, Light, and a City

In Matthew 5:13-16, Jesus employed three images to describe the messianic community. These images are particularly crucial for our understanding of the character and mission of God's people as Jesus and the early Christian community perceived them. However, to grasp the impact of its message, we must view this passage in its immediate context: in the light of what precedes (the Beatitudes, Matt. 5:3-11) and of what follows (Jesus' attitude toward God's covenant law, Matt. 5:17-20).

The exclusive use of plural pronouns in this paragraph (Matt. 5:13-16) shows that these images are used in an essentially collective sense. They reflect the kind of community which is described by the Beatitudes. This body lives and proclaims a message characterized by the values summarized with singular clarity in the Sermon on the Mount. Only this kind of restored community will be truly missionary in a way which corresponds to Jesus' vision for the mission of God's people.

The following paragraph (Matt. 5:17-20) contains Jesus' perception of the relationship of the messianic community to covenant law. This statement is often perceived as an introduction to

Jesus' call to the practice of a higher righteousness which follows (Matt. 5:21-48). However, this juxtaposition of missionary images which describe the messianic community and Jesus' attitude toward covenant law can hardly be coincidental. It is undoubtedly intended to enrich our understanding of the identity and role of the messianic community perceived in terms of salt, light, and a mountaintop city.

OT Background

All three of these metaphors are drawn from the OT. Salt was a symbol associated with Yahweh's gracious covenant as well as the cultic practices of his people. The references to light and the mountaintop city were a part of the prophetic vision of the restoration and mission of God's people in the messianic era.

The image of salt, as used in Matthew's text, may imply, as interpreters have suggested, that a function of the disciple community is to season society as well as to preserve it from decay. But the roots of the image undoubtedly go deeper. In the OT, salt fulfilled a cultic function. "You shall not omit from your grain offerings the salt of the covenant with your God; with all your offerings you shall offer salt" (Lev. 2:13). Apparently salt contributed to sanctifying Israel's offerings. Salt was a sign of covenant relationship, and "salt of the covenant" is matched with the term "covenant of salt" (Num. 18:19; 2 Chron. 13:5). This reflects an oriental custom of parties sealing a covenant by eating a meal seasoned with salt. Thus salt symbolizes the covenant relationship between the Lord and his people, upon which the sacrificial system was based.

Salt was

a bond that united the Lord to both the . . . priests and the . . . kings, and through them to the people. All generations were covered by these bonds, all being viewed as one in their obligation to and dependence upon God. . . . In short, these covenants of salt were intrinsic to the entire economy of nationhood, priesthood, kingship, worship, forgiveness of sin, national identity, and destiny. (Minear, 1997:37)

In light of this background, the text of Matthew 5:13 probably points to the sanctifying mission of God's people in the world (cf. Mark 9:49-50; Luke 14:34-35). Through the mere fact of its existence as a distinctive covenanted community, God's people fulfill the task of inviting others into covenant fellowship and sanctifying the rest of the world (cf. 1 Pet. 2:9). The salt metaphor points to the messianic community as God's contrast-community for the salvation of others. As "salt of the earth," the community restored in the Messiah anticipates cosmic restoration, in which all creation, including the earth, will participate (Minear, 1997:37-40).

According to the prophetic vision, the Servant of Yahweh is to be a light to the nations: "I have given you as a covenant to the people, a light to the nations" (Isa. 42:6cd), "that my salvation may reach to the end of the earth" (49:6d). God's saving mission to the nations will be carried out through the restoration of his people according to his saving covenant intention. In his use of this image, Jesus identifies the messianic community with the ancient prophetic vision of restoration and witness.

A decisive element in this prophetic vision is that Gentiles, attracted by the visible expression of salvation in Israel, will be freely drawn to the people of God. This is to happen not so much from the result of missionary activity as from their fascination with God's people. God's restored people are perceived as the center from which the light of God's glory itself radiates in a dark world. "The Lord will be your everlasting light, and your God will be your glory" (Isa. 60:19cd). "Nations shall come to your light, and kings to the brightness of your dawn" (60:3). God's saving intention will shine so brightly upon Israel that others will be enticed to the life of God's people. "O house of Jacob, come, let us walk in the light of the Lord!" (Isa. 2:5).

The prophets also described the messianic restoration and

mission of God's people in terms of a mountaintop city to which the nations will be attracted. "The mountain of the Lord's house shall be established as the highest of the mountains; . . . all the nations [or peoples] shall stream to it" (Isa. 2:2-3; Mic. 4:1-2; cf. Zech. 8:20, 22). In line with this vision, Jesus described how the messianic community of the Beatitudes would be different. Like a mountaintop city which others will see, it will be a powerful attraction: "[People will] see your good works and give glory to your Father in heaven" (Matt. 5:16). The restoration of a people who walk in the paths of the Lord and the fulfillment of the life envisioned in the law and the prophets will be a magnet which attracts the peoples of the earth (see Yoder, 1982:9).

These images all point to the existence of a community which is different. It is God's restored people of the prophetic vision. Its quality of life oriented by God's gracious Torah (law, which in biblical thought was a guide for living) is plausible because it is truly lived in the restored community. By conserving its unique character as God's contrast-community, the people of God truly become a people in mission. Jesus charges the disciple community of the Beatitudes and the new messianic Torah with its higher justice, to make disciples of all nations. The missionary vision of Matthew 5:13-16 and Matthew 28:19-20 are not really contradictory. Both envision people coming under the lordship of Jesus Christ in the context of the messianic community.

The images of the salt, light, and city on the mountaintop are all drawn from the biblical background of the prophetic vision of God's restored people among whom his righteous reign is a gracious reality. Jesus' use of these images in Matthew's Gospel means that God's reign has begun to become a reality in the messianic community—it is visible and tangible and capable of being experienced even though it is not yet perfected. And this is a fact of redemptive consequence for all humanity.

Matthew 5:13-16

The fundamental relationship of the images of salt, light, and a city is highlighted by the repeated use of the plural pronoun "you." (Unfortunately, English versions do not make this clear.) It is presupposed in each of the Beatitudes ("Blessed are [you] poor in spirit," etc.) but is made specific only in the last one. The plural pronoun "you" which appears six times in Matthew 5:11-12 is the point of departure for introducing the salt, light, and city metaphors in the verses which follow. The use of "you" is especially emphatic. It is as if Jesus had said, "It is *you*, the messianic community of the Beatitudes; *you* who therefore suffer persecution at the hands of evildoers; it is precisely *you*. *You* are the salt of the earth. . . . *You* are the light of the world."

This pairing of suffering and witness should not surprise us. In the NT, the same term is applied to both martyr and witness. Suffering and testimony are two sides of the same coin among God's people. It is a suffering messianic community gathered by its suffering Lord which is salt and light and a mountaintop city in the midst of the world.

We often overlook the fact that the principal verbs in Matthew 5:13-14 are in the indicative mood rather than in the imperative. Jesus does not command his disciples to be salt and light. He simply declares that this suffering community described by the Beatitudes is, by the very nature of the messianic mission, salt and light and a city on a hill. There are no techniques for becoming salt, light, and a mountaintop city apart from the spiritual values and resources of the kingdom described in the Sermon on the Mount.

Our presence and proclamation will carry kingdom substance if by God's grace we are the kind of community described by the Beatitudes. This can happen if, in the power of God's Spirit, we live the life described in the Sermon on the Mount. Such a community will season and purify and enlighten relationships within human society. However, if we are not this kind of community, and if our works do not really correspond to the teachings of Jesus, then we fail. No matter how hard we try, our saltiness will become insipid and worthless, the light will grow clouded and dim, and the city will be hidden from view.

Jesus' insistence on the missionary visibility of the messianic community may have also been a response to the strategy of the Essenes of his time (see Bonnard: 96). They lived together in communities in the Judean desert with an appealing integrity. They dedicated themselves to a purity of life which was both moral and religious, as they awaited the coming Day of the Lord when the reign of Yahweh would be established. But Jesus' words, in line with the prophetic vision (Isa. 2:2) of the "mountain of the Lord's house . . . raised above the hills" round about, stand in contrast to the self-centered otherworldliness of the Essenes.

The messianic community anticipates the restored life of the New Era in a visible way, and it does so "on behalf of the nations." In short, Jesus saw the missionary task of the people of God as anticipating concretely and visibly the kingdom of God with saving intent. The life and works which correspond to God's saving intention are the clearest testimony that God has truly intervened in human history in the form of messianic restoration. His universal reign is thereby inaugurated. So by means of the being and doing of God's restored people as well as the verbal proclamation of his reign, we are to be instruments of his saving activity in the world.

The idea is false that there are only two alternatives open to the people of God in our life and mission in the world: either to conform to the values which characterize society because we need to be in the world to give our witness; or to maintain a different style of life by withdrawing from the world and living in geographic or spiritual isolation. The alternative which Jesus envisioned for his community is life characterized by the Beatitudes of restored communion with both God and others. We are called to live and witness radically under God's reign in the midst of the world.

Matthew 5:17-20

The next paragraph (Matt. 5:17-20) shows that there is an intimate relationship between covenant law—God's gracious intention for the life of his people—and the mission of the Messiah and his community. We have already noted the prophetic vision upon which Jesus based his understanding of mission. An essential aspect of this vision has to do with the function of law in relation to the mission of God's people. The prophets caught a glimpse of how God would "teach his ways" to all, including the Gentiles (Isa. 2:3-4). They saw how the "instruction and the word of the Lord" would lead to the establishment of *shalom* among the peoples of the earth (Mic. 4:2-3). In the Hebrew Bible, Torah did not mean so much rules as it did guidance or instruction. In other words, according to the prophetic vision, God's covenant law plays a fundamental role in the mission of God's restored community.

In the prophetic view, the missionary message of God's restored people is his law which goes forth out of Zion (Isa. 2:3; Mic. 4:2). Similarly, the missionary proclamation of the messianic community is not an amorphous message of mystical type without concrete ethical substance. It is not a message which merely helps us feel better about ourselves, although this may well be one of the important side effects. Instead, it is the announcement of a kingdom which has come; a kingdom in which the reign of God is recognized; a kingdom in which Jesus is already worshiped and obeyed as Lord; a kingdom in which interpersonal relationships correspond to God's covenant intention for his people; a kingdom which will one day be manifested in all of its glory.

Our Protestant heritage through Pietism and movements of revival has fogged our eyes. We evangelicals have a difficult time seeing evangelization as having anything to do with biblical law. We have generally viewed law in terms of legalism and conceived of it as a mortal enemy of true evangelization. Where existentialism has been influential, it has simply served to nurture these negative attitudes toward the function of covenant law.

Jesus, however, rejected the idea that his messianic mission was to lead God's people away from the authentic and legitimate authority of covenant law over them. On the contrary, God had commissioned him to "give fullness" to the "law and the prophets," to fulfill them (Matt. 5:17). As the Messiah, Jesus is the new Moses, described in the typology in Matthew's Gospel (Jeremias, 1967b:867-873). He is the ultimate lawgiver. For Jesus, the category of covenant law was as native and congenial as "the good news of the kingdom" which he proclaimed.

Jesus understood God's law as the expression of the divine saving intention for the life of his people. He offered his teachings not as a substitute for the law but as the culmination or full flowering of God's covenant purpose. From the examples which follow in the Sermon on the Mount (Matt. 5:21-48), we note that Jesus radicalized the law. He gave it its fullest meaning by taking as his point of departure its root in the intention of God. In this sense we use the term "radical," from the Latin *radix*, "root."

To judge from the examples listed in Matthew 5:21-48, we may say that Jesus took the category of covenant law more seriously than did his Jewish contemporaries. He deepened the common understanding of law by discerning its essential spirit through an appeal to its radical intention. In this, Jesus' activities corresponded to the prophetic vision which looked forward to the last times when there would be an authoritative and definitive interpretation of the law of God (Jer. 31:31ff.; Ezek. 36:26ff.; Isa. 2:3; Bonnard: 99). Jesus is perceived not as a replacement for the law but as the fulfillment of God's saving purpose for his people, once expressed in covenant law.

The challenge of Jesus to his community is this: "Unless your righteousness exceeds that of the scribes and Pharisees, you will never enter the kingdom of heaven" (Matt. 5:20). This is not merely a call to a life which is spiritually motivated in contrast to the legalism that characterized the scribes and Pharisees. In a fundamental sense, this passage also contains a penetrating critique of contemporary Jewish missionary practice.

Jesus did not denounce the scribes and Pharisees because they lacked missionary zeal, while his followers were zealous missioners. And in this particular passage, Jesus did not condemn their legalism, in contrast to the spirit marking the messianic community. In what may appear to evangelicals to be a remarkable reversal of roles, Jesus was condemning the lack of moral content in the Jewish mission. For missionary reasons, as well as for their own salvation, the righteousness of the messianic community must exceed that of the scribes and Pharisees.

Rabbinic Mission

The missionary activity of first-century Judaism must have been truly remarkable in its scope. It is also apparent that they were reasonably successful in their efforts. The number of converts or proselytes and God-fearers grew particularly among the Jews of the dispersion. It has been suggested that conversion to Judaism was one of the three principal reasons why the number of Jews living in the diaspora was so high (see Hegermann: 307-308).[1]

The missionary activity of Judaism was notable in a number of ways. (1) They proclaimed the one true God, whose worship was absolutely incompatible with the many forms of pagan cult which abounded in the empire. (2) They proclaimed what they considered to be the true path to spirituality through obedience to the precepts of God's law, a thing which was highly scandalous to enlightened pagans of the period. (3) They shared the conviction that hope for humankind was to be found in faithful worship of the one true God and zealous observance of his law. In the light of this seemingly laudable missionary activity, Jesus' scathing condemnation is all the more remarkable. "Woe to you, scribes and Pharisees, hypocrites! For you cross sea and land to make a single convert, and you make the new convert twice as much a child of hell as yourselves" (Matt. 23:15).

To judge from the evidence in Matthew's Gospel, there must

have been, among the various reasons for this energetic denunciation, at least two principal ones. First of all, these missioners lacked an authentic practice of the piety which they preached. Jesus had an incisive comment to make about this fact: "Do whatever they teach you and follow it; but do not do as they do, for they do not practice what they teach" (Matt. 23:3).

The second reason was their apparently well-intentioned concern for the practical relevance of the law. This led them to reformulate covenant precepts to make their practices more accessible to the people of their time. An example of such adaptation can be seen in the provision for contributing funds for religious purposes rather than using them for the support of elderly parents, as the law intended (Mark 7:9-13). Another was the liberal provision for divorce and remarriage, which responded more to the exigencies of the social situation than to God's covenant intention (Mark 10:2-9). Yet another example was the fine distinctions made to determine liability in the swearing of oaths, while covenant law was intended to protect relationships of faithfulness and veracity among God's people (Matt. 23:16-22).

So the difference between the messianic mission and the rabbinic mission in the first century was not delineated in terms of gospel and law, as in traditional Protestant interpretation. It was rather the question of how the role of covenant law was to be followed in shaping the life and mission of God's people. It had to do with the fundamental matter of discerning its radical intention and, having done this, taking it with utter seriousness. The rabbinic method for interpreting and applying Mosaic covenant provisions was the opposite of that which Jesus used. While the casuistic interpretations of the scribes and Pharisees were aimed at making their observance more generally accessible, Jesus insisted on radicalizing covenant precepts in terms of God's true intention. To do this, he went deeper into the saving will of God as he discerned it. Jesus' condemnation of the rabbinic mission was not aimed at their works, as such, but rather at their tragic lack of authentic moral seriousness.

The spector of the traditional salvation-by-works versus salvation-by-faith debate need not haunt us here. The ethical seriousness which Jesus insisted on presupposes, in the context of Matthew's Gospel, God's gracious forgiving love and the renewing power of his Holy Spirit. In their setting in the Sermon on the Mount, the figures of salt, light, and the mountaintop city tell us something important about the church. Only that community which incarnates the true Spirit and values of the kingdom of God is in a position to proclaim with any degree of credibility the gospel of the kingdom to the surrounding world. According to Jesus, the good works which characterize the messianic community are essential to the communication of the gospel in a way which brings glory to God (Matt. 5:16). Hence, for missionary reasons Jesus denounced the Pharisaic tendency to "relax" the commandments which reflected God's intention for the life of his people. He insisted that the righteousness of kingdom missionaries must exceed that of the scribes and Pharisees if they or their converts expect to enter the kingdom of heaven.

The Legacy of Protestantism

The spiritual legacy of the Protestant Reformation has recovered a more biblical vision of salvation by grace. Thus it has served as a necessary corrective to the ancient and pernicious idea of salvation by works. An important part of the gospel message is the good news that God receives repentant sinners just as we are and forgives us out of love rather than in response to any personal merit. However, the typical Protestant version of this gospel of salvation by faith without works is not fully adequate when measured from Jesus' perspective.

As evangelical Christians, we are quick to proclaim that we live by grace and not by law. Furthermore, we believe that the salvation offered by the new covenant is far superior to that experienced by God's people under the Mosaic covenant. But we need to compare the concrete expressions of the salvation which characterizes our life and witness with the life of the Beatitudes and of obedience to covenant law, as they were radicalized by Jesus in the messianic community. Then we must confess that something has gone awry. The tendency to have our missionary message stress almost unilaterally the Protestant doctrine of salvation by faith alone has somehow severed a vital nerve, leaving us with a message which is more mystical than real.

The concrete social substance of salvation among God's people under the old covenant is described in the Decalogue, the Sabbatical and Jubilee provisions, and the messages of the prophets. However, since the incarnation of Jesus, salvation in the new covenant is superior to that experienced under the old for two principal reasons: the Messiah himself has come, and his Spirit indwells his community. Messianic salvation, which Jesus announced in terms of Jubilee liberation and restoration (Luke 4:18-19), is richer, both in moral content and in spiritual motivation, than the experience of salvation under the old covenant.

However, we need to review the missionary history of the Christian church, among the new churches as well as the sending congregations. With a few notable exceptions, the concrete experience of salvation (in terms of righteousness, *shalom*, communion) has generally been poorer than that which is set forth in the provisions of the old covenant. This places the church and its missionary enterprise more in line with the scribes and Pharisees of first-century Judaism in their life and mission. We have fallen short of the restored community of the Messiah described in the Sermon on the Mount.

Jesus challenges us with his use of the missionary images of salt, light, and the mountaintop city in the context of the Beatitudes and the relationship of the messianic community to covenant law. He calls us to take a new and more penetrating look at the missionary enterprise as it is being carried out by evangelicals in our time. As Jesus reminds us in Matthew's Gospel, the missionary task calls both for the renewal of the church to more authentic peoplehood under God and for making "disciples of all nations" (Matt. 28:19).

14

A Spiritual House

The spiritual house image enhances our understanding of the church's structure and mission (1 Pet. 2:5; cf. Eph. 2:22). Related images include "God's building" (1 Cor. 3:9), "God's temple" (1 Cor. 3:16-17; 2 Cor. 6:16; Eph 2:21), "the household of God" (Eph. 2:19; 1 Pet. 4:17; 1 Tim. 3:15), "the family of faith" (Gal. 6:10), "God's house" (Heb. 3:2-6; 10:21), and dwelling of the Holy Spirit (1 Cor. 3:16; cf. 6:19). Other references include (Matt. 16:18; Mark 14:58—*oikodomeō*; John 2:19—*egeirō*), even though the image itself does not appear in the passage.

The term "house" (*oikos*) is used in a variety of figurative senses in the OT. These include "family" or "race" (e.g., Gen. 7:1) and "dynasty" (2 Sam. 7:11; 1 Kings 2:24). More important for us is the use of the term as a metaphor for the people of God (Num. 12:7) and the fact that it became a technical term for the sanctuary in the Septuagint (Michel, 1967b:120). This usage is continued in the NT. And no other sacred or ecclesiastical structure is called the "house of God" in the NT (Michel, 1967b:121). The Christian community itself is called "house of God" (1 Tim. 3:15; Heb. 3:6; 1 Pet. 4:17), "spiritual house" (1 Pet. 2:5) and "temple of God" (1 Cor. 3:16-17; 2 Cor. 6:16). The metaphoric use of "house" and "temple" as images for the Christian community takes precedence over the literal meanings of the terms.

While the term "edification" (*oikodomeō/oikodomē*) in the experience of the church has come to refer principally to the inner religious life of Christians, in the NT it was an important term for understanding the nature of the Christian community. Essential aspects of Paul's vision of the church are found in the concept of mutual upbuilding which we call edification (1 Thess. 5:11).

The roots of the Christian usage of this image lie in the OT, especially in the prophet Jeremiah. "To build up" and "to destroy" are two themes which run through the book (Jer. 1:10; 12:14, 17; 24:5-7; 31:27-28). In these texts it becomes especially clear that God's intention is to build Israel into a new community following the exile (Jer. 31:27-28). God's building activity is related directly to the restoration of a people who will live under his reign.

> Thus says the Lord, the God of Israel: . . . I will set my eyes upon them for good, and I will bring them back to this land. I will build them up, and not tear them down; I will plant them, and not pluck them up. I will give them a heart to know that I am the Lord; and they shall be my people and I will be their God, for they shall return to me with their whole heart. (Jer. 24:5-7).

Paul understood his vocation in the light of Jeremiah's call (Rom. 1:1-7; Gal. 1:15; Jer. 1:5). He understood his mission, in keeping with the prophetic vision, as authority from the Lord "for building up and not for tearing down" (2 Cor. 13:10; cf. 10:8; cf. Jer. 1:4-10). Paul's apostolic mission consisted in the edification, or upbuilding, of messianic communities, a restored people of God. In keeping with this metaphor, he distinguished between the task of laying the foundation for new communities and their ongoing edification. His task was laying the foundation (Messiah), upon which others would build (1 Cor. 3:6, 10; Rom.

15:20). Edification is essentially restoring messianic people-hood.

This Pauline concept of the edification of God's new messianic people is analogous to Jesus' own vision for gathering and restoring the true people of God. While Paul took his model from Jeremiah, Jesus appears to have drawn more on Ezekiel for his vision. "I will . . . bring you out from the peoples, and gather you . . . where you have been scattered; and I will manifest my holiness among you in the sight of the nations, . . . for my name's sake" (Ezek. 20:41-44). "For the sake of my holy name, . . . I will take you from the nations, and gather you from all the countries, and bring you into your own land. . . . A new heart I will give you, and a new spirit I will put within you; . . . and you shall be my people, and I will be your God" (Ezek. 36:22-28).

Both Jesus and Paul were concerned with gathering and building up the new people of God, restored under his reign of righteousness. In keeping with their common vision, Jesus set out to gather Israel (Matt. 12:30; 23:37). Paul's part in the edification of God's new spiritual house was calling the Gentiles to faith (Rom. 14:20; 15:18; 1 Cor. 3:8).

In light of this OT background, edification does not refer primarily to individuals who need help to become more mature and more spiritual persons. Instead, the concern is to build up the Christian community as God's restored people. The creation of God's spiritual house, the church, is the primary object of edification in Paul's thought and activity. Paul speaks often of the edification of the community as the responsibility which all members share toward one another (1 Cor. 14:3-5, 12, 26; Eph. 4:12, 16, 29; 1 Thess. 5:11).

According to this image, the church is both the object of the creative activity of God's Spirit as well as a testimony to his presence. The church is both sign and instrument of the saving power and presence of the Spirit of God. The church is the temple of the living God. According to the NT passages which use this metaphor, the church is God's building through the activity of

Christ and the Holy Spirit. The spiritual dimensions of the church and its mission are especially prominent in three classic texts with the house image (1 Cor. 3:16-17; Eph. 2:17-22; 1 Pet. 2:4-7).

In 1 Corinthians 3:9-17 Paul declares that the concrete local Christian community in Corinth is "God's building," "God's temple," and the dwelling place of God's Spirit. The fact that Paul can pass from one image to another, from "God's field" to "God's building," in the scope of a single phrase indicates that the basic message of the two metaphors is the same. Both point to the Christian community as a process. The sequence of planting, watering, and growing through which the church is perfected culminates in the field metaphor (1 Cor. 3:6-8). The building image also includes a series of sub-images.

The whole process of building has its foundation in Jesus Christ (3:11). Attention is focused on the process of construction and the crucial relationship between the one essential foundation and what workers build upon it (Minear, 1960:49-50). The shape of the completed house, which includes a wide variety of materials, "gold, silver, precious stones, wood, hay, straw" (1 Cor. 3:12), is not the center of attention. Our attention is directed to the continuing process by which both God and his "gifted" builders carry on the construction. The integrity of the builders' activity will not be finally revealed until that "day" (3:13).

The focus is upon the fact that "you are God's building" and upon the process by which this comes about. In the Greek NT, the term used here for "building" is translated in other contexts as "edification" (e.g., 1 Cor. 14:3, 5, 17, 26; Eph. 4:12, 16, 29). While most English readers would scarcely recognize a relationship between these terms, in the biblical vision, the people of God are built into a building by means of God's edifying work. To edify the people of God is to build the church (1 Thess. 5:11; Col. 2:7). The principal NT passages which apply this term to the church also highlight the charismatic nature of the church (1 Cor. 14; Eph. 4).

The image is fundamentally a charismatic one. Paul self-consciously described his participation in "God's building" as charismatic activity. God has bestowed grace on him by means of the *charis* (1 Cor. 3:10). God's people are "a spiritual house" (1 Pet. 2:5; cf. Eph. 2:22) and a "dwelling of the Holy Spirit" (1 Cor. 3:16; cf. 6:19). All forms of ministry within the "household of God" are charismatic gifts aimed at upbuilding the church (Eph. 4:7-12). In this passage, it is not primarily the maturing of the individual which is in view, important as this may be for the well-being of a congregation. Instead, it is a concern for the social and corporate dimensions of communion which result when all parts of God's building are joined together by bonds of love and mutual responsibility.

All of the spiritual gifts are shared out and designed to serve the purposes of this process of edification: prophecies (1 Cor. 14:3), tongues and their interpretation (14:5), any or all of the "manifestations of the Spirit" (14:12, RSV), and the spiritual gifts which enhance the corporate worship of the community (14:26). This is also the context in which love is described as the most excellent gift or "way" for every believer to exercise any gift (1 Cor. 13). Love provides that cohesive force which is so fundamental to the Christian community. This is true no matter whether the image employed is that of a building under construction or a growing body (1 Cor. 8:1; Eph. 4:16; cf. 2:21).

The charismatic processes by which people are "built into a spiritual house" (1 Pet. 2:5) are fundamental to the church's self-understanding. They virtually define the Christian community. The church exists where people edify one another in their common relationship to Christ (Minear, 1960:164-165). The building image in the church's self-understanding is not an imposing edifice. Instead, it is the humanly precarious process by which the Spirit's gifts edify God's people in their common life.

This is the sense in which the building image makes its initial appearance in the NT (1 Cor. 3:9, 16-17). The metaphor is not applied to a Christian community with any claims to greatness or being an ideal church. It is applied to the church in Corinth, with its factions, strife, and self-centeredness. It is concretely this local assembly which Paul calls "God's building," "God's temple." The metaphor is more an invitation to become "God's temple" through the charismatic process of the Spirit's building activity than it is a description of what it already is. "Do you not know that you are God's temple and that God's Spirit dwells in you?" is more a warning than a statement of fact. The divisive character of the Corinthians, as well as the contentiousness of certain apostolic messengers, threatened "God's building" in Corinth with destruction (1 Cor. 3:16-17, 9).

The metaphor of "God's temple" or "dwelling of the Spirit" need not be understood as a spiritualization of the church, as though the true church were invisible. The "dwelling of the Spirit" in Corinth was highly visible.[1] The spirituality of the church is based on the presence of the Spirit of God within it. God's Spirit is most manifestly present here, although the Spirit cannot be held captive by any human community. The Christian community is called to anticipate the kingdom. God's Spirit is the spirit by which the church lives. The spirituality of the church means that this community, among all human collectives, is inspired in its life and mission by a different Spirit, the Spirit of God.

With their backgrounds in first-century Judaism and Hellenism, the Corinthian believers could well understand this Pauline metaphor. For the Greeks the term "temple" (*naos*) carried the meaning of the "abode of the gods" (Michel, 1967a:880). However, among the religious and moral philosophers in the Hellenistic world, there was also the idea that God made his dwelling in the human heart rather than in buildings made of stone (Barrett: 90). For the Jews, grounded in the OT, the sanctuary and later the temple were held to be the special locus of God's meeting with his people. Jewish apocalyptic writings also offered the idea of a new or renewed temple to be established in the last days (Isa. 28:16-17; 1 Enoch 91:13; Jubilees 1:17; Barrett: 90).

However, the biblical image moves beyond anything found in the Hellenistic or Jewish roots of the Corinthian believers. Only once does Paul view the individual Christian as the temple in which God's Spirit abides (1 Cor. 6:19). Otherwise, the stress is on the messianic community, the church as God's temple, the dwelling place of his Spirit (1 Cor. 3:16-17; 2 Cor. 6:16; Eph. 2:19; cf. 1 Cor. 6:19). The church is the eschatological temple "not made with hands." And the Holy Spirit is the sign or mode of God's presence among his people.

Because of the fundamentally social character of "God's temple," relationships are important. Strife among God's ministers and dissension among God's people constitute an assault on his temple. To form factions among God's people is to drive away God's Spirit. It is not merely a matter of destroying God's temple; it is the destruction of the congregation and the self-destruction of its members. True spirituality means to "discern the body," relationships with other believers (1 Cor. 11:29). It means to edify one another through the exercise of spiritual gifts, to be joined together by the most excellent way of serving —through love.

Built on the Saving Work of Christ

In Ephesians 2:19-22, peoplehood and family images are used together with the building-temple metaphor to describe the new community arising from the saving work of Christ. First, the Gentiles are welcomed into God's people and become a part of God's household (2:19). Then they, together with the Jews, become materials for building "a holy temple, . . . a dwelling place for God in the Spirit" (2:20-22, based on NRSV note). This happens through the charismatic apostolic and prophetic ministries which the Spirit bestows on the church (2:20-22).

The context of the building-temple image in Ephesians 2 shows that the construction of the building is a central result of the saving work of Christ. In this passage we find the richest concentration of atonement imagery in the NT.[2] The building-temple motif along with the peoplehood and family images describe the results of Christ's saving work.

In contrast to the building metaphor in 1 Corinthians, where the allusion is to a concrete local community, the image here carries a universal dimension. In the early chapters of Ephesians, Paul refers four times to "a mystery" (1:9; 3:3, 4, 9; cf. Col. 1:26-27). In common first-century understanding, this mystery had to do with some esoteric secret known only to certain privileged devotees especially initiated into its realm. In contrast, Paul says the mystery has become an open secret since Jesus Christ revealed it.

Until the coming of Christ it had been, indeed, a mystery in the sense that humankind had been incapable of understanding God's plan of salvation for humanity. But in the mission of God's Messiah, the humanly inconceivable is made manifest. "The Gentiles have become fellow heirs, members of the same body, and sharers in the promise in Christ Jesus through the gospel" (Eph. 3:6). God is determined to draw Gentiles into his house, and he has carried out his plan through Jesus Christ (Eph. 1:10; 3:9). God is building a "holy temple" of universal dimensions, "a dwelling place of God in the Spirit." The secret of its coherence is the keystone,[3] Jesus Christ in his saving work, and the ongoing edifying work of apostles and prophets (Eph. 2:17-20).

Three terms emphasize the communion of Jews and Gentiles in this new creation—"fellow citizens," "joined together," and "built together" (Eph. 2:19, 21-22).[4] To be "fellow citizens with the saints" means to share in salvation history. The story of God's ancient covenant people becomes the church's story. Those who are "members of the household of God" are no longer outsiders but a part of God's family. In that family the Messiah's Father is our Father, and all people—Jews and Gentiles —are brothers and sisters. Jews and Gentiles together become God's holy temple, his spiritual dwelling place.

Even though the vision of the church here carried universal dimensions, the spirituality of this temple built by God need not be thought of as something ideal, invisible, or abstract. It is as visible and concrete as the people who have been reconciled by Christ and edified by the gifts of God's grace (*charis*), the apostolic and prophetic ministries in their midst. In this text the emphasis is not so much on the building as such as it is on the process by which God builds the temple, using the charismatic ministries he gives his people. The term used to describe the process of being "joined together" (*sunarmologoumenē*) and growing into a holy temple (Eph. 2:21) is used in Ephesians 4:16 in relation to the body image, in which members are "joined together."

The building image underscores the charismatic nature of the church's structure. The whole structure is "joined together" in the living Christ, in his Spirit. The presence of the Spirit in the church sustains its life and orients its mission. The presence of the Spirit of Christ makes possible the ongoing reconciliation of Jews and Gentiles, even such diverse and antagonistic peoples and persons. In the church both the people far off and those near have access to God by virtue of the Spirit. The building-temple image underlines the spiritual (pneumatic) nature of the church. The structure and mission of the church are not determined by strictly dogmatic or rational or psychological considerations. Instead, they are determined by the Holy Spirit who, although sometimes using these elements for strengthening the church, is never bound by them.

In 1 Peter 2:4-7 Christ is the "living stone," the foundation on which Christians, as "living stones," are incorporated into the "spiritual house." The verb, "be yourselves built" (*oikodomeisthe*), may be either indicative or imperative. In fact, the indicative, "you are being built," is the necessary presupposition to the imperative, "be yourselves built into a spiritual house" (1 Pet. 2:5). This is not an abstract doctrinal statement about the relationship between Christ and believers. It is an invitation to be incorporated into a spiritual house (*pneumatikos oikos*) as "living stones."

Jesus, who was rejected and crucified, is the risen and the living One. He is the One in whom Christians are likewise raised to newness of life, to become "living stones." Built upon the living Christ, believers are formed into a "spiritual house." This is no mere abstraction, because the church is a spiritual house animated by the Spirit of the living Christ.

This image tells us that God's people are joined to "the living stone." The "living stone" is an eschatological and messianic symbol in Judaism and early Christianity (see Jeremias, 1967a:271-280). The figure describes the expected Messiah and the eschatological age which he inaugurates. He is the foundation stone upon which God will build his kingdom (Isa. 28:16). Here the "living stone" is the crucified and risen Jesus, and the people of God are those who are joined to the risen Messiah.

In this community Christians are being built up. More literally, the verb in 1 Peter 2:5 calls on Christians to "continue building yourselves up." In its context the statement is an encouragement to spiritual activity. The "spiritual house" or temple was the place in ancient Israel where the glory of the Lord shone forth. Now this has become the mission of the Christian community.

The image of the spiritual house, together with the figure of "a holy priesthood," underscores the holy character of the people of God. The images also clarify the role of the church in relation to the temple and the priestly hierarchy in Jerusalem. Due to the work of Christ, believers are the true temple, the sanctuary where the glory of God is present.

God's people are charged with a unique function, "to offer spiritual sacrifices acceptable to God through Jesus Christ" (1 Pet. 2:5). This spiritualization of sacrifice does not mean that whereas the sacrifices of Israel had been visible and material, the sacrifice of the new people of God becomes invisible. The change is from cultus to life. As Paul reminded the Christians in Rome, "living sacrifice" implied reordering life according to the will and Spirit of God (Rom. 12). The writer to the Hebrews commends "sacrifice of praise to God, . . . the fruit of lips that confess his name, . . . to do good and to share what you have, for such sacrifices are pleasing to God" (Heb. 13:15-16). This is genuine biblical spirituality, the whole life of a people lived in tune with the Spirit of God.

The "spiritual house" image underscores the fact that the church owes the basis of its life and the shape of its structure to the power of God present in the community in the person of his Spirit. The church is a charismatic community in the NT sense of the term. As the spiritual house-temple image reminds us, the church owes its ongoing edification to the exercise of spiritual gifts in it.

Pneumatic and Charismatic Structure of the Church

The building-temple image underscores the pneumatic and charismatic structure of the church. According to this metaphor, the early church understood itself more as a spiritual building in the process of being edified by charismatic builders than as a finished construction, constitutionally and institutionally complete. Traditionally the church has understood its ministries—*presbuteros, episcopos, diaconos,* pastors, teachers—through the lens of the more institutionally developed church of the second, third and fourth centuries. However, this is an anachronistic way to read the NT texts. It is more appropriate to understand these ministries in the light of the earliest NT views of spiritual gifts, reflected in Paul's early writings, as essentially charismatic.

The idea that spiritual gifts are extraordinary, sensational, occasional happenings has contributed to this traditional distinction between church ministries and spiritual gifts. Tongues, together with expelling demons and other ecstatic and spectacular gifts, are taken as the point of departure for classification and evaluation of charismatic phenomena. In this, Paul's attitude is particularly instructive. While he wholeheartedly accepts the gift of tongues as a special manifestation of God's grace, he does not hesitate to relativize the exercise of this particular spiritual gift. If the gift of tongues is used in the church assembly, it must be interpreted so that it can edify the community (1 Cor. 14).

According to Paul, the exercise of the gifts is not autonomous. There are certain basic criteria by which their authenticity and usefulness may be measured. The first of these is consonance with the lordship of Jesus (1 Cor. 12:3). Only through the work of the Holy Spirit can Jesus be confessed as Lord and all of life subjected to his lordship. God's Spirit is present and active in the church only where Jesus is concretely recognized and obeyed as Lord (1 John 4:2-3). A second criterion for discerning the usefulness of spiritual gifts is their contribution to the edification of the community (1 Cor. 14:3-5, 12, 19, 26, 31; Eph. 4:12). For this reason, no doubt, fraternal love is the essential context in which spiritual gifts are exercised (1 Cor. 13; Eph. 4:2; Rom. 12:9-10). These criteria are, of course, applicable to the entire gamut of charismatic gifts, those which are listed (1 Cor. 12; Rom. 12; Eph. 4) as well as others which are useful but which are not specifically mentioned.

Charismatic gifts can be recognized and ordered within the congregation (1 Tim. 4:14; 2 Tim. 1:6). But by nature spiritual gifts resist efforts to institutionalize them. In his early epistles, Paul emphasizes the free activity of God's Spirit in abundantly gifting his people for their life and mission. While there is a concern for order in these epistles, practically nothing is said about formally ordaining their exercise. The Spirit "allots [grace gifts] to each one individually just as the Spirit chooses" (1 Cor. 12:11; cf. 12:7, 27; Rom. 12:3; Eph. 4:7). In these texts we are confronted with a vision of universality (all of God's people are gifted) and variety (the Spirit gives as the Spirit wills). Some gifts may be for leadership, and others fill auxiliary roles. The exercise of some gifts depends more on the spoken word and others more on the deed. Yet all of the gifts are charismatic, and all are useful insofar as they edify (see Yoder, 1992:47-60).

The charismatic structure of the church defies attempts to order its life and mission in a strictly hierarchical or institutional sense. There can be plurality of gifts in which one person may exercise more than one gift; Paul himself is an example of this.

Their free and universal distribution by God's Spirit makes it impossible to limit them to any particular group within the Christian community (1 Cor. 12:29-30). The gift of administration (*kubernēseis*, literally the ability to pilot the ship) appears next to last in the list of gifts in 1 Corinthians 12:28. This should discourage any hierarchical ambitions in the community.

The building image reminds us that the church is essentially a charismatic community. The Spirit of the living Christ within the community bestows on the church in a multiform and universal way all of the spiritual gifts necessary for its life and mission. The church is a charismatic community in relation to its mission or ministries (1 Cor. 12:4-5) as well as its life or vocation (Rom. 11:29; 1 Cor. 7:7, 17). In the biblical vision, a charismatic ordering of the church brings unity to the community in which there is a wide variety of gifts. Order is respected in the context of liberty (1 Cor. 12:4, 7). The twin polar temptations of anarchic egalitarianism and petrifying uniformity can be overcome only through the supernatural gifts of the Spirit of God in a charismatic community.

A Fallen House

This apostolic view of the church as God's building-temple, "the dwelling of the Holy Spirit," a charismatic community, soon proved to be too humanly precarious to be sustained. The Didache, probably written during the last quarter of the first century, is an exception. Here we find the charismatic ministry of apostles, prophets, and teachers described, even though it was necessary to warn against the activity of false prophets. *Episcopos* and *diaconos* take their place alongside prophets and teachers as charismatic ministries (Didache 11, 13, 15). However, under the duress of strained relationships in the church, church leaders veered from the Pauline course of mutual submission and the recognition of variety. They soon called for submission to the bishop (Ignatius of Antioch, Eph. 5.1-3; Smyrna 9.1-2; Tral. 2.1; 3.1-3; and Clement of Rome, 1 Clem. 40-42; 54; 60.2, 4).

These experiences which characterized the church at the turn of the first century have marked the ongoing life of the church. As a result the church has largely lost the vision of itself as God's building in the process of being charismatically edified. Instead, it sees itself as an institution of salvation and a depository of sound doctrine. Needless to say, this has well nigh incapacitated the church for God's mission in the world. This is so because the church's life and mission depend on the charismatic gifts of the Spirit in a house which is in the process of becoming the temple of the living God.

15

A Witnessing Community

The church in the New Testament viewed itself as a witnessing community. This is especially clear in the book of Acts.[1] The apostolic community was witnessing to the reality of Christ and the coming of God's kingdom in their midst. The *martus* (witness) word group in the New Testament has not traditionally been given major attention as an image for the church's self-understanding. Yet the relatively frequent use of this metaphor in the NT with reference to the community of disciples indicates that this is an important image for understanding biblically the nature and mission of the church.[2]

It has frequently been noted that Jesus, in the Lukan version of the great commission, charged his disciples to be his witnesses throughout the whole world (Luke 24:48; Acts 1:8). However, our paradigms for understanding this commission to witness have been drawn largely from the heyday of the missionary enterprise of the church in the West. We have tended to overlook those periods in which the meaning and experience of witness and martyrdom blended into a common experience. Furthermore, especially among evangelicals in North America, witness has come to be a term applied to programs of personal evangelism. These typically employ psychological techniques of marketing, which may have contributed more to our understanding of mission than the biblical background.

There have been many efforts to correct the rampant individualism so characteristic of Western Protestantism. One example of this concern is the excellent study in biblical theology by the French Reformed theologian, Suzanne de Dietrich. In her book she underscores the corporate nature of the vocation of God's people as a "witnessing community," a body of witnesses (13-20). Important as this insight has been, in practice it has often meant little more than the enlistment of "every member" in the evangelistic task of the church.

But even with all of its new insights into the importance of witness and its fundamentally corporate character, the church has more often than not fallen far short of the biblical understanding of this image. We have been "a witnessing community" more in name than in reality. Scarcely, if ever, have we had the insights (or the courage) to penetrate to the roots of witness in the NT, to Jesus Christ himself, "the faithful witness." The radical character of the authentic witness-martyr always proves illusive to a church infatuated by the temptation to prestige, power, and wealth.[3]

If we are to recover the biblical vision of the nature and mission of the church as "the witnessing community," we need to bypass contemporary concepts. We need to question even the classic expressions of the missionary enterprise by going all the way back to the original faithful witness. Our understanding of the Lord's commission to be witnesses needs to be based on Jesus' own witness, illuminated by its biblical background (especially by the prophetic vision found in Isaiah 40ff.). That witness is illustrated in the pages of the NT, especially in the graphic portrait of this witnessing community of the first century found in the book of Revelation.

The Witness Image

The *martus* family of terms generally translated in the NT as "witness" or "testimony" is used often in the technical sense of witness to ascertainable facts. But in the NT, the meaning of these terms moves beyond this common secular sense. They are used to express witness to truths and realities experienced, to make confession, and finally to refer to suffering and death as a result of witness to this reality. The double meanings of witness and martyrdom in the NT use of this image in reality complement one another.

Revelation 1:2, 5, 6 offers an especially clear example of the multiple meanings of the image. John "bore witness (*martureō*) to the word of God and to the testimony (*marturia*) of Jesus Christ" (1:2, RSV). John witnesses to what he has seen and experienced: Jesus' inauguration of the kingdom and his death and resurrection. Jesus' testimony includes his witness to the coming of the kingdom of God as well as giving his life in faithfulness to his saving mission as God's Messiah. This is clear in verse 5, where Jesus Christ is described as the "faithful witness" (*ho martus ho pistos*).

The NT presents Jesus maintaining his faithful witness to the coming of the kingdom of God even to the point of death on the cross. Jesus is the authentic witness-martyr in both of these principal senses of the term. In addition to understanding the meaning of the work of Christ in terms of witness-martyrdom, the NT community found this image useful in understanding its own life and mission. The roots of the image are found in the OT.

Old Testament Background

In the Greek OT the *martus* family of words is used widely in the legal sense of witness in a judicial trial. This is also its popular nonbiblical meaning. However, in Isaiah 40ff. we find the terms used with new shades of meaning. In Isaiah 43:8-13 (see also Isa. 41:21-29; 44:18-25) the prophet pictures Yahweh staging a court trial in the presence of the nations. In this trial it will be shown that Yahweh alone is truly God and that the gods of the Gentiles are not.

This is more than a contest between monotheism and polytheism. Yahweh alone is able to save his people. He is more powerful than the gods of the nations. Furthermore, the power of Yahweh is of a radically different genre than that of the gods of the Gentiles, who seek to exercise control by means of coercion. In contrast, Yahweh will do a "new thing" (Isa. 43:19) for the salvation of his people, in keeping with his covenant promise. In spite of their bitter experience in exile, God's people are called upon to bear witness to his saving acts.

> Bring forth the people who are blind, yet have eyes,
>   who are deaf, yet have ears!
> Let all the nations gather together,
>   and let the peoples assemble.
> Who among them declared this,
>   and foretold to us the former things?
> Let them bring *their witnesses* to justify them,
>   and let them hear and say, "It is true."
> You are *my witnesses*, says the Lord,
>   and my servant whom I have chosen,
> so that you may know and believe me
>   and understand that I am He.
> Before me no god was formed,
>   nor shall there be any after me.
> I, I am the Lord,
>   and besides me there is no savior.
> I declared and saved and proclaimed,
>   when there was no strange god among you;
>   and you are *my witnesses*, says the Lord.
> I am God, and also henceforth I am He;
>   there is no one who can deliver from my hand;
> I work and who can hinder it? . . .
> Do not fear, or be afraid;
>   have I not told you from of old and declared it?
>   You are *my witnesses*!

> Is there any god besides me?
>> There is no other rock; I know not one.
>>>> (Isa. 43:8-13; 44:8; emphasis added).

In contrast to the witnesses of the gods, Israel is told three times, "You are my witnesses." In the same context, Israel is called Yahweh's servant (41:8, 9; 43:10; 44:1-2, 21). Israel, God's servant, will declare to the nations the reality of Yahweh's saving activity in their midst. His saving power is so different from the ways of the nations. The meaning of witness in these texts moves beyond the strictly legal sense of the term. It carries the meaning of confession based on the experience of salvation, the mission of God's witnessing community in the midst of the nations. This is a witness which surpasses by far mere verbal declaration. It is the proclamation of the living God, whose saving activity is reflected in the conduct and very existence of Israel.

The dual motifs of witness and servanthood are intensified in the Servant poems of Isaiah (42:1-6; 49:1-6; 50:4-9; 52:13—53:12). The identity of the servant first seems to be Israel as a people. Then it focuses on a prophetic figure called "Servant of Yahweh," who represents and fulfills the purpose of all of God's people. Vicarious suffering becomes an integral part of his witness. His witness is specifically set forth in several passages (Isa. 42:4, 6; 49:1, 6; 52:15; 53:11-12; 62:10; cf. 9:2; 11:9). These passages tell us that the prophetic (or messianic) figure must die for his witness. We must refrain from reading more into the texts than is there, in light of developments in later Judaism and early Christianity. Yet in Isaiah 40ff. we find the beginnings of a witness-martyr vision as essential to the prophetic mission of the people of God in the world (Strathmann, 1967b:485).

Jesus: The Original Witness-Martyr

Both Jesus and the early church interpreted his messianic witness in terms of the prophetic vision found in Isaiah 40ff. To judge from the NT evaluation of the prophets' witness, the expected fate of the prophets was martyrdom (Matt. 23:34-37 et par.; Luke 13:33). Martyrdom was considered an integral part of the prophetic calling. This is the tradition in which Jesus placed himself and his followers (Matt. 5:11-12; 23:34). He referred to salvation history as a succession of witness-martyrdom from Abel to Zechariah, in which he and his followers were also participants (Matt. 23:35). Jesus was persecuted and expected his followers to suffer likewise (John 15:20).

The Gospels tell a story of Jesus, who was faithful in bearing witness to the kingdom of God which had erupted in their midst. He was constantly haunted by the possibility of a violent death. Jesus was accused of blasphemy and Sabbath desecration, offenses which carried the threat of capital punishment. The Gospels report that Jesus was repeatedly in danger of being stoned (Luke 4:29; John 8:59; 10:31-36; 11:8). These perceptions of his situation were realistic.

Jesus' teaching concerning the true authority of servanthood is reported in all four Gospels (Matt. 20:25-28; Mark 10:42-45; Luke 22:24-27; John 13:12-16). The most obvious meaning of this passage is that among the people of God, authority derives from service. Only those who renounce the primacy of their own self-centered interests and live for the welfare of others exercise authentic authority.

There are examples of selfless sacrifice for others in the rest of society, though it is somewhat rare. Some rulers put the interests of the common good first in the exercise of their office. But in the last analysis, even these think they have to use force to stay in power and defend the social welfare they promote. However, in the Christian community which these texts envision, this so-called "just" dependence on coercive force is disallowed. The authority which characterized the messianic community may not even compel what is judged to be legitimate and right. By its very nature all that this authority can do is bear witness to the cause of righteousness and in extreme cases die for it.

It is certainly not a coincidence that both Matthew and Mark conclude the passage with Jesus' sacrifice of his own life for many. Jesus resisted the temptation to use force even for the establishment of God's righteous rule. He did not even personally organize the movement which has come to bear his name.

Jesus was simply a witness. He called his disciples also to be witnesses. In the face of the violence which threatened his life, Jesus preferred to let himself be killed rather than to respond in kind to the violence of his enemies. This paradoxical authority, in its vulnerability, turns all other kinds of authority upside-down. But as the disciples eventually learned, authentic witness is grounded concretely on the authority of Jesus. Witness, as defined by Jesus' example, must characterize God's people in mission in the world.

According to the NT, Jesus himself was the source of the early church's understanding of witness (*martus*) as witness-martyrdom. Matthew's Gospel organizes the teachings of Jesus into five discourses; the second cycle of discourses is a key passage for understanding both the fundamental significance of the witness of the messianic community as well as the witness-martyr dimension of their mission. The early community's missionary vision was an essential component of their self-understanding (Matt. 10:5-23). To judge from the way in which the martyrdom motif permeates this passage, suffering is an essential ingredient of witness (10:18). Just as Jesus was delivered up to the council (10:17) and taken before the "governors and kings . . . as a testimony to them" (10:18), so also the twelve would be witnesses (10:22, 24-25, 28, 38).

We assume that the first readers of Matthew's Gospel were a witnessing community in the same sense. Matthew makes it clear that Jesus' followers are also witnesses, confessors, martyrs (10:26-39). At the deepest level the designation "witnessing community" refers neither to a strategy for evangelism nor a campaign for engaging all the membership in the church's mission. It first is the description of the community which takes its reason for being from Jesus Christ, the original witness-martyr.

The power and strategic value of this radical biblical under-standing of witness should not be underestimated. This is the witness-suffering which eventually broke imperial persecution and brought Roman emperors to their knees before the Lord and Savior. At his name "every knee should bend, in heaven and on earth and under the earth, and every tongue should confess that Jesus Christ is Lord, to the glory of God the Father" (Phil. 2:10-11).

The Early Church's Conception of Witness

The Lukan version of the great commission (Luke 24:48; Acts 1:8) takes the idea of witness *to* the facts of Jesus' life, death, and resurrection—and combines it with witness in the sense of evangelistic confession. This confession lies beyond the realm of observable facts and includes the living experience of the wit-ness who has grasped the significance of Jesus. The book of Acts shows the development in the meaning of witness from eyewit-ness testimony, to observable facts, to confession based on expe-rience.

The writer, Luke, treats both Paul and Stephen as witnesses of Jesus in the latter part of the book (Acts 22:15, 20; 26:16). Ob-viously, neither can have been a witness in the sense of the term as it is used in the early part of the book of Acts (1:22; 2:32; 3:15; 5:31f.; 10:39, 41). Stephen's suffering and death are the crown-ing evidence of the seriousness of his confessional witness. We note in the book of Acts the way in which the meaning of wit-ness moves from one sense to another: first, its original literal meaning as those who give eyewitness testimony to the fact of the incarnation (1:22); second, confessional witness based on the witness's experience of the risen Christ (22:15); finally, wit-ness includes participation in suffering and death as the crown-ing expression of that witness.

Peter, one of the witnesses to the fact of the incarnation, also refers to witness in the expanded sense. He addresses his peers in the early church "as an elder myself and a witness of the sufferings of Christ, as well as one who shares in the glory to be revealed" (1 Pet. 5:1). Clearly he refers to more than simply being an eyewitness of the crucifixion. A witness is one who bears similar suffering for similar reasons—faithful witness to God's righteous reign. Witness is personal participation in Christ's mission, "sharing Christ's sufferings" (1 Pet. 4:13). One who bears the name of Christ, as his witness, is ready to suffer for the sake of his name (Acts 9:15-16). This motif was widespread in the early church (cf. 2 Cor. 1:5; Col. 1:24; 1 Pet. 2:21; Matt. 10:38; 16:24).

Jesus, indeed, died for us, as the early tradition recognized (1 Cor. 15:3; et al.). But, according to Matthew 10:32-33, Jesus also died to show those who confess him before the world how to make this same confession and how to die in their witness when necessary. This understanding is by no means limited to Matthew. Paul's counsel in Philippians 2:5-8, among other things, serves as instruction for witness. In its broader sense, it is both testimony and suffering. During his lifetime Paul pointed in the same direction. He invited people to "be imitators of me, as I am of Christ" (1 Cor. 11:1). After his martyrdom, these words encouraged his readers to think of the death of Jesus, as well as the death of Paul and other apostles, as examples for them. In contrast to Gnostic spiritualizing, the Apostolic Fathers (Ignatius, Polycarp, Irenaeus, Origen, et al.) insisted that to be "in Christ" meant to be ready to die like Christ.

The New Testament Witness of the Early Church

Jesus himself is emphatically described in the book of Revelation as "the faithful witness" (1:5; 3:14). His revelation of God's character and saving intention is called the "testimony of Jesus Christ" (1:2, 9), and he is pictured as having fulfilled his mission obediently. Jesus showed himself faithful to his mission as God's anointed witness to the nations, even to the point of giving his lifeblood (1:5). Antipas, who was killed in Satan's realm at Pergamum, is identified by the same designation, "the faithful witness" (2:13). In line with Jesus' own self-understanding as a witness (John 18:37), he showed himself to be utterly faithful in his mission even unto death. The fact that the same designation is applied to Antipas shows that the crucified Lord is the model for Christian witness.

The phrase translated "the testimony (*marturia*) of Jesus" is a striking feature of the book of Revelation. The phrase appears six times (1:2, 9; 12:17; 19:10, twice; 20:4; cf. 6:9) and offers a clue to the meaning of the term in the book. We should probably understand the genitive case employed here as subjective—Jesus' testimony, or witness, rather than a witness to Jesus (Strathmann, 1967b:500-501). In four of these passages, the phrase "the testimony of Jesus" accompanies the phrases "word of God" or "commandments of God" (Rev. 1:2, 9; 12:17; 20:4). In a fifth text, the reference is to the witness of martyrs who have been slain "for the word of God" (6:9). They are evidently complementary expressions referring to one and the same reality, God's saving revelation. So the phrase "the testimony (witness) of Jesus" becomes a formula for gospel.

The process of development in the meanings of the *martus* word family, noted in earlier writings in the NT, is completed in the book of Revelation. The witness of Jesus is linked to his passion. The meanings of witness as attestation to facts and the confession of experienced reality—these culminate in suffering and death which demonstrate the ultimate faithfulness of the witnesses in their testimony. The book of Revelation, taking its clue from the "witness of Jesus," also understands the witness of Jesus' servants as martyrs.

This understanding of witness is especially clear in the graphic figure of cosmic warfare portrayed in Revelation 12. Satan is overcome "by the blood of the Lamb"—through the witness of Jesus unto death—"and by the word of their testimony (witness), for they did not cling to life even in the face of death" (12:11). The enemy is particularly enraged by the faithful obedience of God's people and by their Jesus-like testimony (12:17).

The church takes part in this "war of the Lamb," participating in the witness of Jesus. This witness unto death is not limited to the Messiah, nor to the so-called martyrs (12:11). Instead, it is incumbent upon the whole community of witness (12:17). Suffering and death are integral parts of the "witness of Jesus" in which all members of the messianic community are potentially participants.

The use of the *martus* family of terms in the book of Revelation illumines both the biblical understanding of the meaning of Jesus' witness unto death and its perception of the mission of his witnessing community. The revelatory-saving mission of the Messiah required a faithfulness to the Father even to the point of suffering and death at the hands of the enemies of God. The community of the Messiah is called to faithfulness to their Lord in his mission in a world which has fallen under the domain of Satan. This calls for a witness of attestation and confession sealed by suffering and even death.

Bright Spots in a Fading Image

The roots of this image for understanding the nature of the church—a community of witness-martyrs—can be traced to the NT and to Jesus himself. The offering of life was seen as the way of life (Matt. 16:24ff.). Suffering for the "name" was occasion for rejoicing (Acts 5:41). Paul sees his suffering as completing "what is lacking in Christ's afflictions for the sake of his body" (Col. 1:24). The complementary nature of witness and suffering was foundational to Paul's understanding of mission. These elements build up to a climax in the book of Revelation. Jesus Christ is the Lamb (Servant) slain, the faithful witness, the original martyr in a community of martyrs (Rev. 2:13).

However, the image of the witnessing community has played a relatively minor role in the Christian church's self-understanding. In recent times, the image of a witnessing community has sometimes been recovered in the church's articulation of a biblical theology and its evangelistic strategies. Yet the image has lacked the radical depth of the NT's understanding of witness-martyr.

This fact, however, comes as no surprise when we recall the history of the church. From the beginning of the fourth century, the established church has enjoyed a position of relative power and prosperity; suffering and martyrdom became anomalies. The Christian church, which for three centuries had been a persecuted minority, became a persecuting majority in the fourth century. From that time, the witness-martyr image became largely irrelevant for the church's self-understanding. Confessors and martyrs of the earlier period were venerated, and the church found other images for its self-understanding more consistent with its ongoing stance in the world.

However, those radical movements of renewal that were persecuted by the established church often found themselves in situations akin to those of the pre-Constantinian communities. In these groups, the witness-martyr motif has again proved useful in understanding both the meaning of the work of Christ as well as their own nature and mission as communities of witness. These communities have produced martyrologies characterized by a similar spirit of witness and suffering as those produced by the early church.

The predominant social and spiritual climate usually has more influence than the Bible. The current climate generally determines which of the biblical images the church finds meaningful for the articulation of its self-understanding. Yet sometimes the church, like the Christian communities of the first century, finds itself living under the cross. Then it also discovers that the witness-martyr motif is a powerful image for understanding the nature of its life and for orienting its mission in the world.

The
Church
in Mission

16

A Community of Transformation

The church is God's mission in the world, as it understands God's purpose for it so to be. This is different from what it has come to be in its Constantinian tradition. The images by which the NT community articulated its self-understanding contain their vision of this divine intention. From these images a normative vision emerges which is foundational for our churchly self-understanding and our view of mission. When the church neglects the insights into the nature and mission of the church which the biblical images afford, its self-understanding becomes deformed and God' missionary intention in the world is truncated.

This chapter revisualizes the church in light of the biblical images we have studied. In these images are clues which point toward an ecclesiology more congenial to God's essential missionary intention for his people. When we follow these clues, we should restore a missiology more solidly based in the biblical vision of the church.

Church and Mission

In its ancient creed, Israel confessed that God has made an essentially non-people his people (Deut. 26:5-9; cf. Hos. 2:23). This distinctive peoplehood established Israel's identity and determined the shape of its mission. Sometimes Israel lived according to the charismatic principle as God's contrast-community in the midst of the nations; thus it reflected faithfully his saving intention and fulfilled obediently its divine mission. When Israel became like the nations, it denied its essential character and failed in its mission.

Israel was to have a "social holiness" based on the distinctive character of God himself (Lev. 9:2; 11:45; et al.). This social holiness was not merely cultic, nor simply creedal. It was manifested fundamentally in covenant relationships of righteousness and peace. These are the elements which characterize the classic missionary texts of the OT (Isa. 2:2-5; Mic. 4:1-4; et al.).

God once created a distinctive people to reflect his character and fulfill his mission among all the peoples of the earth in the vocation of Abraham (Gen. 12:1-3) and in the exodus-Sinai event (Isa. 43:15-21). So also the NT views the formation of the messianic community, the church, as a new creation (Gal. 6:15-16; 2 Cor. 5:17). This new humanity, restored according to the image of the Messiah, lies at the center of God's saving purposes for all humanity as well as for creation itself (Eph. 3:3-11; cf. Col. 1:13-14). In the biblical view, peoplehood is central to the church's self-understanding as a community of salvation and to its view of mission. This dimension has been largely lost in the modern missionary enterprise, but its importance in the biblical understanding can scarcely be overestimated.

Inspired by images drawn from the OT understanding of God's people, the early church found the roots of mission in its peoplehood (1 Pet. 2:9-10). To be without a people is to be without God. To know God is to be part of a people, God's holy people. Peoplehood is a part of the good news as well as an essential instrument in mission.

The biblical vision of mission, rooted firmly in God's people, frees the church from the dual dilemma of individualism and institutionalism in its mission. In its evangelization, the church has tended to fall prey to one or the other of these temptations because its sense of peoplehood has become so tenuous. Rather than simply trying to communicate abstract eternal truths in its evangelization, the church has a history of salvation to share, a story to tell. In this perspective, salvation can be neither ahistoric nor amoral. It will be vital and relational, consisting of new life in the family of God.

The Church—a Sign of Salvation

The purpose of God's people was to be a source of blessing to all the peoples of the earth (Gen. 12:1-3). The prophets envisioned the restoration of God's people to serve as "an everlasting sign" of his saving intention (Isa. 55:13). This understanding colors the NT perception of the church's identity and role.

The lordship of Christ is proclaimed in the context of a confessing community that lives under his lordship. As firstfruits of the kingdom, the church can testify with credibility to the power of God's restored reign. By living out kingdom values, the church is a sign of the reality of God's kingdom. The firstfruits of the new creation must be visible in the church. It is the new humanity being restored in the image of its Creator. Simply *being* the living community of the Spirit of God is to participate in God's mission in the world.

The credibility of the gospel which the church proclaims is directly related to the authenticity of its life. Unbelievers have asked Christendom for eighteen centuries, "How can the church speak of redemption when nothing has really changed since the coming of the Redeemer?" The saving power of the Christian message shines forth convincingly through the practices of the Christian community. This is what characterized the early church. In its entire existence, it was a *sign* of the truth of the gospel. The growth of the early church was due to "the radiance of the sign." This was the missionary theory of the early church. They drew this vision from the history of God's people, and above all, from the Messiah himself. During its pre-Constantinian period, the church owed its amazing growth far more to its dynamic presence as a saving contrast-community in the midst of pagan society than it did to organized mission (Lohfink: 176-177).

The Greek apologist, Athenagoras, writing around A.D. 177, revealed the secret of the success of the early Christian mission:

> But among us you will find uneducated persons, and artisans, and old women, who, if they are unable in words to prove the benefit of our doctrine, yet by their deeds exhibit the benefit arising from their persuasion of the truth: they do not rehearse speeches but exhibit good works; when struck, they do not strike again; when robbed, they do not go to law; they give to those who ask of them, and love their neighbors as themselves. (Athenagoras: 134)

God's honor and the credibility of the gospel message were validated by the early church's practice. In its very life, the church was a sign and presence through whom God was glorified in the world. The early church saw itself as God's contrast-community whose life is itself a gift of grace. The images with which the church understood its identity and role were powerful symbols of its life as a new creation, a new humanity, the family of God, a city set on a hill as a light before all humanity, a living demonstration of God's intention for all of humankind.

The vocation of the twelve was a symbolic and prophetic act pointing to a restored people, to the creation of a people charged with the mission of accompanying God in his saving purpose. This people is gathered from among the nations to become God's sign of salvation to the nations. According to the biblical vision, when God's people shine forth as a sign among the peoples of the earth, those peoples will be attracted to come and learn the secret of their salvation. The good news is that God loves his enemies and offers his love to the unjust as well as to the righteous. Such news was credible because this was the way God's people lived (Athenagoras: 134).

The missionary visibility of the church as "a city built on a hill" (Matt. 5:14) has more than once been distorted into a triumphalistic image. At times the church has naively identified itself with the kingdom of God. A recent reaction has called for the church to be scattered and dissolved and become absorbed in society. However, this immersion in social and political structures has not really contributed to the transformation of society; Christians have generally acted within society's structures much like anyone else. The expendability of the church is a valid sacrifice only insofar as its witness is authentic, according to the mold of the Master. Christ calls the church to be different, a contrast-community in the world and for the world.

The primary issue in the mission of the church is not simply a matter of personal activism. In 1 Peter 2:9 the private holiness of individual Christians is not in view. The point of the passage is that it takes an entire people to give witness to God's saving plan for the world. As salvation history reminds us, this people can be a small minority, indeed, as long as its witness grows out of the authenticity of its life. Rather than allowing itself to become secularized, the primitive church preferred to remain a prophetic minority in its witness. In God's strategy, the renewal of all creation begins with this "new creation," the restored people of God. The size of the city is not decisive. The essential thing is that it be built on the mountain of God's saving intention where it becomes a light that can transform the world.

Because the church does not exist for itself but for the world, it is necessary that the church be the church. The church dare not become like the world. It must retain its contrast identity. When the church loses this distinctive character, it loses the power to transform society. In that case, neither missionary activity nor social action will be of lasting benefit (Lohfink: 146).

Early in the third century, Origen believed that Christians

best served society by participating in the church. An essential ingredient of this vision of the church is the absence of all desire to exercise coercive power over others. In the messianic community, the domination of others was simply out of the question. Therefore, the best possible service to a society possessed by the demons of power was to be a contrast-community freed from a thirst for power. Only in this way could the demons be cast out. Origen said,

> We know of the existence in each city of another sort of country, created by the Logos of God. . . . We do not accept those who love power. But we put pressure on those who on account of their great humility are reluctant to hastily take upon themselves the common responsibility of the church of God. . . . If Christians do avoid these responsibilities [service of the state], it is not with the motive of shirking the public service of life. But they keep themselves for a more divine and necessary service in the church of God for the sake of the salvation of men. (Origen: 75)

The church serves the world best by taking with utter seriousness its call to be "a holy nation, God's own people" in the midst of society (1 Pet. 2:9-10). Since the time of Constantine, Christians have felt called to accept responsibility for the social order largely on the world's terms. That these Christians have often rendered relatively useful services cannot be questioned. What the NT and the early church questioned was that the essential mission of Christians consists of this. "The most important and most irreplaceable service Christians can render society is quite simply that they truly be the church" (Lohfink: 168).

Prophetic Renewal and Mission

The biblical context of mission is conflict. Truly radical renewal of the people of God is apparently impossible without conflict. The powers committed to the conservation of deformed structures resist change. The clearest biblical descriptions of Is-

rael's identity and role come from prophetic and priestly reform-
ist writings which were in conflict with the religious and political
establishment. Jesus' evangelical parables were essentially parables of conflict (Glen). In John's Gospel, the conflict between Jesus and the Jews reflects a community in conflict with the synagogue late in the first century. Pauline mission and theology
were influenced by confrontation with the Judaizers. And the
book of Revelation celebrates the triumphant witness of a martyr
church in mortal conflict with the powers of evil.

OT prophets bewailed the lack of an authentic presence of
Yahweh in the midst of his people. It was as if God had been
driven out of his sanctuary and even forced to abandon his holy
city (Ezek. 8:6, 12; 11:23). Jeremiah lamented the fact that the
hope and savior of Israel had become a stranger in the land (Jer.
14:8). According to the prophetic burden, the restoration of Israel to their roots is the divine intention expressed in the
Abrahamic and Mosaic covenants. God's purpose was essential
to their survival as God's people and instrumental in their participation in God's saving mission to the nations.

Jesus linked the recovery of mission to a radical restoration
of God's people. His concern for the restoration of covenant law
to its biblical function brought him into conflict with Jewish legalism as well as with their extensive missionary enterprise. Jesus and the primitive community saw themselves in the prophetic tradition. They were in the line of those who suffered persecution at the hands of the establishment for their insistence on
the necessity of the radical renewal of God's people. They
wanted God's people to recover their divinely intended identity
and role.

The relationship between the radical renewal of God's people and their faithfulness in God's mission has been difficult for
the church to grasp. Those who are most vocal in their call for
the radical renewal of the church often fail to see its implications
for mission. It is as though the church needed to be renewed
merely for its own sake.

On the other hand, many of the most active proponents of increased missionary activity fail to perceive the relevance of the radical renewal of the church for the missionary task. They continue to call for increased activism and commitment to programs which have demonstrated their inability to transmit an authentic gospel.

As a result, radical Christian communities may become ingrown and self-serving. And the missionary enterprise continues in the hands of Christian activists who seem to be more concerned for the discovery of more effective missionary strategies than in the authenticity of the message communicated. Meanwhile, the world awaits a clear, uncompromised, undistorted word of salvation. As the Lausanne Congress on Evangelism reminds us all, the church is called to "let the earth hear *His* voice" (emphasis mine).

Liberation and Mission

The exodus-liberation motif is found in a number of the images for the church. It is impossible to conceive of the people of God biblically apart from the exodus-Sinai experience of salvation. Israel's peoplehood was rooted in their deliverance from Egypt (Exod. 6:6-7a). This constitutive element in the life of God's people became a paradigm for the church's understanding of its salvation, as liberation from all forms of servitude.

At Sinai, Israel heard the promise, "Now therefore, if you obey my voice and keep my covenant, you shall be my treasured possession out of all the peoples. Indeed, the whole earth is mine, but you shall be for me a priestly kingdom and a holy nation" (Exod. 19:5-6a). Being liberated from Egypt meant becoming free to experience relationships of righteousness and peace under God's gracious covenant. Israel was redeemed from Egyptian bondage, not on its own merits but as part of God's saving purpose for all nations. Liberation is for mission.

When Israel found itself suffering from new forms of bondage under the monarchy, the prophets called for a return to the desert. They wanted a new liberation, the restoration of a people equipped to carry out God's saving intention. When Israel's unfaithfulness rendered the exodus-Sinai experience of liberation inoperative, the prophets spoke of a new covenant with God's law written "on their hearts." The new covenant would restore Israel to peoplehood under God (Jer. 31:31-33). This renewed people is the context for the prophetic vision of a new covenant universal in its scope.

In the shepherd-and-flock image, the historic exodus liberation of God's people is related to their vocation to mission. The image speaks of liberation from all forms of oppression by the powers of evil. It speaks of a restored messianic community in which the enslaved find freedom and the outcasts become fully a people. In the exodus, the enslaved Hebrews became a people. In the new exodus of messianic salvation, the hated Samaritans and Israel's outcasts found salvation in the flock of God.

The way out (literally, *ex-hodos*) of Egyptian bondage became a primary paradigm for the new way (*hodos*) of salvation offered by the Messiah. This image speaks powerfully in our time to Christians who suffer from economic and political oppression, particularly in third-world countries subjected to the exploitation of neocolonial imperialisms. In an earlier century, this image served to articulate the experience of many who were enslaved to drunkenness as an escape from the brutal working conditions to which they were subjected by the industrial revolution.

The same image can describe the liberating resources of the Spirit of God to be found among his people for those who suffer from chemical dependencies in our generation. Wherever persons are being liberated from their slavery to evil powers, the exodus-liberation metaphor stirs the church's imagination, helping it to understand its life and mission. But when the church falls into the sterility of theological abstractions and doctrinal debates, the image loses its attraction and even becomes the object of suspicion, just as it was in Jesus' time.

This biblical paradigm continually reminds the church of its vocation to be an agent of transformation in a world enslaved by all sorts of evil powers. The church's mission is to name courageously the evil powers and to expel them by the power of Jesus Christ. In many instances demon possession is personal and congregations will be able to cast out the evil spirits in the name of Christ. The church can offer the oppressed a safe habitat within the family of God, where evil powers have been broken.

In other instances, demonic oppression is systemic, causing untold suffering to groups within society, or the oppression of entire peoples. Here too, the mission of God's people is to name the demons, such as nationalism, racism, militarism, materialism, sexism, hedonism, totalitarianism, exploitation. Believers need to cry out to God, who delivers the oppressed and welcomes them into communities of refuge. There these demons have already been cast out and people are freed to worship God alone.

Wholistic Mission

The images used in the NT to articulate the church's identity and role enrich our vision of the church. They give greater substance to our understanding of the gospel. These images reflect a more full-orbed understanding of salvation. They furnish us with a more wholistic vision of God's saving mission in the world.

In the prophetic vision of mission, the life of God's people is marked by covenant justice and *shalom*. This is so attractive that the nations are drawn to serve the God of Israel. Jesus and the early Christian community took over this vision and expanded it. The life of the restored community prompts humankind to "give glory to [their] Father in heaven" (Matt. 5:16). It involves the creation of a new humanity characterized by concrete relationships of justice and peace (Eph. 2:14-16). Authentic mission issues in a new social order of *shalom*. It leads to a new kind of humanity, liberated from the choking idolatries of materialism and religious exclusivism, of nationalism and individualism.

Recognition of the primacy of the kingdom of God will contribute to wholeness in the life and mission of the church. To "strive first for the kingdom of God and his righteousness" means subordinating all else to the overriding concerns of God's reign. The priority of the kingdom will save the church from petty concern for its own preservation. Even legitimate aspects of mission such as gospel proclamation, social service, church planting, and church growth will not occupy the church's sole attention. Its mission will be as deep and broad as God's, and as far-reaching as God's saving intention. All aspects of God's righteous will and reign, as Jesus made them known to us, are legitimate aspects of the church's missionary concern.

The family image frees us from tendencies to conceive of salvation as primarily or exclusively inward or spiritualistic. Authentic mission leads to relationships of social and spiritual wholeness—healed relationships with the Father as well as with brothers and sisters in God's household. Integrity of life in God's family is saving and instrumental in the healing of all the other families of the earth. The family metaphor makes especially clear the integrity of life and mission which mark the church. Life in the Father's house is both the mission and the goal of mission.

This unity of life and witness—of deed and word—facilitates truly saving evangelization.

The communication of the Evangel in its fullness to every person worldwide is a mandate of the Lord Jesus to His community. There are times when our communication may be by attitude and action only, and times when the spoken word will stand alone, but we must repudiate as demonic the attempt to drive a wedge between. Men will look as they listen and what they see must be at one with what they hear. There is no biblical dichotomy between the word spoken and the word incarnated in the lives of God's people. (Lausanne)

It has often been imagined that ministries of reconciliation and of justice and peace belong to the sphere of social activism. Others hold that the mission of the church is to share the good news or gospel in word. However, the NT reminds us that in authentic mission, a peacemaker must also be an evangelist. And if we really are to share the whole gospel, evangelists must also be peacemakers.

Mission Is Cruciform

The church's mission is shaped by the prophetic vision of the Servant of Yahweh. Israel, God's servant, was a witness to the nations, a witness about Yahweh's saving activity in their midst. The proclamation of God's people was based on their experience of God's covenant grace. The Servant Songs of Isaiah present the double motif of witness and servanthood. Suffering for others or vicarious suffering is an integral aspect of witness. These are the roots of the witness-martyr understanding of the mission of God's people.

Jesus was the original witness-martyr (Rev. 1:5; 3:14). He is also the prototype for a witness-martyr community. The image of the church as a witnessing community permeates the entire NT. It is essential to the early Christian understanding of mission presented in the Gospels (cf. Matt. 10; Mark 10:42-45). The witnessing community is also a key for understanding the church's witness in the book of Revelation. This is the same missionary vision that underlies Paul's basic conviction that Christians share in the sufferings of Christ, and that somehow their participation in Christ's sufferings can be of benefit for others.

The story of the church is a story of the power of vicarious suffering in witness. Wherever the Christian church has been willing to suffer on behalf of their oppressors as well as the oppressed, the saving intention of God has been communicated with unusual persuasiveness. In Jesus, they had experienced the power of suffering for others to achieve the reconciliation of enemies (Rom. 5:10). And in the church, victory over the enemies of God was achieved through vicarious suffering (Rev. 12:11). It was soon noted that "the blood of the martyrs is the seed of the church" (cf. Tertullian: 55, 60). In the church's experience (including our own generation), the suffering witness of Christians communicates God's love with amazing power.

Christians gratefully confess that there is a cross at the center of God's saving mission to humankind. While this cross is certainly unique, it was no accident. The cross was not only essential for our salvation; it is also essential to God's ongoing mission. Calvary should remove all doubts that God's mission is cruciform. However, as humans, the temptation to avoid personal suffering is overpowering. The temptation to use power in the interests of the church's mission is almost irresistible. Therefore, Christendom has relegated the meaning of the death of Jesus to the spheres of ritual and dcgma, thereby denying the ongoing saving efficacy of vicarious suffering. In times of material and spiritual peril, Christendom has been tempted to "save" itself by shedding the blood of its enemies.

Mission Is Charismatic

God's activity in the world, in creation and in a new creation, is essentially pneumatic, dependent on his Spirit. The church's participation in God's mission must also be pneumatic and charismatic, in the power of this Spirit and dependent on the gifts of his grace. The ancient people of God were able to survive their Egyptian sojourn as well as the contemporizing pressures of their own monarchy due to the charismatic principle, their dependence upon God's grace. A people willing to live and survive by the grace of God, whose character bears the stamp of God's Spirit, will by the very nature of things be an effective witness.

The charismatic processes by which people are "built into a spiritual house" (1 Pet. 2:5) are so essential to the church's self-understanding that they virtually become a definition for the Christian community. The church exists where persons are mutually edified in a common relationship to the living Christ.

Some mission strategies distinguish neatly between the processes whereby the church is edified and the ways in which it participates in God's mission in the world. But such strategists forget the pneumatic-charismatic vision of the NT church. Passages which speak of the charismatic gifts bestowed by the Spirit on the church for its edification do not distinguish neatly between nurture and evangelization, between edification and mission. A truly nurtured community will be genuinely evangelistic, and a really edified people will participate effectively in God's mission. The structure and mission of the church are not determined by strictly dogmatic, ritual, rational, sociological, or psychological considerations. They are determined, rather, by the dynamic presence of the Spirit of God, who makes use of structures but refuses to be bound by them.

Attempts to order the life and mission of the church in strictly hierarchical, institutional, or even logical senses often represent a denial of the nature of its pneumatic-charismatic structure. Mission has often been institutionalized, no doubt, because the pneumatic-charismatic character of the church in mission seemed too elusive and too humanly precarious to be sustained. The NT envisions a community that depends on the Spirit of God alone for the resources to support both its life and mission. The church is often unwilling to depend on the charismatic gifts of God's Spirit for its life (Rom. 11:29; 1 Cor. 7:7, 17) and its mission (1 Cor. 12:4-5; cf. Eph. 4:11). This has often led the church to depend excessively on management techniques, on psychological and sociological strategies, on pragmatic activities, and on other methods which do not necessarily foster the life and mission of God's people.

Apostolic Poverty

Jesus' mission was directed essentially to "the poor, the crippled, the blind, and the lame" (Luke 14:21). This motif runs throughout the Gospel reports of Jesus' ministry. The same theme was already in the OT. Yahweh himself was the Protector, who cared for orphans and strangers, the poor and widows, for all who for one reason or another were dispossessed and victims of oppression in ancient Israel.

Parallel to this concern for the poor and the oppressed in both Testaments is a vision of God's people as poor. One of the strands running through the OT pictures Israel as "the fewest of all peoples" (Deut. 7:7); as "aliens and tenants" with Yahweh (Lev. 25:23); as "a people humble and lowly" (Zeph. 3:12); and as God's "suffering ones" (literally, poor; Isa. 49:13). In the Gospels the messianic community is identified with the poor, and in the epistles the term is applied to the Christian church.

In a special way, through the incarnation of Christ itself, apostolic poverty became embedded in the very nature of the church's life and mission. The early church caught this vision from Jesus. Meekness, humility, and generosity were especially prominent among believers. Not surprisingly, the economic practices of the community bore a close relationship to its effective evangelistic witness (Matt. 5:13-16; Acts 2:42-44, 47b; 4:32-33; 5:12-14; 6:7).

After the Constantinian shift, however, this vision has survived in the church only marginally and occasionally. Mission was left to the mendicant orders while the church enjoyed power, prestige, and wealth. This was the context in which movements of mission renewal emerged. Among the Waldensians and the Franciscans, missioners voluntarily assumed apostolic poverty in order to communicate an authentic gospel message.

According to Jesus and the early church, the good news can be given *to* the poor best by a church *of* the poor. The experience of God's people in mission substantiates this. The gospel is communicated with most clarity and credibility to those who are tempted toward power, prestige, and wealth from a position of weakness, humility, and simplicity.

The modern missionary movement arose during the period of imperial expansion of the powers of the northern hemisphere. Hence, it has been unable effectively to shake off the image which Protestant missionaries in general reflect in the third world. There they are often viewed as agents of wealth and power. Faithfulness to the biblical metaphors calls for reversing this image. It is difficult to see how methods which, in effect, deny the incarnation can be used to carry out God's mission with integrity. The most challenging forms which mission will take in the years ahead will not be characterized by modern Western gadgetry, nor by more and better electronic techniques, nor through increased activism on the part of the missionary enterprise. Instead, mission needs Christlike weakness and apostolic poverty, assumed in the interests of communicating more authentically the gospel of Jesus Christ.

Mission and Eschatology

A strong biblical sense of eschatology is essential to the church's self-understanding as God's people in mission. The "pull of the future" determines the shape of mission in the present. The kingdom of God has already come into our midst. In Christ, the power of the age to come is already manifest. In Christ, the goal of history has been revealed, filling the church's life and mission with meaning and hope. The biblical vision of eschatology requires that hope be intimately and concretely linked to Jesus the Messiah. Where this link is missing, eschatology can become either archaism, with dreams of restoring the golden age of a distant past; or futurism, in which the past is forgotten and a utopian future is imagined; or escapism, in which salvation is sought through flight into another world (Bosch: 235).

As the church reads the signs of the kingdom and its vision of the shape of God's reign, it always runs the risk of being conditioned by life in "the present evil age" (Gal. 1:4). Our reading of signs must be constantly corrected by a lively expectancy of the coming kingdom, anticipated radically in Christ. The church's experiences of the new order, even at best, are of themselves insufficient sources of hope.

If we are to set the life and mission of the church in an eschatological frame of reference, we need to live and witness in hope. This Christian hope inspires the church and offers a source of expectancy to the world. Too often this hope has been incomplete and therefore distorted. At times Christians have looked only for a new heaven. Other believers, in periods of optimism, have looked only for a new earth. The NT church carried out its mission in the confident hope of a new heaven *and* a new earth (Rev. 21:1).

The NT closes with a vision of "the holy city, the new Jerusalem, coming down out of heaven from God" (Rev. 21:2). God is "making all things new" (Rev. 21:5). In absolute contrast to Babylon, the city of humanity's own making, this new creation is a gift of God. This certainty sustains the people of God in mission in the face of seemingly overwhelming odds. God's community in mission is called to practice obedience and faithfulness to Christ and thereby anticipate the new creation which God will perfect. Christians are to live the present in the light of God's future.

Conclusion

The messianic movement to restore God's righteous reign over his people originated in "Galilee of the nations." From this place on the geographic and social periphery, it moved to Jerusalem, the center of Judaism. The apostolic mission of the primitive church began in Palestine, on the eastern edge of the Roman empire. From there it moved to the east, south, north, and west until it reached the center of the empire, Rome.

However, in notable contrast, the main currents of mission have since then flowed from centers of imperial power to outlying colonies. This inevitably came to mean that the mission was carried from the rich and powerful centers of the world to the poor and the oppressed peoples. This represents a sociological and missiological reversal of the Christian apostolate of the first century. In this process the metaphors which most stirred the missionary imagination of the early church became largely irrelevant.

The pilgrimage images of the NT no longer spoke to the church in its mission, since it had become established in the Empire. In fact, in this transition the early meaning of *paroikos* (sojourner, alien) became "parishioner," to fit the new situation. New-order images had stirred the early Christian community to undertake its apostolate, but they also lost their power to inspire. The NT vision of a new creation and a new humanity was relegated to the world-to-come beyond the scope of history. From that distance, the pull of the future was all but lost as a source of authentic missionary vitality. Peoplehood images became less useful because the church was no longer a holy people—God's contrast-community. Images of transformation also largely lost their symbolic power because the church had ceased to be a witnessing (martyr) community, dependent on the Spirit of God alone.

But even so, this is the church which has monopolized mission in its institutionalized forms for the past eighteen centuries. The people of God have lived under the burden of having the mission of the church carried out largely by the part of the church least prepared for the apostolate, judged by its primary biblical images. Traditionally, power and wealth, which all but disqualify the church for participation in true apostolate, have been concentrated in the hands of the part of the church that has formally felt called to carry out the missionary enterprise. When mission flows from centers of power and prestige, a certain kind of gospel is communicated, different from when the gospel is shared in weakness from the social periphery. Different images are required to express the church's self-understanding. Political, juridical, organic, anatomical, and commercial images have been found more useful for reflecting the self-understanding of a rich and powerful church.

The story of the church is largely a story of God's faithfulness in the midst of the unfaithfulness of his people. The crisis of missions in our time may well be a sign of hope pointing a way out of the contradictions which have besieged the modern missionary enterprise. The monopoly of the northern-hemisphere church over mission is crumbling. The Spirit of God has been able to use even the church's imperfect obedience to its mission mandate to bring it into conformity with God's will. Ironically, through the missionary efforts of the churches in the north, the center of vital Christian presence and effective mission has shifted from post-Christian Europe (and North America) to the third world. Relationships of interdependence in life and mission are coming to characterize the churches throughout the world. God is creating a new thing in our midst.

Out of their particular experiences and vision, third-world churches are calling us to a renewal which promises to greatly enrich our understanding of the nature and mission of the church. The comfort of the humanly precarious pilgrimage images, the challenges of the new-order images of God's counter-kingdom, the priceless values of peoplehood images, and the spiritual power of images of transformation all furnish inspiration and encouragement to a humanly weak and suffering church, a church that lives and witnesses under the cross in faithfulness to its Lord.

Notes

Chapter 2.   A People in Mission: The Biblical Record

1. This is the sense of the biblical term translated "holy." The original meaning of the root was apparently "separated" or "cut off" from other peoples and practices (Craigie: 179).

2. The biblical texts are not fully unanimous in their evaluation of the theological and ethical implications of kingship. Compare, for example, 1 Sam. 8; 10:17-24; 12; Deut. 17:14-20 with 1 Sam. 9:1-10; 16.

3. Rom. 5:8-11; 6:15-23; 11:30-32; 1 Cor. 6:9-11; Gal. 1:13-17, 23; 4:3-7, 8-10; Eph. 2:1-22; 5:8; Col. 1:21-22; 2:13; 3:7-11; 1 Tim. 1:13; Titus 3:3-7; Philem. 11; 1 Pet. 2:10; 2:25.

4. Cf. Rom. 1:7; 16:15; 1 Cor. 1:2; 2 Cor. 1:1; 13:12; Phil. 1:1; 4:22.

Chapter 3.   Church and Mission: The Constantinian Legacy

1. "In order to validate its existence, the church looked increasingly, not to the future illuminated by the imminent parousia of its Lord, nor to the present, illuminated by the extraordinary gifts of the Holy Spirit, but to the past illuminated by the composition of the Apostolic canon, the creation of the Apostolic creed, and the establishment of the Apostolic episcopacy. These were the norms for measuring orthodoxy" (Pelikan: 107).

2. Kingdom and temple are examples of this (cf. Augustine, *City of God* 15.1; 18.49).

3. Likewise, Augustine's insistence that sacraments celebrated by unworthy clergy are valid implies that effective holiness is not really essential to the church's life and mission (Gonzalez: 50).

Chapter 4.   The Way

1. A representative listing of these texts includes Matt. 22:16; Mark 12:14; Luke 1:79; 20:21; Acts 2:28; 13:10; 16:17; 18:25-26; Rom. 3:16-17;

11:33; 1 Cor. 4:17; 12:31; 1 Thess. 3:11; Heb. 3:10; James 1:8; 5:20 (RSV); 2 Pet. 2:2, 15, 21; Rev. 15:3.

2. In the NRSV, *peripateō* is not always translated literally, "to walk," but rather dynamically, "to live." The verb appears in the following texts in a figurative sense to refer to the character of life in the Christian community: Rom. 6:4; 8:1, 4; 13:13; 14:15; 2 Cor. 5:7; Gal. 5:16, 25; 6:16; Eph. 2:10; 4:1, 17; 5:2, 8, 15; Col. 1:10; 2:6; 1 Thess. 2:12; 2 Pet. 3:11; 1 John 1:7; 2:6; 2 John 6; 3 John 3-4; Rev. 21:24.

3. But for another conclusion, see Michaelis: 78-79.

4. See note 2, above, for a listing of representative texts.

Chapter 5. Sojourners

1. *Paroikeō,* Heb. 11:9; *paroikia,* Acts 13:17; 1 Pet. 1:17; *paroikos,* Acts 7:6, 29; Eph. 2:19; 1 Pet. 2:11.

2. *Parepidēmos,* Heb. 11:13; 1 Pet. 1:1; 2:11.

3. *Xenos,* Heb. 11:13; *allotrios,* Acts 7:6; Heb. 11:9.

4. *Diaspora,* James 1:1; 1 Pet. 1:1.

5. *Politeia,* Eph. 2:12; *politeuma,* Phil. 3:20; *politeuomai,* Phil. 1:27; *sumpolitai,* Eph. 2:19.

6. A similar reversal of meaning has occurred in the case of the term "minister" (*diakonos*), who is generally anything but this in the exercise of governmental functions, secular or ecclesiastical. The term "Christian" has suffered a similar transformation of meaning.

Chapter 6. The Poor

1. This interpretation is suggested by Bammel (909, 912). For another view, see Fitzmyer (1968b:867).

2. This is seen in the Magnificat (Luke 1:46-55), in the precarious conditions of Jesus' birth (2:1-7), in the announcement to the shepherds, unclean by ritual definition (2:8-21), and in the offering of the poor (two doves) in the rites of purification (2:22-24). In the genealogy given in Matthew's gospel, all five women mentioned (Tamar, Rahab, Ruth, the wife of Uriah, and Mary) qualified as outcasts and poor.

3. Against this interpretation is Fitzmyer (1968a:784; 1968b:867).

4. Remarkably, in some cases these have been designated as "the poor" and "the humble."

Chapter 7. The Kingdom of God

1. The approximate number of occurrences of *basileia* (kingdom) in the NT is as follows: Matthew, 51; Mark, 16; Luke, 41; John, 5; Acts, 8; Pauline epistles, 14; Hebrews and Catholic epistles, 4; Revelation, 4.

2. The biblical term "kingdom of God" or "reign of God" is liable to be misunderstood due to the secular meaning of the term "kingdom." Hans Küng defines the kingdom of God simply as "God's cause" in the world (1976a:215). Bruce Chilton has suggested that the kingdom of God is, in effect, "God come in strength" (126). "Kingdom" is funda-

mentally a political term and implies a wide range of social relationships. "Kingdom of God" refers to a new social order, God's new order, rather than to a specific geographical territory. In Sinai, we witness the coming of Yahweh to rule over his people. In Jesus' proclamation of the kingdom of God, we perceive the saving activity of God present in the person and word-deeds of the Messiah (Luke 11:20; cf. Matt. 12:28). The essential element in the messianic proclamation of the evangel is "your God reigns" (Isa. 52:7).

3. An example of increased interest in the kingdom of God image may be seen in "A Response to Lausanne: Theological Implications of Radical Discipleship" (Lausanne). This document was drawn up by an *ad hoc* group made up largely of third-world, Australian, and young evangelical participants. The four-page statement contains ten references to the "kingdom of God." In contrast, "The Lausanne Covenant," the ten-page official statement of the 1974 Lausanne Congress, contains only four references to the "kingdom of God."

4. Jesus' response to Pilate, "My kingdom is not from this world" (John 18:36), has often been interpreted to mean that the kingdom has nothing to do with social structures. Therefore, the kingdom is viewed as a reality to be experienced in the world to come, in a future which lies beyond the scope of history and is in contrast to this world. The kingdom of God is also perceived as an inner, spiritual reality, the right relationship of an individual with God. Jesus' words in Luke 17:21 are misinterpreted, as some translations have done: "the kingdom of God is within you" (cf. KJV and NIV). Many take this as referring primarily to an inner personal experience. But it is more in line with the intent of Jesus here to interpret Luke's text, "The kingdom of God is among you" or "in the midst of you" (cf. NRSV, RSV). From the context of John 18:36, the meaning of Jesus' words become clear. His kingship is not of this world: he does not resort to coercive violence, either for self-protection or for the establishment of the kingdom. Yet God's reign does affect the political, social, and economic decisions of his people. They hold values that offer a radical alternative to those of the world. Such believers do not withdraw into the inner spiritual nature of the person or project the kingdom only into a future beyond history (Driver, 1993a:90-91).

5. The primary sense of the Greek verb *phthanō* is to "come before, to precede" (Bauer: 856). Thayer suggests the following translation of Matthew 12:28 and Luke 11:20: "The kingdom of God has come upon you sooner than you expected" (652).

Chapter 8. New Creation
1. This is the primary meaning of the Greek verb *phthanō*.
2. The phrase "on the third day" undoubtedly introduces a new symbolism. It is certainly a reference to the resurrection.

3. "Eternal life" here is an equivalent for God's kingdom, or his new creation (cf. Gal. 5:21; 6:15).

4. For the following paragraphs, see Driver, 1986:235-241.

5. Whether the term translated "creation" (*ktisis*) refers to nature, or to humanity, or to both, is open to question. Traditional interpretations of this passage see "creation" as referring to the world of nature. However, Walter Gutbrod (Foerster: 1029, n. 196) and Juan Mateos (1984:1761) prefer to interpret the term as a primary reference to humanity. In 2 Corinthians 5:17 and Galatians 6:15, as well as in this passage, humanity seems to be in focus. Furthermore, the context of all three passages, the suffering witness of God's people, also points toward a primary interest in the world of humanity. Humanity is the central element of the created universe according to the biblical vision. Therefore, it seems best to understand "creation" in these texts in the inclusive sense.

Chapter 9. New Humanity

1. Tamar and Rahab were of Canaanite origin. Ruth was a Moabitess who had cast her lot with a new people and their God. Bathsheba was the wife of Uriah the Hittite.

2. This is true for "new humanity" in Ephesians 2:15; 4:24; and for "new creation" in 2 Corinthians 5:17 and Galatians 6:15.

3. Colossians 3:10; 1 Corinthians 5:7; and Hebrews 12:24 are exceptions which show that the two terms may occasionally be used synonymously.

4. The basic meaning of the word "Adam" is "man" or "humanity."

5. For the following section, see Driver, 1986:130-139.

6. "Just as we have borne the image of the man of dust, we will also bear the image of the man of heaven" (1 Cor. 15:49). The primary meaning of this text may well be a reference to spiritual bodies to be received in the future. This interpretation is favored by C. K. Barrett (377). However, in some ancient manuscripts, including p[46] and Aleph, the text reads as follows: "Just as we have borne the image of the man of dust, *let us also bear* the image of the man of heaven" (italics mine). In addition to being the source of our resurrection bodies at the last day, Jesus Christ, the New Man, is also source of life in the eschatological new humanity, already present in the messianic community.

Chapter 10. The People of God

1. *Laos* appears 140 times in the NT. It is not always clear just when the term is only literal, or if it is used in an imaginistic sense to refer to

the people of God (see Strathmann, 1967a:50).

2. In the first three, the absence is probably not significant, and its rare use in John leads one to wonder if the image might not have been uncongenial to the Johannine tradition, due perhaps to the conflict of the Johannine community with the synagogue (see Minear, 1960:272, n. 1).

3. Minear offers the following list of passages where the people of God has a marked significance for the self-consciousness of the Christian church: Matt. 1:21; 2:6; 4:16, 23; John 11:50; 18:14; Rom. 9:25-26; 11:1-2; 15:10; Titus 2:14; Acts 3:23; 7:34; 13:17-31; 15:14; 18:10; 2 Cor. 6:16; Heb. 2:17; 4:9; 8:10; 10:30; 13:12; 1 Pet. 2:9-10; Luke 1:17, 77; 2:10, 31-32; 7:16; Rev. 18:4; 21:3 (Minear, 1960:272, n. 1).

4. "Israel" probably meant originally "God reigns" (Küng, 1967a:114).

5. Amos and Hosea in Israel; and Isaiah, Micah, Zephaniah, Jeremiah, Nahum, Habakkuk, and Ezekiel in Judah (and finally in exile).

6. Acts 15:14; 18:10; Rom. 9:25-26; 2 Cor. 6:16; Titus 2:14; 1 Pet. 2:9-10; Heb. 4:9; 8:10; 10:30; 13:12; Rev. 18:4; 21:3.

7. Among these images are "the twelve tribes" (Matt. 19:28; James 1:1; Rev. 7:4); "the circumcision" (Phil. 3:3; Rom. 2:25-29; Col. 2:11-12; "the Israel of God" (Gal. 6:16); "the house of Israel" (Heb. 8:8); "the commonwealth of Israel" (Eph. 2:12).

8. Eventually the term "laity" (*laos*) has come to refer to all those who are not of the clergy; but this is entirely out of touch with its biblical meaning as an image for the whole church.

Chapter 11. The Family of God

1. Ephesians 2:19 (*oikeioi tou theou*); 1 Timothy 3:15 (*oikos theou*); 1 Peter 4:17 (*oikou tou theou*); Hebrews 3:1-6 (*oikon autou*); 10:21 (*oikon tou theou*).

2. Galatians 6:10 (*oikeious tēs pisteos*).

3. Direct and indirect NT references to house churches include Acts 2:46; 5:42; 8:3; 10:2, 22; 16:15, 31, 34; 18:8; 20:20; 21:8; Rom. 16:5, 14-15; 1 Cor. 1:16; 16:19; Col. 4:15; 1 Tim. 3:4-5, 12; 2 Tim. 1:16; 4:19; Titus 1:11; Philem. 2.

4. Following paragraphs are based largely on Minear, 1960:165-169.

5. For additional fruits of sonship, see Minear, 1960:170.

Chapter 12. The Shepherd and the Flock

1. Similar language is used in John 10:3 to describe Jesus, the Good Shepherd, who "calls his own sheep by name and leads them out."

2. *Poimnē* and *poimnion*: Matt. 26:31; Luke 2:8; 12:32; John 10:16; Acts 20:28-29; 1 Cor. 9:7; 1 Pet. 5:2-3. In the following paragraphs, I am indebted to Minear, 1960:84-89.

3. *Arnion, aren, probaton*: Matt. 7:15; 9:36; et par.; 10:6, 16; et par.;

15:24; 25:32; Luke 10:3; John 10:1-27; 21:15-17; Rom. 8:36; Heb. 13:20; 1 Pet. 2:25.

4. *Poimēn:* Matt. 9:36; et par.; 25:32; 26:31; et par.; Luke 2:8, 20; John 10:2-16; Eph. 4:11; Heb. 13:20; 1 Pet. 2:25.

5. Following the prologue (John 1:1-18) and the description of Jesus' activities during an inaugural week (1:19—2:12), the Gospel is set in the context of a first Passover (2:13—4:54), an unnamed feast (5:1-47), a second Passover (6:1-71), the Feast of Tabernacles (7:1—10:21), the Feast of Dedication (10:22—11:54), a final Passover (11:55—20:31), and the epilogue (21:1-25; Boismard: 1501).

6. The other two were Passover, and Pentecost (Exod. 23:14-15; Lev. 23:15-22).

7. Scholars quite generally see them as a reference to the Gentiles. However, a good case can be made for identifying them with the Samaritans (see Zorrilla: 52, 63).

Chapter 13.   Salt, Light, and a City
1. The other two reasons adduced are large Jewish families and a relatively favorable social situation. It has been estimated that there were approximately four to six million Jews living in the diaspora, while fewer than two million Jews lived in Palestine in the first century.

Chapter 14.   A Spiritual House
1. The same concrete visibility can be claimed for the "spiritual house" described in 1 Peter 2:5.

2. Vicarious suffering (Eph. 2:14, 17), martyr motif (2:14; 3:1), conflict-victory motif (1:21; 2:14, 16; 6:12), sacrificial imagery (1:7; 2:13; 5:3), expiation motif (2:14, 18), redemption-purchase motif (1:7; 4:30), reconciliation (2:16), justification (2:10; 4:24; 6:14), adoption-family image (1:5; 2:19; 5:1), archetypal imagery (1:10; 2:1, 5, 6, 10, 15, 16; 3:16-17; 4:13, 20, 24; 5:18).

3. Hans Küng (1967a:171) suggests that "keystone" is a better translation than "cornerstone." See also Jeremias (1967a:275).

4. The Greek terms make this relationship clearer: *sumpolitai, sunarmologoumenē,* and *sunoikodomeisthe.*

Chapter 15.   A Witnessing Community
1. A representative list of texts includes Luke 24:48; Acts 1:8; 2:32; 3:15; 5:32; 10:39, 41; 13:31; 22:15, 20; 26:16.

2. The frequency with which these terms appear in the NT in a metaphorical sense is approximately the following: *martus,* 20; *marturein,* 60; *marturia,* 30; *marturion,* 15.

3. See Juan Mateos (1975:29-32). The same material appeared in English translation in *Sojourners,* July 1977:12-13.

Bibliography

Note
Information is given in boldface type as needed to distinguish books.

Abbreviations
ANF   *The Ante-Nicene Fathers.* 10 vols. Ed. A. Roberts, J. Donaldson, et al. New York: Christian Literature Co., 1885-1887; vol. 9, 1896-97. Repr., New York: Charles Scribner's Sons, various dates.
TDNT   *Theological Dictionary of the New Testament.* 10 vols. Ed. G. Friedrich and G. Kittel. Trans. G. W. Bromiley. Grand Rapids, Eerdmans, 1964-76.

Books and Articles
Athenagoras. "A Plea for the Christians." In *ANF*, vol. 2.
Augustine: 1886. *City of God.* In *Nicene and Post-Nicene Fathers of the Christian Church,* vol. 2. Ed. Philip Schaff. New York: Charles Scribner's Sons. Repr., Grand Rapids: Eerdmans, 1956.
Augustine: 1979. "Soliloquies." In *Augustine: Earlier Writings.* Library of Christian Classics, vol. 6. Ed. John H. S. Burleigh. Philadelphia: Westminster.
Bammel, Ernst, et al. "*Ptōkos,* et al." In *TDNT*, vol. 6.
Banks, Robert. *Paul's Idea of Community: The Early House Churches in Their Historical Setting.* Grand Rapids: Eerdmans, 1980.
Barth, Markus. *Ephesians: Introduction, Translation, and Commentary on Chapters 1-3.* Anchor Bible. Garden City, N.Y.: Doubleday, 1974.
Barrett, C. K. *A Commentary on the First Epistle to the Corinthians.* New York: Harper & Row, 1968.

Bauer, Walter. *A Greek-English Lexicon of the New Testament and Other Early Christian Literature.* Trans. and adapt. William F. Arndt and F. Wilbur Gingrich. Chicago: Univ. of Chicago. 1979.

Behm, Johannes. "*Kainos,* et al." In *TDNT,* vol. 3.

Bettenson, Henry, ed. *Documents of the Christian Church.* London: Oxford Univ. Press, 1967.

Boismard, M., ed., et al. *Biblia de Jerusalén.* Bilbao: Desclée y Brouwer, 1984.

Bonnard, Pierre. *Evangelio Según San Mateo.* Madrid: Ediciones Christiandad, 1976.

Bosch, David. *Witness to the World: The Christian Mission in Theological Perspective.* London: Marshall, Morgan and Scott, 1980.

Bright, John. *A History of Israel.* Philadelphia: Westminster, 1959.

Catholic Institute for International Relations. *The Road to Damascus: Kairos and Conversion.* London: Catholic Institute for International Relations; Washington: Center for Concern, 1989.

Chilton, Bruce. *The Kingdom of God in the Teaching of Jesus.* Philadelphia: Fortress, 1984.

Clement. "The First Epistle of Clement to the Corinthians." Trans. John Keith. In *ANF,* vol. 9.

Craigie, P. C. *The Book of Deuteronomy.* London: Hodder and Stoughton, 1976.

De Dietrich, Suzanne. *The Witnessing Community: The Biblical Record of God's Purposes.* Philadelphia: Westminster, 1958.

De Vaux, Roland, ed., et al. *Biblia de Jerusalén.* Bilbao: Desclée y Brouwer, 1984.

Driver, John: *Understanding the Atonement for the Mission of the Church.* Scottdale, Pa.: Herald Press, 1986.

Driver, John: **1993a.** "The Kingdom of God: Goal of Messianic Mission." In *The Transfiguration of Mission.* Ed. Wilbert R. Shenk. Scottdale, Pa.: Herald Press.

Driver, John: **1993b.** "The Kingdom of God: A Key to Understanding Mission." In *Mission Focus,* vol. 1. Ed. Wilbert R. Shenk. Elkhart, Ind.: Mission Focus.

Eichrodt, Walter. *Theology of the Old Testament.* Vol. 2. Philadelphia: Westminster, 1967.

Eusebius. *Ecclesiastical History.* Trans. C. F. Cruse, London: Henry G. Bohn, n.d. Grand Rapids: Baker Book House, 1962.

Fitzmyer, Joseph A.: **1968a.** "The Letter to the Galatians." In *The Jerome Biblical Commentary.* Ed. Raymond E. Brown, Joseph A. Fitzmyer, and Roland E. Murphy. Englewood Cliffs, N.J.: Prentice-Hall, 1968.

Fitzmyer, Joseph A.: **1968b.** "The Letter to the Romans." In *The Jerome Biblical Commentary.* Ed. R. E. Brown *et al.* Englewood Cliffs, N.J.: Prentice-Hall, 1968.

Foerster, Werner. "*Ktizō,* et al." In *TDNT,* vol. 3.

Fox, Robin Lane. *Pagans and Christians.* New York: Alfred A. Knopf, 1987.

Glen, J. Stanley. *The Parables of Conflict in Luke.* Philadelphia: Westminster, 1962.

Gonzalez, Justo L. *A History of Christian Thought.* Vol. 2. Nashville: Abingdon, 1971.

Grundmann, Walter. *"Tapeinos,* et al." In *TDNT,* vol. 8.

Hauck, Friedrich, et al. *"Ptōkos,* et al." In *TDNT,* vol. 6.

Hegermann, Harald. "El Judaísmo Helenístico." In *El Mundo del Nuevo Testamento.* Ed. Johannes Leipoldt and Walter Grundmann. Madrid: Ediciones Cristiandad, 1973.

Hooker, Morna D. "Interchange and Suffering." In *Suffering and Martyrdom in the New Testament.* Ed. William Horburg and Brian McNeil. Cambridge: Cambridge Univ. Press, 1981.

Jeremias, Joachim: **1964.** *"Adam."* In *TDNT,* vol. 1.

Jeremias, Joachim: **1967a.** *"Lithos,* et al." In *TDNT,* vol. 4.

Jeremias, Joachim: **1967b.** *"Mōusēs."* In *TDNT,* vol. 4.

Jeremias, Joachim: **1968.** *"Poimēn,* et al." In *TDNT,* vol. 6.

Jeremias, Joachim: **1969.** *Jerusalem in the Time of Jesus.* Philadelphia: Fortress.

Jeremias, Joachim: **1971.** *New Testament Theology.* New York: Charles Scribner's Sons.

Justin Martyr: **1885a.** *The First Apology.* In *ANF,* vol. 1.

Justin Martyr: **1885b.** *Dialogue with Trypho.* In *ANF,* vol. 1.

Küng, Hans: **1967.** *The Church.* New York: Sheed and Ward.

Küng, Hans: **1976.** *On Being a Christian.* Garden City, N.Y.: Doubleday.

"Lausanne, Response to." Unpublished typescript. n.d.

Lohfink, Gerhard. *Jesus and Community: The Social Dimensions of Christian Faith.* Trans. John P. Galvin. Philadelphia: Fortress, 1984.

Mateos, Juan: **1975.** *El Nuevo Testamento.* Edicíon para Latinoamérica. Madrid: Ediciones Cristiandad.

Mateos, Juan: **1984.** *Nueva Biblia Española.* Madrid: Ediciones Cristiandad.

McKensie, John L. "Aspects of Old Testament Thought." In *The Jerome Biblical Commentary.* Ed. R. E. Brown *et al.* Englewood Cliffs, N.J.: Prentice-Hall, 1968.

Michel, Otto: **1967a.** *"Naos."* In *TDNT,* vol. 4.

Michel, Otto: **1967b.** *"Oikos,* et al." In *TDNT,* vol. 5.

Minear, Paul S.: **1960.** *Images of the Church in the New Testament.* Philadelphia: Westminster.

Minear, Paul S.: **1997.** "The Salt of the Earth." *Interpretation* (Jan.): 31-41.

Michaelis, Wilhelm. *"Hodos,* et al." In *TDNT,* vol. 5.

Murphy, Roland E. "Salmos." In *Comentario Biblico "San Jeronimo."* Vol. 2. Madrid: Ediciones Cristiandad, 1971.

Origen. *Contra Celsum.* In *ANF,* vol. 4.

Pelikan, Jaroslav. *The Christian Tradition: The Emergence of the Catholic Tradition (100-600)*. Chicago: Univ. of Chicago Press, 1971.

Pikaza, Javier, and Francisco de la Calle. *Teología de los Evangelios de Jesus*. Salamanca: Ediciones Sígueme, 1977.

Polycarp. "The Epistle to the Philippians." In *The Apostolic Fathers*, vol. 1. Trans. K. Lake. Cambridge, Mass.: Harvard Univ. Press, 1912.

Quadratus? "The Epistle to Diognetus." Trans. James A. Kleist. In *Ancient Christian Writers*, no. 6. Ed. by Johannes Quasten and Joseph C. Plumpe. New York: Newman Press, 1948.

Reicke, Bo. *"Pro."* In *TDNT*, vol. 6.

Schlier, Heinrich. *"Hairesis, et al."* In *TDNT*, vol. 1.

Schmidt, Karl Ludwig: **1964.** *"Diaspora."* In *TDNT*, vol. 2.

Schmidt, Karl Ludwig, and Martin Anton Schmidt: **1967.** *"Paroikos, et al."* In *TDNT*, vol. 5.

Smyrna, Church of. "The Martyrdom of Polycarp." In *The Apostolic Fathers*, vol. 2. Trans. K. Lake. Cambridge, Mass.: Harvard Univ. Press, 1913.

Strathmann, Hermann: **1967a.** *"Laos."* In *TDNT*, vol. 4.

Strathmann, Hermann: **1967b.** *"Martus, et al."* In *TDNT*, vol. 4.

Tertullian. *Apologeticum*. ANF, vol. 3.

Thayer, Joseph Henry. *A Greek-English Lexicon of the New Testament*. Chicago: American Book Company, 1889.

Vawter, Bruce. "Evangelio según San Juan." In *Comentario Biblico "San Jeronimo."* Vol. 4. Madrid: Ediciones Cristiandad, 1972.

Westminster Study Bible. New York: Wm. Collins Sons, 1965.

Yoder, John H.: **1980.** "The Apostle's Apology Revisited." In *The New Way of Jesus*. Ed. William Klassen. Newton, Kans: Faith & Life Press.

Yoder, John H.: **1982.** "The Prophet (Is. 2:1-4; Mi. 4:1-4)." *Church and Peace* 6.1 (Dec.).

Yoder, John H.: **1992.** *Body Politics: Five Practices of the Christian Community Before the Watching World*. Nashville: Discipleship Resources.

Yoder, John H.: **1994.** *The Politics of Jesus*. Rev. ed. Grand Rapids: Eerdmans.

Zorrilla, Hugo. *La Fiesta de Liberación de los Oprimidos: Relectura de Jn. 7.1—10.21*. San José, Costa Rica: Ediciones SEBILA, 1981.

The Author

John Driver, from Hesston, Kansas, holds a B.A. degree from Goshen (Ind.) College, a B.D. from Goshen Biblical Seminary, and a S.T.M. from Perkins School of Theology. He and his wife, Bonita Landis, are the parents of three children.

John (1945-48) and Bonita (1947-48) worked under Mennonite Central Committee in Puerto Rico. They served under the Mennonite Board of Missions during 1951-89: in Puerto Rico (1951-66), Uruguay (1967-74, 1985-89), Spain (1975-80, 1983-84), and Argentina (1981). John was professor of church history and New Testament at the Seminario Evangélico Menonita de Teología in Montevideo and academic dean until the seminary closed in 1974. The Drivers returned to Montevideo in 1985 at the invitation of the Centro de Estudios of the Mennonite Church in Uruguay, where John was teaching and writing.

Driver is the author of many books in Spanish and English (see page 2, above). Since their retirement in 1989, the Drivers have made their home in Goshen, where they are active members in East Goshen Mennonite Church. John has continued to teach in the Hispanic ministries program at Goshen College, in the Central American theological education program of Seminario Anabautista Latinoamericana centered in Guatemala, in 1993 as visiting professor at Instituto Bíblico de Buenos Aires, and in 1995 at Seminario Menonita de Colombia in Bogotá.